FEMINISMS AND DEVELOPMENT

Disrupting taken-for-granted assumptions, this expert series redefines issues at the heart of today's feminist contestations in a development context. Bringing together a formidable collective of thinkers from the global South and North, it explores what it is that can bring about positive changes in women's rights and realities.

These timely and topical collections reposition feminism within development studies, bringing into view substantial commonalities across the countries of the global South that have so far gone unrecognized.

Series editor
Andrea Cornwall

Forthcoming titles

Changing Narratives of Sexuality:
Contestations, Compliance and Women's Empowerment
Charmaine Pereira

Women in Politics:
Gender, Power and Development
Mariz Tadros

About the Editors

Andrea Cornwall is the director of the Pathways of Women's Empowerment programme and professor of anthropology and development in the School of Global Studies at the University of Sussex. She has written widely on gender issues in development, sexuality and development and participatory governance. Her publications include *Women, Sexuality and the Political Power of Pleasure* (co-edited with Susie Jolly and Kate Hawkins, 2013), *Men and Development: Politicizing Masculinities* (co-edited with Jerker Edström and Alan Greig, 2011) and *The Politics of Rights: Dilemmas for Feminist Praxis* (co-edited with Maxine Molyneux, 2009).

Jenny Edwards has been the programme officer for the Pathways of Women's Empowerment programme at the Institute of Development Studies since 2006. She studied cultures and communities at the University of Sussex and her dissertation was on the politics of stepmothering as portrayed in children's literature. Her interests are in the issues of gender stereotyping, particularly in popular culture, and women's political representation.

Feminisms, Empowerment and Development

Changing Women's Lives

edited by
Andrea Cornwall and Jenny Edwards

Zed Books
LONDON & NEW YORK

*To Andrea's mum, Ilse Cornwall-Ross,
and to the memory of Jenny's mum,
Shirley Skepper*

Feminisms, Empowerment and Development: Changing Women's Lives was first published in 2014 by Zed Books Ltd, 7 Cynthia Street, London N1 9JF, UK and Room 400, 175 Fifth Avenue, New York, NY 10010, USA

www.zedbooks.co.uk

Typeset in Monotype Bembo by Kate Kirkwood
Index by John Barker
Cover designed by www.alice-marwick.co.uk
Printed and bound by CPI Group (UK) Ltd, Croydon, CR0 4YY

Distributed in the USA exclusively by Palgrave Macmillan, a division of St Martin's Press, LLC, 175 Fifth Avenue, New York, NY 10010, USA

A catalogue record for this book is available from the British Library
Library of Congress Cataloguing in Publication Data available

ISBN 978 1 78032 584 2 hb
ISBN 978 1 78032 583 5 pb

MIX
Paper from responsible sources
FSC   FSC® C013604

Contents

Acknowledgements

. . . .

This book brings together contributions from the regional hubs and thematic working groups of the international research and communications initiative Pathways of Women's Empowerment (www.pathwaysofempowerment.org). We would like to thank our wonderful colleagues in the Pathways programme for their friendship, support and the stimulating exchange of ideas over the past eight years. Our interactions have been truly inspirational, and we really appreciate the bonds of collegiality that have been formed. In particular, we would like to thank our Pathways colleagues who have contributed to this book for their patience and endurance during the process of the book's evolution. We would also like to thank Rosalind Eyben, Naila Kabeer, Mariz Tadros, Cecilia Sardenberg and Tessa Lewin for their insightful feedback at various stages as we developed this manuscript.

We're very grateful to Zed Books, to Kim Walker, Tamsine O'Riordan, Kika Sroka-Miller, Jakob Horstmann, Dan Och, Mike Kirkwood and all the others at Zed who have made it possible to bring this series into being and who have been involved in the production of this book. We would also like to thank Wiley-Blackwell, Palgrave Macmillan and Sage Publications for their kind permission in allowing us to publish updated versions and segments of articles previously published in the *IDS Bulletin*, *Development* and *Current Sociology*.

We'd like to express our sincere thanks to our donors, who

have played such a vital role in supporting our work. We are appreciative to the Department for International Development (DFID) for the Research Programme Consortium model that permitted us to develop a genuinely mutual and democratic approach to international research collaboration and for challenging us to be creative and imaginative in our approach to communications. We thank the Norwegian Ministry of Foreign Affairs for believing in what we were doing and trusting us to know how best to achieve our goals. And we'd like to extend our gratitude to the Swedish International Co-operation Agency (Sida) for providing support that allowed us to realize our publication promises.

Andrea would like to thank her children, Jake and Kate Cornwall Scoones, for all the stimulating conversations and disagreements about gender, feminism and difference that we've had as this book was in the making. Jenny would like to thank her daughter, Indiana Edwards, for the thought-provoking conversations which made her question and challenge assumptions and ideas she had previously taken for granted.

Preface

● ●

Andrea Cornwall

Feminisms, Empowerment and Development brings together a constellation of studies from an international research and communications initiative, Pathways of Women's Empowerment (www.pathways-of-empowerment.org). Pathways began in 2006, with support from the UK government's Department of International Development and the Norwegian Ministry of Foreign Affairs, with the bold assertion that international development agencies were pouring resources into constructing motorways – one-size-fits-all programmes and interventions – that may lead to nowhere in terms of actually addressing the structural gender inequalities that are such a powerful source of disempowerment.

We set out to explore how women in different contexts, cultures and circumstances experience power, empowerment and change in their lives. Our focus was not only on the policies and programmes, feminist movements and organizations that explicitly sought to bring about changes in women's lives. We were interested in discovering what we called 'hidden pathways', the otherwise invisible routes that women travel on journeys of empowerment, as we sought to get to grips in a more holistic way with what makes positive change happen in women's lives. These were to include a focus beyond the conventional emphases in work on women's empowerment – enabling more women to gain an independent income, getting more women into politics, securing women's sexual and reproductive rights

– on other dimensions of women's lives that are a source of empowering pleasure and leisure.

A network of regional hubs in Latin America, the Middle East, South Asia and West Africa – with partners across the regions – and a hub that took as its focus 'Aidland' and global development policy, Pathways drew together researchers from more than a dozen countries. Cross-hub thematic groups on work, voice and sexuality worked on collaborative research projects, conferences and workshops. This gave rise to a series of volumes in the Feminisms and Development series, as well as special issues of journals, monographs and other edited collections, working papers, documentaries, digital stories, photographic competitions and exhibitions, short stories, and performative events. An interactive learning platform repurposed our work for use by secondary school teachers and trainers (http://learning-platform. pathwaysofempowerment.org/), and in an online forum, Contestations, we sought to engage activists and practitioners in debating contentious issues in gender and development. Over the eight years since Pathways came into being, the network has expanded to embrace other researchers and activists working on women's rights and empowerment, and to explore new avenues for engagement.

This book marks an important point in our journey. It brings together a diversity of contributions from across the Pathways network, reflecting some of the regional and thematic diversity of our work. Together, these studies offer a perspective on empowerment that complicates the conventional narrative, and that takes us off the motorways of current gender and development policy to the roads less travelled that take us further into the everyday realities of women's lives. The contributions enrich our understandings of the dynamics of power, empowerment and change, and serve as a vital reminder that empowerment is not a destination, nor something that can be 'delivered', but a journey that is neither linear nor predictable in terms of its outcomes. We came to understand, with these studies, that pathways of positive change do not only involve extending the boundaries of what we are able to do – physically, economically or politically. Empowerment also involves shifts in the way in which we perceive the world and our place within it. Pathways of empowerment, then, can be as much about routes that ignite our indignation and invite new ways of imagining what might be and expanding our horizons of possibility – about shifts in consciousness that make other kinds of changes possible. These are journeys that can be taken alone, but that may become more possible, and more productive, when taken in company.

Some of the most powerful stories of empowerment that we came across in our work involved shifts of consciousness and forms of collective action that came about as part of women's rights activism, facilitated and supported by women's movements and organizations. These are pathways that have been travelled by hundreds of thousands, if not millions, of women around the world. And yet the international development enterprise has been profoundly neglectful of the role that women's movements, small and large, have in making change happen to bring about greater gender justice and equality. It's time for that to change, and it is our hope that this book, and our work in the Pathways network, can make a small contribution to making more visible the vital role of women's rights in the struggle for a fairer and more equitable world.

INTRODUCTION
Negotiating Empowerment

● ●

Andrea Cornwall and Jenny Edwards

From its origins as a feminist strategy for social transformation, women's empowerment has come to be championed by corporate CEOs, international NGOs, powerful Western governments and the financial institutions they preside over – and, or so it would seem, the entire global development apparatus. 'Gender equality is smart economics', the phrase coined by brilliant marketeers at the World Bank to promote investment in women and girls, has become a meme whose traces can be found in a thousand echoes across the landscape of corporate and international development institutions. Extravagant promises are made talking up the 'value-added' of such investments: 'stopping poverty before it starts' by investing in adolescent girls; 'lifting' economies; stemming the effects of the financial crisis; driving economic growth. This embrace of women's empowerment centres on women's entrepreneurship but also accommodates a focus on women's leadership, and extols women's contributions to a host of other development goods.

Bringing together a diversity of studies from a variety of locations, this book offers insights from empirical research that complicate the picture painted in these narratives of women's empowerment. It weaves together fine-grained ethnographic studies of processes, perceptions and institutions with macro-level analyses of shifts in law and policy, ranging across sites as diverse as family courts in Cairo, the meeting rooms of international

1

development agencies in London and New York, and slum dwellings in which Bangladeshi women watch television. Together, contributors ask questions about how positive change in women's lives is brought about and experienced. Drawing on rich empirical and conceptual work produced over a period of five years by an international network of researchers – the Pathways of Women's Empowerment research programme (Pathways) – this book seeks to restore to discussions of women's empowerment a consideration of the complexities of change and the lived realities of women's lives in diverse contexts.

Understanding change in women's lives

A key question for Pathways was: what makes change happen for the better in women's lives? Our interest went beyond planned intervention to broader and more diffuse social, cultural and economic changes that wrought effects in the lives of women in all their diversity. Part of our work was oriented at mapping the effects of interventions that have a deliberate focus on women's empowerment, such as laws, policies and programmes aimed specifically at women. As a corollary, we also sought to explore the role of relationships in facilitating women's access to legal, social, economic or political institutions. Shaped by and shaping our recognition of the relational nature of empowerment, much of this work focused on women's organizations and on front-line workers, activists and bureaucrats in government and the aid apparatus involved in mediating women's empowerment. A third dimension of our work explored what we called 'hidden pathways' – unusual, unexpected and commonly unseen pathways that we sought to find and make visible. Many of these hidden pathways took us into terrains that are under-explored in development: television, popular music, faith and religious practice, everyday domesticity, pleasure in leisure and in sexual relationships. They provided us with diversions that were rich in insight, adding more significantly than we anticipated at the outset to our understanding of processes of and preconditions for empowerment.

This book takes shape from these different approaches to understanding processes of change. In this introduction, we explore the backdrop to today's enthusiasm for women's empowerment via a consideration of foundational feminist writing and a brief account of contemporary development policy. We go on to address a number of salient themes emerging from reflection on the disjunctures that come into view, weaving into this discussion elements from the chapters in this book that highlight important dimensions of empowerment in practice. A central thread that runs through this diversity of experiences and examples is the relational understanding of empowerment that Pathways came to recognize as critical to making sense of what was needed to bring about change – whether through direct efforts to produce particular kinds of change or more diffuse shifts in mindset, confidence and consciousness that underpin broader societal change. What emerges are powerful tales of the dedication and ingenuity of those who persist against all odds, the tactics that are resorted to in fields of power in which there may be little overt room for manoeuvre, the rallying points, the alliances, the compromises and the disappointments. In doing so, we seek to restore some of the complex richness of women's experience to discussions of women's empowerment.

Tracks and traces: women's empowerment in development

The concept of empowerment has a long history in social change work, in fields such as popular education, community psychology and community organizing. Feminist consciousness raising and collective action informed early applications of the concept to international development in the 1970s. Women's empowerment came to be articulated in the 1980s and 1990s as a radical approach that was concerned with transforming power relations in favour of women's rights and greater equality between women and men (Batliwala 1993, 2007; Kabeer 1994, 1999). As Bisnath and Elson observe, it was explicitly used to frame and facilitate the struggle for social justice and women's equality through a transformation of economic, social and political structures at national and international levels. (1999: 1)

In the writings of the 1980s and early 1990s, empowerment was cast as an unfolding process, a journey that women could take alone or together that would lead to changes in consciousness and collective power. Common to many of these writings was an insistence that empowerment was not something that could be bestowed by others, but was about recognizing inequalities in power, asserting the right to have rights, and acting individually and in concert to press for and bring about structural change in favour of greater equality (Batliwala 1993; Kabeer 1994, 1999; Rowlands 1997; Sen 1997).

As early as 1994, Srilatha Batliwala expressed concern about the growing popularity of the term, which had virtually replaced, she argued, terms such as welfare and community participation. Warning that empowerment was in danger of losing its trans-formative edge, she called for a more precise understanding of both power and empowerment. Defining power 'as control over material assets, intellectual resources, and ideology' (1994: 129), Batliwala defined empowerment as 'the process of challenging existing power relations, and of gaining greater control over the sources of power' (1994: 130). Challenging a tendency in the discourses of the day (Moore 2001) to limit the concept to purely local, 'grassroots' participation, Batliwala pressed for the potential of what she called an 'empowerment spiral' to mobilize larger-scale transformative political action.

Out of this earlier feminist engagement with international development, then, a narrative of empowerment emerges that is bound up with both collective action ('power with') and the development of 'power within' and 'power to' at the level of consciousness. These two facets of empowerment – consciousness and collective action – are represented in writings from this period as deeply mutually imbricated. Gita Sen draws on Srilatha Batliwala to argue:

Empowerment is, first and foremost, about power; changing power relations in favour of those who previously exercised little power over their own lives. Batliwala (1993) defines power as having two central aspects – control over resources (physical, human, intellectual, financial, and the self), and control over ideology (beliefs, values and attitudes). If power means control, then empowerment therefore is the process of gaining control. (1997: 2)

What feminist work from this period emphasizes – a point that tends to be lost in today's policy narratives of women's empowerment – is that there is a complex reciprocal relationship between women's 'self-understanding' (Kabeer 1994) and 'capacity for self-expression' (Sen 1997) and their access to and control over material resources. That is to say, providing women with loans, business opportunities and means to generate income may in and of itself bring about some changes in their lives, including enabling them to better manage their poverty. But to see really *substantial* changes, the kind that can transform the root causes of that poverty and begin to address the deep structural basis of gender inequality, conditions need to be fostered for shifts in consciousness so that women begin to understand their situations and come together to act to bring about change that can benefit not only them, but also other women. As Hania Sholkamy (2010: 257) puts it:

Alleviating poverty and enabling women to make some income can better lives, but the enabling environment that confirms the right to work, to property, to safety, to voice, to sexuality and to freedom is not created by sewing machines or micro-credit alone.

What lies at the heart of these differences and disjunctures is how power is conceived. The individualist perspective of contemporary neo-liberal empowerment policies, dubbed 'liberal empowerment' by Cecilia Sardenberg (2009) following Ann Ferguson (2004), sees power as an asset: something that can be acquired, bestowed and wielded. Feminist conceptions of power and empowerment are altogether more nuanced. Naila Kabeer, for example, wants us to see power as 'more fluid, more pervasive and more socially embedded than the conventional focus on individual decision making would suggest', and goes on to argue that

> the multi-dimensional nature of power suggests that empowerment strategies for women must build on 'the power within' as a necessary adjunct to improving their ability to control resources, to determine agendas and make decisions. (1994: 229)

As evoked so eloquently in Batliwala's (1993) and Kabeer's (1994) accounts of grassroots conscientization and mobilization in India and Bangladesh, such processes engage people in making sense of their worlds, their relationships, their assumptions, beliefs, practices and values – and in questioning that which they have come to take for granted, with potentially transformatory effects. Batliwala notes:

> One unique feature of this approach is the stress placed on changing women's self-image: the argument is that unless women are liberated from their existing perception of themselves as weak, inferior and limited beings, no amount of external interventions – whether in the form of resource access or economic power – will enable them to challenge existing power equations in society, the community or the family. (1993: 31)

Such a process involves denaturalizing 'truths' that diminish the humanity of some to the advantage of others, and making strange those familiar social norms that surround us and which are such a potent source of inequity and disempowerment. Kabeer describes how:

> Strategies of 'empowerment from within' provide women with these other perspectives. They entail reflection, analysis and assessment of what has hitherto been taken for granted so as to uncover the socially constructed and socially shared basis of apparently individual problems. New forms of consciousness arise out of women's newly acquired access to the intangible resources of analytical skills, social networks, organizational strength, solidarity and sense of not being alone. (1994: 245–6)

Three important insights emerge from feminist writings on empowerment from the 1990s. The first is that empowerment is fundamentally about changing power relations. It is not just about improving women's capacities to cope with situations in which they experience oppression or injustice. It is about enabling women to bring into view and into question what they might previously have considered 'natural' or 'normal', and to begin to act to change that reality. Kabeer (1994), citing Dighe and Jain (1989: 87), describes how, while 'a state of powerlessness ... manifests itself in a feeling of "I cannot", empowerment contains an element of collective self-confidence that results in a feeling of "we can"'. Following from this, the second insight is that empowerment is relational in (at least) two senses: it concerns the relations of power in which people are located, within which they may experience disempowerment or come to acquire the 'ability to make strategic life choices' (Kabeer 1999), and it is contingent on a prior or future state to which a person's current situation is related.

Thirdly, we learn from this work that empowerment is a process, not a fixed state, status or end-point, let alone a measurable outcome to which targets can be attached. Although interventions such as legal changes, education policy or microfinance initiatives favouring women can be measured, as Malhotra *et al.* 2002 contend, these should be seen as 'enabling factors' or 'outcomes' but cannot be interpreted as a proxy for empowerment. Empowerment cannot simply be bestowed on others (Rowlands 1997). It is a process best captured in the metaphor of a journey along pathways that can be travelled individually or together with others, in which the nature of the terrain is significant in determining progress. The work of external actors and interventions, then, may be conceived not as 'empowering women' – because, as feminist writers assure us, empowerment is not something that is 'done to' women but is done by them for themselves – but as clearing some of the obstacles from the path, providing signposts, stiles, bridges, sustenance and company for those making these journeys.

Motorways and pathways

Turning to the arena of contemporary development policy, how readily can we identify these insights from feminist writings on empowerment? The versions of empowerment that appear in contemporary international development policy and in the promotional material produced by international development agencies primarily concern the acquisition of material means through which women empower themselves as individuals, and of the benefits that come when they direct their earning and spending power to the service of their families, communities and national economies (Eyben and Napier-Moore 2009; Eyben 2010). There is an interchangeability in these representations: what might once have seemed like a disparate array of corporate and development actors with quite distinctive positions – the likes, for example, of Walmart, Oxfam, DfID, the Nike Foundation, Plan International and the IMF – are all apparently purveying the same message, sometimes even in the same words. We see a familiar series of tropes – most commonly the pronouncement of the intrinsic value of women's empowerment – before proceeding to the real business at hand: 'unleashing potential' and harnessing the power of billions of women workers and their transformative economic effects as the producers and consumers who will drive growth.

At the heart of this discourse is a belief that women's business success is enough to overcome all other barriers to equality; once women hold the purse strings, their spending power will automatically translate into a capacity to be those 'agents of change' in their communities and countries that we hear about in speeches by prominent development officials. This version of 'women's empowerment' is more appealing than traditional feminist concerns with the more 'nebulous' inequality and oppression – to international donors and banks, and indeed to the publics invited to 'invest in' rather than give charity to support women entrepreneurs and girls as 'agents of change'. What has come to be known as the 'business case' for women's empowerment emerges from this; there is a version of the mantra that appears in many of these glossies and speeches that speaks in one breath about women being important in and of themselves, and also a means to enhance economic efficiency. Writing in 1997, Gita Sen cautioned:

> It is a short step from thinking of governments or agencies as 'empowering' people through programmes to viewing empowerment as another handout, something governments do for or on behalf of people. The danger here is that the focus will shift entirely to the provision of access to external resources, assets, or services, and away from methodologies that will create spaces for people to build confidence and self-esteem. (1997: 3)

That very danger is all too evident in today's 'empowerment lite' (Cornwall 1997). Important elements of the version of women's empowerment that gained prominence in the 1990s are sloughed away in this repackaged version; the chains of equivalence (Laclau 1990) that once held 'women's empowerment' together with 'rights', 'equality', 'justice' and 'collective action' are replaced with new attachments to 'efficiency', 'investment' and 'returns'. Empowerment becomes an individual resource to be maximized for efficiency.

What falls out of the frame is the very relational dimensions that were so fundamentally part of feminist conceptualizations of empowerment and their central focus on transforming the power relations that sustain inequitable gender relations. This is not a simple act of omission. Looking more closely at the ways in which feminist work on empowerment has been taken up by development institutions, we can see the stripping away of foundational dimensions through a series of discursive moves. We see, for example, what happens to the influential definition of empowerment developed by Naila Kabeer (1999) with its emphasis on the *ability* to make *strategic* life choices by those who were *previously denied* such an ability. This is transmuted, in the World Bank's selective adoption of her work, into:

> Empowerment is the process of enhancing the capacity of individuals or groups to make choices and to transform those choices into desired

actions and outcomes. Central to this process are actions which both build individual and collective assets, and improve the efficiency and fairness of the organizational and institutional context which govern the use of these assets.[1]

The empowerment framework produced for the World Bank by Alsop *et al.* (2005), and adopted by a range of other development actors, offers a guide to identifying, itemizing and measuring 'assets' and 'opportunity structures'. In the process of reducing empowerment to measurable outcomes, the relational dimensions of empowerment disappear and with them that which is constitutive of the concept itself. Individuals and groups may acquire assets, and institutions may improve their governance, but these elements in themselves do not necessarily produce empowerment. Empowerment lies in the ways in which those constituent elements come *together*, a dynamic process that is all about these interactions. Gergen provides us with an analogous example in his exploration of relational agency through the metaphor of a baseball game:

> What we traditionally view as 'independent' elements – the man with the bat, the bags, the men in the field – are not truly independent. They are all mutually defining.... Alone they would [all] be virtually without meaning. It is when we bring all these elements into a mutually defining relationship that we can speak about 'playing baseball'. Let us then speak of the baseball game as a confluence, a form of life in this case that is constituted by an array of mutually defining 'entities'. (2009: 54)

Gergen's notion of 'confluence' provides a useful way of conceiving of the interplay of elements in the process of empowerment. Like the bat and the player in a game of baseball, material resources and the means to make use of them are not in themselves constitutive of empowerment. They only become part of the process of empowerment when they are brought together relationally; when someone uses their material resources and capacities to do something that changes the way they relate to others in their social world and the way those others relate to them. And, as has been shown by a number of studies, this cannot be prejudged, nor is empowerment in one area of a woman's life necessarily transferable to other areas of her life (Malhotra and Mather 1997 and others, cited in Malhotra *et al.* 2002). Much, then, comes to depend on context.

Contexts of choice

Writing in the field of health promotion, Barbara Israel and colleagues contend that

> for empowerment to be a meaningful concept, distinct from others such as self-esteem and self-efficacy, the cultural, historical, social, economic and political context within which the individual exists must be recognized. It is possible to develop a program aimed at individual empowerment, but if this does not consider the context in which the individual is embedded ... there is less likelihood that actual increases in influence and control and concomitant improvement in health and quality of life will occur. (1994: 153)

It is a well-accepted feminist dictum that 'real' empowerment is something that women can only do for themselves (Rowlands 1997). Yet, while there is general acceptance of this axiom, less attention is paid to the fact that women's pathways of empowerment are pursued – to paraphrase Marx – under conditions that are not of their own choosing. Development agencies often evoke images of the empowered autonomous subjects produced as a result of their interventions – women who are able to choose, make and shape their own directions of travel. In reality, very few of us have the capacity to make independent choices and to follow them through. The 'structures of constraint' referred to by Marx and highlighted by many feminist economists (Folbre 1994; Kabeer 2008) act as a brake on women's ability to choose their own paths. And the very nature of empowerment is something far more contingent and contextual, and ultimately far less predictable, than allowed for in the quick-fit solutions purveyed by development agencies.

Studies in this volume demonstrate how context is crucial in making sense of empowerment. Historical shifts in societal and cultural norms and practices – as well as in institutions in politics and the economy, current and previous political conjunctures, the density of donor engagement and the nature of the state, the broader landscape of organizations and social movements, and many other contextual factors – impinge on the possibilities for women's empowerment, facilitating and enabling but also blocking and restricting possibilities. Akosua Adomako Ampofo and Awo Mana Asiedu's study of popular music culture in Ghana (Chapter 7) discusses how prevalent sexual stereotyping of women in pop music plays a role in shaping society, reinscribing gendered power relations which in turn 'straitjacket' women within traditional norms and expectations. Hussaina Abdullah's analysis of peace building in Sierra Leone (Chapter 3) shows how vital history is to understanding women's struggles to gain visibility and voice. In her analysis of girls' education, an intervention that has become one of development's magic bullets, Akosua Darkwah (Chapter 4) shows that for older generations of Ghanaian women education *did* provide a pathway of empowerment. For younger women, however, the route map has changed, as have their means of enhancing their prospects in the contemporary labour market. This leads Darkwah to conclude that 'context is key in determining whether or not an educated girl will grow up to become an empowered woman'.

Terezinha Gonçalves' account of the gains made by the domestic workers' movement in Brazil (Chapter 11) illustrates just how much context matters. To understand the story of the domestic workers' movement, she points out, we need to recognize deep-rooted patterns of discrimination and exploitation from the era of slavery. Equally, to make sense of what the movement has achieved, we need to locate their activism in the current political conjuncture. Brazil's left-of-centre Workers' Party government has had a major influence on the gains secured by workers' movements of all kinds, especially those of the marginalized. To grasp how significant these gains are, we need to know about the dynamics of difference in this context – gender, race and class – and the distinctive tensions and contradictions their intersection provokes. Gonçalves shows how these play out in all aspects of domestic workers' lives, from the workplace to the home, and to engagement with union, feminist and black movements. What these and other chapters affirm is the folly of a one-size-fits-all approach to empowerment that pays little or no attention to the actual social, cultural and political backdrop of planned intervention.

Exercising voice

Whether women's empowerment is conceptualized as an individual journey or as a collective struggle, women finding and using their voice to instigate changes in societal structures, values and behaviour is central. There is as little disagreement among development actors about the need to promote women's political empowerment as there is with the benefits of women's economic empowerment (Eyben *et al.* 2008). Yet quite *which* women are the beneficiaries of empowerment interventions, who they represent, and what they voice raises a host of thorny issues (Goetz and Nyamu Musembi 2008; Tadros 2010). Much attention has been focused on the domain of formal politics, and on increasing the numbers of women in office. Quota systems are a relatively recent innovation – many dating from the period after the 1995 Beijing conference, where the 30 per cent target for female representation in political office was set. Ana Alice Costa, in Chapter 3, draws on Latin American experience to reflect on lessons learnt from the contrasting experiences of countries achieving relatively high proportions of women in public office, and those where numbers remain very low.

Quotas may get more women into political office, where they are implemented effectively – and that remains a huge challenge, as Costa points out. But changing politics calls for more than a few individual women finding a path into political office. Experience has shown us that even having a female leader doesn't necessarily create chances for other women: the UK's Margaret

Thatcher only had one female cabinet minister during her 11-year reign, and it was only under the male leadership of the subsequent Labour government that things began to improve, with 18 female cabinet ministers over 13 years (Duckworth and Cracknell 2013). As the slogan of the Argentinian Political Feminist Network cited by Costa puts it, 'with a few women in politics, women change; with a lot of women in politics, politics change'.

For feminist and women's movements in many countries, the highly exclusionary, patriarchal arena of formal politics has often been one of the least promising pathways to power. Costa notes how few women have made it to the top on merit, rather than through family connections. Pathways research across a diversity of contexts in the global South – Bangladesh, Brazil, Ghana, Palestine, Pakistan, Sierra Leone, Sudan – shows that women seeking political office have faced obstacles not only of their gender, but also of their class: family connections and support are shown in these studies to be a vital factor in women's political success (Tadros 2010, 2014). In contexts where there has been a widening of political opportunity beyond a clutch of privileged women, it is often due not only to changes in the institutional design of electoral systems, but to public policies and to the active engagement of women's movements. Costa notes that

> quota systems alone are not sufficient to create the conditions for women to empower themselves politically: quotas are not automatic pathways of political empowerment for women. But when quotas are complemented with public policies to promote equality that can create deeper transformations in the patriarchal structure in society, with a view to expanding democracy, then they can serve as a route to change. (p. 62)

Development goals and targets, especially those established as indicators for the achievement of Millennium Development Goal 3, have focused more attention on formal politics than on the myriad of other spaces that exist for decision making and influence.

And yet women's marginalization from formal institutions of politics and the economy has meant that women's organizing has often focused on other means of being heard: through movement building to gain public presence and influence public opinion, through engaging the media, and through alliances with other movements – and, as Rosalind Eyben points out in Chapter 8, supportive bureaucrats. As Mulki Al-Sharmani's analysis of the family court reforms in Egypt (Chapter 1) highlights, this calls for a multi-stranded process of dialogue that must necessarily extend beyond the usual actors and arenas:

> reform strategies need to go beyond lobbying the government. What has been lacking in the processes and efforts of reforming Egyptian laws thus far has been the building of support among different sectors of the society (religious scholars, Islamic NGOs, legislators, families and communities) through dialogue and awareness raising, and partaking in the process of imparting to new generations of children and young people enlightened religious knowledge and sensibilities that are appreciative of justice, equality, and acceptance of and respect for others. (p. 46)

A common thread running through these very different contexts and struggles is the significance of the kinds of relationships that can serve advocacy and mobilization, in particular alliances and coalitions. What emerges is the strategic importance for feminist action of a multi-layered constituency of potential allies, located within, as well as outside, government and other agencies for policy making and implementation.

Emerging from this work is recognition of the need to look more closely at the different arenas in which women gain and claim voice. Hussaina Abdullah's chapter tells a story, familiar from other contexts, of the role played by women's mobilization and voice in Sierra Leone's struggle for peace and women's marginalization after the war was over. And yet, as she shows, there can be a cumulative effect of efforts to gain public and political space, as tactics are honed and networks are strengthened, lending women opportunities for political apprenticeship that they may otherwise be denied. Sohela Nazneen and Maheen Sultan make an observation that holds for other settings. In their comparative analysis of three Bangladeshi women's organizations (Chapter 9), they note how feminist and women's movements have been as reluctant to engage in party politics as they have been unsuccessful in engaging political parties with their concerns.

This work points to the need to think critically about the extent to which opportunities to participate and influence in one arena translate into a broader willingness on the part of powerful institutions to listen to women – and about a more holistic approach to women's political empowerment that can go beyond the narrow cycle of support to women politicians and instead support women's organizing at all levels.

Expanding horizons of possibility

Empowerment is not just about enlarging the boundaries of action. It is also about expanding the horizons of possibility, of what people imagine themselves being able to be and do. Mainstream empowerment discourses reduce the complexity of this process to a simple equation, in which there is a linear connection between choice, action and outcome (Buvinic and King 2007). The rich empirical material presented in this book reveals some of the limitations of thinking about empowerment in such a linear way.

A deliberate action that contravenes a social norm may constitute an act of empowerment. But such acts may or may not have any effect on the acts of others; similarly, they may or may not make any difference in the longer term to the situation either of the actor or of other women. Acts may have entirely unintended outcomes, just as outcomes may be produced by entirely unrelated acts. Actions presumed to lead to empowerment – taking a loan, for example – may simply sustain women in their existing situation. External interventions aimed at producing empowerment may, similarly, fail to achieve the desired results precisely because there is a failure to understand the social dimensions of constraint, as well as the cultural limits of choice (Kabeer 2008). As Kalpana

Wilson (2008) notes, within this there is a reduction of women's exercise of agency to strategies for individual self-improvement, rather than struggles for transformation: 'liberal' as opposed to 'liberating' empowerment (Ferguson 2004; Sardenberg 2009). Looking beyond the obvious – towards hidden pathways of women's empowerment – becomes crucial if we are to understand change in women's lives. Aanmona Priyadarshini and Samia Afroz Rahim's account of what Bangladeshi slum women gain from watching TV (Chapter 14) is a good example of what can be learnt by looking beyond deliberate efforts to 'empower women' to what is happening in women's lives that is bringing about change. What comes to constitute a (potentially empowering) 'choice' is very context-specific. It depends not only on broader social, cultural, economic and political environments, but also on the circumstances of particular women.

What is experienced as empowering by one woman is not necessarily going to be so for every woman; empowerment for one can be disempowerment for another, or can even cause disempowerment *to* another. Terezinha Gonçalves, in Chapter 11, discusses how Brazilian domestic workers' rights are often neglected by their middle- and upper-class employers, who, freed from these tasks by their live-in worker, disrespect the role as a profession. In Pakistan, as Ayesha Khan notes in Chapter 5, in some cases in order for women to fulfil the often empowering job of Lady Health Worker, their daughters have to give up their education in order to shoulder the burden of housework. What may be available as a choice to one woman may be out of bounds for others, and it may be a matter of context whether certain kinds of choices can be constructed as 'empowering' at all.

Narratives of empowerment tend to evoke women taking power, doing what they please, shrugging off customs or constraints, making it for themselves. And yet when we look more closely at women's pathways of empowerment, and at what 'choice' may actually mean in their everyday lives, a rather different picture emerges. Sometimes what women actually want and do stray from the paths development organizations expect women to tread. But it is important to recognize and respect women's own perspectives and decisions, even if they may not appear to outsiders to be empowering. In a number of chapters in this collection, the kinds of 'choices' that are being made do not feature in any way in the development narrative. Yet they are no less important in women's lives. We find pathways of empowerment that wend through settings such as the Pakistani religious education classes studied by Neelam Hussain (Chapter 12) or an afternoon in front of the television enjoyed by Priyadarshini and Rahim's informants. Even though the importance of sport and other leisure activities as part of a positive and fulfilling lifestyle is taken for granted in the West, it is difficult for development agencies to countenance that the pleasures of leisure can be empowering. And yet, as UN Women official Anne Marie Goetz put it, 'it is time for us to recognize pleasure and leisure as a measure of women's empowerment'.[2]

Confronting stereotypes and changing norms

How women are portrayed in literature, religion and the media deeply affects how they are perceived and treated. For all the affirmative tone that development agencies take when extolling women's role in uplifting and enriching their communities and societies, these popular representations tell a different story. They include the message that a woman's education is secondary to a man's, that her unmarried state is a crisis, that if she is good she devotes her life to her family, that violence against her is brought on by her own immorality and that her abuse is a weapon of war. Cropping up in a number of chapters is the pervasive notion of what a 'good girl' or 'good woman' is and how she is expected to act; anything that kicks against these expectations is frowned upon, if not actively repressed. As Adomako Ampofo and Asiedu note, gender stereotypes purveyed through popular culture 'may serve as sites where models of behaviour (representation) become models for behaviour (warnings, advice)' (p. 141).

Stereotypes of the 'good woman' are in the stock-in-trade of the mass media. But international development organizations are also complicit in representing the deserving object of development in ways that are strikingly heteronormative, reinforcing a normative version of idealized heterosexual womanhood: the married woman who devotes her resources to sustaining her family. Obscured from view are those women who fail to conform to this norm, be they single, divorced or widowed, lesbian or transgender, or women engaged in businesses like sex work that meet with ambivalence or outright moral opprobrium. Pathways' research on changing narratives of sexuality (Pereira 2009, 2014) brings into view the restrictive effects that development's heteronormativity has on the ways in which women's empowerment can be imagined (Pereira 2009; Jolly, Cornwall and Hawkins 2013).

International NGOs, development banks and donors make much of these normative narratives of the deserving poor woman, deploying them to secure their own funds and legitimacy. Their use of the iconic image of the 'poor, powerless and pregnant' Third World woman (Mohanty 1988; Win 2004) may have given way to the smiling faces of 'empowered' women, but the story is still one in which the development agency plays the part of hero. Women's organizations face difficult choices about how to portray women's issues. In reflections on the dilemmas faced by a Bangladeshi feminist NGO in getting the tone right in advocacy for acid victims, Nazneen and Sultan (Chapter 9) consider the challenges in this context of navigating between representations that play to a sympathy that can be elicited from viewing publics, and the need to show women not as victims but agents.

Yet the limits of this agency become clear once we map representations onto the realities of what international development agencies actually do to address the situations women inhabit. The reduction of empowerment to 'assets' and 'institutional structures' plays a part in producing interventions that may simply provide women with the means to better endure their poverty, precisely because they have not sought the kinds of changes in consciousness and collective agency that are so vital to transformative change.

These are fundamentally about changing the very values and norms on the basis of which gender discrimination continues to thrive in societal, economic and political institutions. As Hania Sholkamy reminds us:

> Changing values and norms is not as simple as creating jobs or building roads. The hundreds of thousands (if not millions) of loans, schemes, health and rights classes and training sessions have bettered the lives of women at certain moments in time, but they have not transformed them or the web of relations in which they live and act. (2010: 257)

But this process of change is not only driven by intervention – indeed, in a number of chapters, we are reminded of the impact of broader economic and societal change on the way women are beginning to see themselves. Priyadarshini and Rahim, in Chapter 14, document conformity with normative ideals of women's position in society, alongside desire among the working-class Bangladeshi women they worked with for more positive and powerful representations of women. They cite students at Jahangirnagar University in Bangladesh:

> We should break with the stereotypes that are portrayed in the media: married women are always shown as busy making a home and tending to children; the good wife is the one looking after her in-laws and tolerating all manner of injustice; dark women are constantly shown trying to become fair and pretty – all this should change and new images and stories of women need to be depicted. (p. 283)

What we can see emerging from these stories are the new pathways of empowerment that are opening up with wider societal and economic change – enabling women to expand their imaginations, and to learn and employ tactics for negotiating power in their lives. As Priyadarshini and Rahim note, 'The space for fantasizing that television offers is limited only by one's imagination' (p. 289). Kabeer (personal comment) reports that the most reliable proxy indicator of empowerment emerging from the analysis of Pathways' large-scale quantitative survey of women in Bangladesh was access to television: not merely for the inspiration that women might gain from watching other women navigate power relations within intimate and domestic settings, so gaining greater control over their lives, but also as a means of opening up women's lives to the world around them and to a wealth of images and information that otherwise might have remained completely out of view.

Relationships matter

Mainstream empowerment narratives tend to neglect relationships, focusing on individual women's trajectories of self-improvement or on the bigger picture of society-wide economic change. Naila Kabeer and Lopita Huq's chapter places relationships at the centre, showing how a social relationship with a women's organization can prove stronger even than familial bonds (Chapter 13). They tell of how an NGO that was suffocated by donor desire for investment in a success story – the Bangladeshi women's organization Saptagram – was revived out of the love of its members. Precisely because it had invested so much in building relationships with the women, they came to see it as a cherished part of their everyday lives. They cite Rashida:

> I have learnt how to stand on my own two feet from Saptagram, the value of unity, how to overcome problems, how to mix with people, how to sign my name. And I have learnt about our rights. (p. 263)

The quote is revealing. Being able to 'stand on my own two feet' is a familiar enough indicator of empowerment, but this is set alongside other gains such as the value of unity, how to mix with people, 'our rights'. It attests to a more relational than individualistic view of autonomy (cf. MacKenzie and Stoljar 2000). Kabeer (1999) makes a point often forgotten by those who pick up more enthusiastically on her framework than on her analysis, cautioning against extracting women from the relational webs that constitute their social and economic lives. In this work, she highlights the centrality of relationships and especially of collective organization in empowerment:

> In a context where cultural values constrain women's ability to make strategic life choices, structural inequalities cannot be addressed by individuals alone.... Individual women can, and do, act against the norm, but their impact on the situation of women in general is likely to remain limited and they may have to pay a high price for their autonomy. The project of women's empowerment is dependent on collective solidarity in the public arena as well as individual assertiveness in the private. Women's organizations and social movements in particular have an important role to play in creating the conditions for change and in reducing the costs for the individual. (1999: 457)

Refocusing our attention on the relational dimensions of empowerment has substantial implications for how agencies and actors seeking to foster empowerment might better orient their efforts to generating the kind of empowering effects they wish to produce.

Hania Sholkamy's analysis (Chapter 6) of the empowering dimensions of a Conditional Cash Transfer (CCT) pilot programme that she was closely involved in designing, and on which she conducted participant observation on implementation in Egypt, reveals another important relational dimension: that between women beneficiaries and those involved in anti-poverty programmes. Rather than focusing only on what women gain from having access to the cash in cash transfer schemes, attention was placed on the quality of the relationships that women have with the front-line workers who administer the programme. Recognizing both the empowering dimensions for them, as workers, of training aimed at changing the ways they work and the empowering effects that this can have for the poor women who are their clients, Sholkamy's analysis points us towards the significance of placing greater emphasis on those who mediate such programmes and their role in transformation.

This emerges very directly in Ayesha Khan's account of front-line Lady Health Workers in Pakistan (Chapter 5). Khan draws on stories of the lives of Lady Health Workers that illustrate the interaction of paid work with circumstance and context to produce situations in which women experience positive change in their lives. This huge government programme, a major employer of women and a vital link between households and health services, offers women the kind of regular, predictable, income that Kabeer *et al.* (2013) find to be an essential constituent of successful economic empowerment initiatives. It also offers the expanded mobility that brings with it a concomitant expansion in their sense of their own horizons of possibility, and, with the growing visibility that this brings for women's paid work, the horizons of others. An important insight in Khan's work is the unevenness of women's experiences of 'empowering' interventions: she shows that what's empowering to one woman isn't necessarily empowering to others. Khan's exploration of what these new working lives have meant for women's individual and collective agency illustrates the centrality of relational agency in making sense of these changes.

Cecilia Sardenberg, in Chapter 15, illustrates other relational dimensions that are important to factor into our understanding of empowerment. Writing about women in a low-income neighbourhood in Brazil, she shows how change can take place amidst apparent continuity, when women's perspectives on their own relationships and entitlements change. Sardenberg illustrates how a tradition of matrifocal domestic arrangements and female employment in this context has offered women a degree of power within an otherwise patriarchal culture. What has changed, she suggests, is women's own recognition of their position. In particular, women have come to recognize the limits of ideals of conjugal relationships that were part of their own discourse in this community a decade ago: they are now freeing themselves from abusive relationships, and making their own decisions about where and whether to work, even if they face opposition from partners. Sardenberg's analysis attests to the significance of consciousness for women's empowerment and affirms the centrality of relationships, of the 'power with' that comes from being embedded in kin and community relationships of solidarity, principally with women, which enable women to gain the power to act.

Negotiating empowerment

Empowerment is a contextual, relational process that does not have predictable outcomes. Much in that process comes to depend on negotiation. Empowerment emerges from the studies in this book as something that is less about clear-cut choices that come to be translated into actions and yield specifiable outcomes, and more about provisional and dynamic relationships and experiences. Much depends on how women approach the situations they find themselves in, and the tools at their disposal to navigate and negotiate the difficulties they experience on their journeys.

Eileen Kuttab's account of strategies of resistance and accommodation that characterize the ways in which Palestinian women's movement actors and NGOs negotiate empowerment in the Palestinian context (Chapter 10) reveals some of the contradictions of conventional approaches. She reminds us of the importance of context, and of the need to situate strategies for women's empowerment on a larger political canvas:

> Women want not only access to resources, but also control over them. They want not only to participate in decision making through quotas for women, but to do so with full rights as equal citizens. Women don't want to work in any employment opportunity, but to be employed in protected and decent work. In such a situation women become empowered, and this is why this kind of empowerment cannot happen under colonial occupation and patriarchal domination. (p. 207)

Journeys of negotiation, accommodation and compromise that women's organizations undertake as they seek out and build alliances are captured in the chapters by Kabeer and Huq, Nazneen and Sultan, and Gonçalves. Rosalind Eyben picks up on this in her exploration of the strategies and tactics used by feminist bureaucrats engaged in 'gender mainstreaming' in aid organizations (Chapter 8), revealing some of the subversive tools feminist bureaucrats can draw on in negotiating empowerment within their organizations.

Contestation may provide women less scope for the exercise of agency than tactical accommodation and, indeed, compromise; choices that transgress societal norms may be especially hard to make, with risks particularly high for women who can least afford to take them. These negotiations are especially interesting for what they tell us about women's own assessment of opportunities and risks, and also for the way in which we make sense of their exercise of agency. They can be an essential part of women living their lives and achieving the most positive outcomes from situations not of their own making. Thus the kind of changes that we see in women's everyday lives is much more subtle, much more incremental, than that portrayed by development agencies in their narratives of empowerment. These come into view, for example, in Cecilia Sardenberg's ethnographic account of changes across generations of working class women in a Brazilian low-income neighbourhood (Chapter 15).

Sardenberg explores how shifting expectations shape women's everyday lives and choices, surfacing a host of inter-locking factors that together conspire to produce a disabling environment for women, but also – as women negotiate power in their intimate, domestic and family lives – open avenues for change that might otherwise remain completely hidden. Such openings also emerge in Neelam Hussain's account of the social life of the *dars*, or religious education classes, in Pakistan, and in excerpts from the lives of some of those who participate in them – an account that reveals empowering experiences that centre around women's negotiation of these spaces as sites for relational agency. Emerging from these chapters is a nuanced account of negotiation, accommodation and compromise that is a welcome corrective to representations that emphasize only the boldest conquests. They paint a rich picture of tactical engage-ment, highlighting the complexities that are part of any process of social change.

Conclusion

This book seeks to shed light on the play of power and empowerment in women's everyday lives in contexts where change is driven by a diversity of factors, from shifts in government policy to more diffuse social and economic changes stemming from new religious practices as well as changing economic opportunities. The lessons that emerge from these studies have a number of implications for those concerned with women's empowerment.

A key insight is that mechanisms for promoting women's empowerment – quotas, education and training, credit, legal reforms – are not in themselves sufficient to bring about women's empowerment. As Mulki Al-Sharmani notes:

> legal reforms (even the most emancipating ones) are not the end result. These reforms are only meaningful in so far as they actually lead to positive and substantive changes in the lives of those who are targeted by the new laws. (p. 46)

This process of transforming a potentially useful instrument into one that actually delivers what is said on the tin involves more than passing a law or adopting a particular kind of programme or approach. The finest policies and laws mean nothing if no one is held to account for their non-implementation, and if those charged with implementing them are themselves disempowered. Hania Sholkamy's exploration of an Egyptian experiment that sought to transform conventional conditional cash transfer programme design into one that could genuinely empower women offers many lessons. One of the most important is that closer attention should be paid to those delivering such programmes and their crucial role in women's empowerment – and indeed, as Ayesha Khan shows for Pakistan, the role of such programmes in their *own* empowerment. This resonates with key insights from empowerment writings of the 1990s, that remind us of a piece that is all too often missing from today's empowerment interventions: the significance of shifting people's consciousness of their own and others' capabilities, of building confidence and the power to act, as well as of expanding horizons of possibility.

Among the lessons to be learned from looking at what might be regarded as development's 'motorways' – magic bullet solutions – one of the most important concerns the implications of neglecting the significance of context. It becomes evident that while there may be merits in institutionalizing quotas and investing in girls' education, carbon-copy solutions cannot be rolled out to every region without looking at the bigger picture and appreciating the factors that might stymie potential benefits. To put it in development-speak: creating an 'enabling environment' within which women can empower themselves calls for the kind of analysis of power relations and cultural practices and dynamics that some agencies are beginning to do, pioneered by the Swedish International Co-operation Agency.

As the diverse studies in this collection show, significant changes in women's lives are taking place outside the range of conventional empowerment interventions. By focusing on understanding change in women's everyday lives, through a multiplicity of methods and entry points, these studies highlight issues that have been neglected by development agencies, such as relationships, leisure, faith, pleasure, love and care. They also illuminate the role that might be played by unconventional approaches to bringing about shifts in people's perceptions of self and other, and lead to changes in social norms and practices that act as a brake on women's – and men's – capacities to take advantage of opportunities and enjoy well-being, support and happiness in their lives. Popular music, creative writing and television soap operas, for example, have the potential to reach wider and deeper than many development interventions, permeating places that may be completely out of range of conventional efforts to change attitudes, beliefs and practices.

Perhaps most of all, what the contributors to this book emphasize is that empowerment is a complex process of negotiation, rather than a linear sequence of inputs and outcomes. Policies that view women as instrumental to other objectives cannot promote women's empowerment, because they fail to address the structures by which gender inequality is perpetuated over time. Women's own voices, analyses, experiences and solutions continue to be disregarded in the rush for results. It is time that more attention was paid to them. Rather than betting on a limited range of institutional interventions, governments and development agencies should invest in tackling deeper-rooted issues of power that impede transformative change. There is a long tradition of working with empowerment in feminist organizing, popular education and health promotion that holds important lessons. By enabling people to reflect critically on their lives, together, these approaches address a vital missing piece in today's empowerment interventions, that of developing a critical consciousness as a precursor to addressing, together, what needs to be done to dismantle those obstacles and create sustainable pathways to a more just and equal world.

Acknowledgements

We would like to thank Rosalind Eyben, Naila Kabeer, Mariz Tadros, Cecilia Sardenberg and Tessa Lewin for their comments on an earlier version of this introduction.

Notes

1   http://go.worldbank.org/V45HD4P100.
2   Speech given at 'Making Change Happen through Women's Collective Action', Pathways of Women's Empowerment/UN Women CSW Event, New York, 28 February 2012.

References

Alsop, R., N. Heinsohn and A. Somma (2005) 'Measuring Empowerment: An Analytic Framework', in R. Alsop (ed.), *Power, Rights and Poverty: Concepts and Connections*, World Bank, Washington, DC.

Batliwala, S. (1993) *Empowerment of Women in South Asia: Concepts and Practices*, Asian-South Pacific Bureau of Adult Education, Mumbai.

—— (1994) 'The Meaning of Women's Empowerment: New Concepts from Action', in G. Sen, A. Germain and L. C. Chen (eds), *Population*

Policies Reconsidered: Health, Empowerment, and Rights, Harvard Center for Population and Development Studies, Boston, MA.

—— (2007) 'Taking the Power out of Empowerment: An Experiential Account', *Development in Practice*, Vol. 17, No. 4/5, pp. 557–65.

Bisnath, S. and D. Elson (1999) 'Women's Empowerment Revisited', background paper for Progress of the World's Women 2000: a UNIFEM Report, UNIFEM, New York, NY.

Buvinic, M. and E. M. King (2007) 'Smart Economics', *Finance and Development*, Vol. 44, No. 2, pp. 7–12.

Cornwall, A. (1997) 'Men, Masculinity and "Gender in Development"', *Gender and Development*, Vol. 5, No. 2, pp. 8–13.

Dighe, A. and S. Jain (1989) 'Women's Development Programme: Some Insights into Partcipatory Evaluation', *Prshasnika*, Vol. 18, Nos 1-4, pp. 77-98.

Duckworth, N. and R. Cracknell (2013) 'Women in Parliament and Government', Standard Note SN/SG/1250, Social and General Statistics Section, House of Commons Library, London.

Eyben, R. (2010) 'What If the Girls Don't Want to Be Businesswomen? Discursive Dissonance in a Global Policy Space', *Development*, Vol. 53, No. 2, pp. 274–9.

Eyben, R. and R. Napier-Moore (2009) 'Choosing Words with Care? Shifting Meanings of Women's Empowerment in International Development', *Third World Quarterly*, Vol. 30, No. 2, pp. 285–300.

Eyben, R., N. Kabeer and A. Cornwall (2008) 'Conceptualising Empowerment and the Implications for Pro-Poor Growth', paper for the DAC Poverty Network, Institute of Development Studies, Brighton.

Ferguson, A. (2004) 'Can Development Create Empowerment and Women's Liberation?', paper presented at the 2004 Center for Global Justice Workshop 'Alternatives to Globalization', http://www.global justicecenter.org/wp-content/dev1.pdf (accessed 5 September 2013).

Folbre, N. (1994) *Who Pays for the Kids? Gender and the Structures of Constraint*, Routledge, New York, NY.

Gergen, K. J. (2009) *Relational Being: Beyond Self and Community*, Oxford University Press, Oxford and New York, NY.

Goetz, A. M. and C. Nyamu Musembi (2008) 'Voice and Women's Empowerment: Mapping a Research Agenda', Pathways Working Paper No. 2, Pathways of Women's Empowerment RPC, Brighton.

Israel, B., B. Checkoway, A. Schulz and M. Zimmerman (1994) 'Health Education and Community Empowerment: Conceptualizing and Measuring Perceptions of Individual, Organizational and Community Control', *Health Education Quarterly*, Vol. 21, No. 2, pp. 149–70.

Jolly, S., A. Cornwall and K. Hawkins (eds) (2013) *Women, Sexuality and the*

Political Power of Pleasure, Zed Books, London.

Kabeer, N. (1994) *Reversed Realities: Gender Hierarchies in Development Thought*, Verso, London.

—— (1999) 'Resources, Agency, Achievements: Reflections on the Measurement of Women's Empowerment', *Development and Change*, Vol. 30, No. 3, pp. 435–64.

—— (2008) 'Paid Work, Women's Empowerment and Gender Justice: Critical Pathways of Social Change', Pathways Working Paper No. 3, Pathways of Women's Empowerment RPC, Brighton.

Kabeer, N. with R. Assaad, A. Darkwah, S. Mahmud, H. Sholkamy, S. Tasneem and D. Tsikata (2013) *Paid Work, Women's Empowerment and Inclusive Growth: Transforming the Structures of Constraint*, UN Women, New York, NY.

Laclau, E. (1990) *New Reflections on the Revolution of Our Time*, Verso, London.

MacKenzie, C. and N. Stoljar (2000) *Relational Autonomy: Feminist Perspectives on Autonomy, Agency and the Social Self*, Oxford University Press, Oxford.

Malhotra, A. and M. Mather (1997) 'Do Schooling and Work Empower Women in Developing Countries? Gender and Domestic Decisions in Sri Lanka', *Sociological Forum*, Vol. 12, No. 4, pp. 599–630.

Malhotra, A., S. R. Schuler and C. Boender (2002) 'Measuring Women's Empowerment as a Variable in International Development', background paper prepared for the World Bank workshop on 'Poverty and Gender: New Perspectives', World Bank, Washington DC.

Mohanty, C. (1988) 'Under Western Eyes: Feminist Scholarship and Colonial Discourses', *Feminist Review*, Vol. 30, Autumn, pp. 61–88.

Moore, M. (2001) 'Empowerment at Last?', *Journal of International Development*, Vol. 13, No. 3, pp. 321–9.

Pereira, C. (2009) 'Interrogating Norms: Feminists Theorizing Sexuality, Gender and Heterosexuality', *Development*, Vol. 52, No. 1, pp. 18–24.

—— (2014) *Changing Narratives of Sexuality*, Zed Books, London.

Rowlands, J. (1997) *Questioning Empowerment: Working with Women in Honduras*, Oxfam Publishing, Oxford.

Sardenberg, C. (2009) 'Liberal vs Liberating Empowerment: Conceptualising Women's Empowerment from a Latin American Feminist Perspective', Pathways Working Paper No. 7, Pathways of Women's Empowerment RPC, Brighton.

Sen, G. (1997) 'Empowerment as an Approach to Poverty', Working Paper Series 97.07, background paper for the UNDP Human Development Report, UNDP, New York, NY.

Sholkamy, H. (2010) 'Power, Politics and Development in the Arab

Context: Or How Can Rearing Chicks Change Patriarchy?', *Development*, Vol. 53, No. 2, pp. 254–8.

Tadros, M. (2010) 'Introduction: Quotas – Add Women and Stir?', *IDS Bulletin*, Vol. 41, No. 5, pp. 1–10.

—— (2014) *Women in Politics: Gender, Power and Development*, Zed Books, London.

Wilson, K. (2008) 'Reclaiming "Agency", Reasserting Resistance', *IDS Bulletin*, Vol. 39, No. 6, pp. 83–91.

Win, E. (2004) 'Not Very Poor, Powerless or Pregnant: The African Woman Forgotten by Development', *IDS Bulletin*, Vol. 35, No. 4, pp. 61–4.

1
Legal Reform, Women's Empowerment and Social Change
The Case of Egypt
● ●
Mulki Al-Sharmani

Feminist legal scholarship over the past three decades has, on the one hand, shed light on the importance of law as a mechanism of oppression of women as well as a pathway to their empowerment, and on the other hand grappled with the complexities and contradictions of the roles that law and legal reform can play in the lives of women both at the macro and at the micro levels (Mackinnon 1987; Smart 1989; Mussman 1991; Thornton 1991; Boyd 1994; Kapur and Cossman 1994; Wang 2004). What this scholarship suggests is that both the potential transformative benefits of the law and the challenges it can pose for women lie beyond its functional role as a tool of claiming or denying rights. This work draws attention to the gendering nature and effects of the legal process itself, and the contribution that this makes to the construction and reproduction of discriminating and marginalizing gender norms.

The literature also suggests the need to pay close attention to processes through which legal reforms are introduced, debated and implemented in order to understand more fully the outcomes of these reforms, and their often mixed and contradictory effects on women. Kapur and Cossman (1994), for instance, argue that the process of legal reform is in fact more important than its outcomes because it is through the process that we can capture (and subvert) the discursive power of law and its complex interplay with other domains of the gendered lives of women and men (normative and social, for example). Writers also underscore the importance of understanding the multi-dimensionality of the process through which legal empowerment or disempowerment works and the need to recognize that multiple actors (rather than merely the state) can have considerable influence on this process and its outcomes (Smart 1989; Boyd 1994).

In Egypt, family laws were reformed in the 2000s with the aim of facilitating and enhancing women's access to legal justice and empowerment. In 2000, a comprehensive procedural law (Personal Status Law, PSL No. 1) was passed, granting women the right to obtain no-fault divorce (*khul*) in exchange for giving up their rights to dower and alimony. In 2004, new family courts were established introducing a mediation-based and family-sensitive legal process. In that same year, PSL No. 11 was passed, which set up a government fund through which female disputants are paid court-ordered alimony. Finally, in 2005, PSL No. 4 was passed, which extended divorced mothers' rights to child custody until their children (boys or girls) reach 15. The outcomes of these reforms, however, have been mixed and for the most part still fall short of addressing the inequalities and vulnerabilities from which women suffer.

This chapter seeks to shed light on the complexities and contradictions of these family law reforms. It draws on ethnographic research carried out in 2007–10[1] that included interviews with female and male plaintiffs, judges, mediation specialists, lawyers, legislators, women's rights activists, public thinkers, religious scholars and members of the religious establishment,[2] observation of court proceedings in family law cases, and a content analysis of court records. My analysis focuses on two issues, which complicate and perhaps diminish the transformative role that the new legal reforms can play in strengthening Egyptian women's rights and achieving gender justice. First, I argue that despite the recently passed laws, the institutional model of marriage that the state continues to uphold through its codes and court system is premised on gendered roles and rights for husbands and wives. This legal model of marriage, however, contradicts the realities of Egyptian marriages. Second, the incongruence between the agendas of different reform actors, their piecemeal approach, and their top-down and non-participatory strategies have had an inevitably mixed impact on the reform outcomes. This has meant that the multi-dimensionality and social embeddedness of the process of law making have not been taken into account adequately in the reform efforts undertaken by both state and non-state actors, thereby undermining the effectiveness and significance of these endeavours.

Constructing marriage in modern Egyptian family laws

Egypt, like all other Middle Eastern countries with the exception of Turkey, adopts family laws that are drawn from the doctrines of classical schools of Islamic law. Reform efforts thus have to engage with the model of marriage and marital relations that is sanctioned by Islamic legal schools. But is the Islamic model of marriage inherently discriminatory against women? [Abu Odeh (2004) and Mir-Hosseini (2003) argue that the main schools of Islamic jurisprudence share a gendered model of marriage in which the relations between husbands and wives tend to be hierarchical. In this model, Islamic marriage is based on a contractual agreement between a man and a woman in which the husband has the duty to provide for his wife and their offspring, and, in return, the wife makes herself available to him and puts herself under his authority and protection. The husband's exclusive right to his wife's sexual and reproductive labour is earned through and conditioned upon his economic role. This model of marriage does not recognize shared matrimonial resources. Whatever possessions and assets the wife brings to the marriage remain hers. Likewise, apart from maintenance for herself and her children, the wife cannot make claims to resources acquired by the husband during marriage. In addition, the husband has a unilateral right to repudiation and polygamy.

Nonetheless, the schools of Islamic jurisprudence show considerable difference in the specificity of spousal rights and duties; this plurality often worked for women, as historical studies of pre-codification eras in the Muslim world show (Tucker 2008; Hallaq 2009). In fact, historians who have studied the trajectories of modern Muslim family laws argue that the gender inequality and biases against women found in present-day family codes cannot be explained away by their religious sources. For example, Abdel Rahim (1996) and Sonbol (2005) have traced the discrimination against women that is embedded in modern laws to modernist notions of building cohesive nuclear families that could be disciplined and controlled by modern nation states. Sonbol argues that the process of codification of Muslim family laws was based not only on the doctrines of one or several Islamic legal schools, but also on borrowings from colonial European laws. She shows that the project of subject making and nation building that was undertaken by modern Muslim nation states in the twentieth century incorporated modernist European notions that perceived nuclear families as the essential building blocks for progressive and well-governed societies. This discourse shifted the purpose of marriage from regulating a contractual relationship between a man and woman to creating nuclear families and maintaining their cohesiveness. Modern nation states saw the nuclear patriarchal family as the institution in which individuals were reproduced as citizens and dutiful members of the nation. To enable families to fulfil their roles in the process of subject making, these states devised family laws that regulated the rights and duties of family members. Husbands were bestowed the responsibility of heading the family and providing for its family members. In return for the protection and financial support that women and children received from the husband/father, they owed him obedience and submission.

Article 1 in Egypt's first codified family code, PSL No. 25 of 1920, defines a husband's main role as being the provider for his wife, while the role of the latter is to be sexually available to the husband. The law, furthermore, makes a wife's right to her husband's financial support conditional on her fulfilment of her sexual role – she is expected to be physically available in the conjugal home. Article 11 in PSL No. 25 stipulates that a wife who is found by the court to be disobedient (*nashiz*) loses her right to her husband's financial support.[3] Disobedience is defined as a wife's refusal to reside in the conjugal home with her husband. The law stipulates that this home has to be adequate and safe and the court needs to ascertain that the wife's desertion was not due to a reason sanctioned by the social norms (*urf*). The law does not spell out what these reasons are, but it is commonly understood that these would include leaving the conjugal home to visit extended family or to seek education or health care. Whether a wife's leaving the conjugal home for work is considered a socially acceptable reason has been contested by litigants and judges. According to law PSL No. 100 of 1985, if a wife has written in her marriage contract that she holds a job, a husband cannot bring an obedience ordinance case against her on the basis of her going out to work.

The subsequent family code (PSL No. 25 of 1929) also granted both spouses rights on a basis that was unequal and discriminatory against women in many aspects. Men had an unfettered right to unilateral repudiation and polygamy, and they enjoyed full guardianship over their children; whereas women had highly restricted access to divorce and could not be the legal guardians of their children even when they were the custodial parents. The new Egyptian Child Law, which was passed in June 2008, grants custodial female parents guardianship over their children. However, existing personal status laws still deny this.

In 1979, the late President Sadat decreed PSL No. 44 of 1979, which included revolutionary reforms. PSL No. 44 protected working women from obedience ordinance suits from their husbands on the grounds of their leaving the conjugal home to work, and affirmed their right to spousal financial support. Other reforms included a wife's automatic right to judicial divorce if her husband enters into a new marriage without her having to prove injury; and her right to the conjugal home in the case of divorce if she has the custody of the children. The new law also legislated *mut'a* (indemnity) for women who are divorced by their husbands without their desire or fault (Fawzy 2004).

To avoid opposition from the religious establishment, Islamist groups and other conservative factions in society, President Sadat decreed the law at a time when Parliament was not in session. PSL No. 44 of 1979, however, was later annulled by the High Supreme Court in 1985 because the process through which it was passed was ruled to be unconstitutional. That same year, its replacement (PSL No. 100) was passed. The new law lacked many of the revolutionary articles of its predecessor.

Thus, marriage as constructed by the Egyptian modern laws is one in which a husband supports his wife and children, provides them with an adequate and safe conjugal home, and is considered by the legal institution as the guardian and leader of this family unit. In exchange, a wife is expected to fulfil the sexual needs of her husband, to be physically available in the conjugal home, and to care for the children, although she cannot claim guardianship over them. Her role is sexualized and her rights are unequal to her husband's. But does this institutional model of marriage fit with the lived experiences of Egyptian women and men?

Lived experiences of marriage

Marriage continues to be an important social institution in which Egyptians invest to seek stability, security and social acceptability as well as to forge social and economic alliances between families. For the women interviewed for this study, the process of getting married involved finding a partner, negotiating each partner's share of the costs of marriage, and entering into marriage with adequate protection against divorce and abandonment. However, these different aspects of the process were not necessarily congruent with one another. Negotiations and compromises had to be made. Some women strategized better than others, but many entered into marriages that were inherently based on precarious foundations such as reliance on meagre resources that were shared with in-laws; the husband's irregular employment status; discrepancy between husband's and wife's perceptions of their financial roles in the marriage and the realities of their economic needs; pursuit of partners with economic assets at the expense of emotional and educational compatibility; as well as the unequal and hierarchical legal rights and obligations of husbands and wives. Many of the interviewed women worked before marriage. Some continued to work after marriage either regularly or intermittently, while others gave up their jobs. But the majority of the women were sceptical about the notion that work strengthened their marital rights and relations.

The legal gendering of marriage takes place through the interplay between different state codes (labour, social security and family), which is often disempowering to women. It is not only the case that gendered notions of men's and women's roles in family laws contribute to labour or social security laws that discriminate against women and their spouses; in addition, labour or social security laws that discriminate against women destabilize their marriages. For example, widowed women are sometimes forced to enter into unregistered marriages (*urfi*), in which they can make no legal claim to financial support or inheritance from their second husbands, in order that they can keep the pensions of their deceased first partners. Also, in the course of this research, I have come across married women in their sixties whose husbands did not support their families because either they earned very little and intermittently from informal labour, or because they were absent partners who repeatedly abandoned and then returned to the conjugal home. The wives engaged in a variety of informal occupations to make ends meet and were at a stage of their lives in which they could no longer sustain work because of poor health. A number of these women were in the process of divorcing their husbands through *khul* because they wanted to be eligible for monthly payments from the state's social aid and assistance programme (SAA). According to SAA regulations, in order to receive monthly cash, female beneficiaries have to prove that they are in dire economic need and that they are divorced, widowed, or have been deserted by their husbands for at least four years. In fact, studies of government welfare in the past decade and a half show that programmes such as the

SAA are operated on the basis of a philosophy and work practice that gender the roles and needs of their female beneficiaries and expect them to be in abject poverty and without a male provider (Bibars 2001; Sabry 2005).

The new family courts: implementation challenges

Effective implementation of the new laws is impaired by a number of shortcomings, which in effect impede women's access to justice. For instance, the failure to obligate disputants to attend mediation sessions results in making pre-litigation mediation an ineffective resolution tool. In addition, lack of resources, enforcement mechanisms and adequate training of court personnel diminish the effectiveness of the alternative mechanisms of dispute resolution that the new court system offers.

Most of all, the legal process in the new court system is gendered through its discourse and practices. In this discourse, women are considered emotional and hasty, and therefore incapable of making rational decisions about ending their marriages. Some of the interviewed mediation specialists and court experts believe that women resort to *khul* hastily over petty reasons such as a disagreement over the colour of upholstery in the conjugal home. This scepticism about women's rationality, particularly when it comes to decisions about divorce, is also accompanied by practices that some mediation specialists and judges use when they attempt to reconcile disputants. A common practice is to warn the female disputant of the difficulties and stigma that await her if she becomes a divorced woman. In one of the observed court sessions, for example, the senior judge tried to persuade a plaintiff to reconsider her divorce claim by warning her that her young daughter would probably have a difficult life with limited marriage prospects and respectability if her mother became a divorcee through *khul*. In addition, this legal discourse depicts female sexuality as the object of her husband's control. It is assumed by lawyers and judges that it is men's legal obligation to guard the sexual honour of their wives. Thus, lawyers' briefs and court judgements often contain legal claims that are based on this notion. However, the texts of the substantive laws, while affirming men's financial obligation towards their wives, do not assign husbands an obligation to protect the sexual honour of their wives.

But women are appropriating the new laws in ways that are advantageous to their individual needs, albeit not necessarily enhancing collective gender equality and justice. For instance, the right to *khul* is being used by female plaintiffs for a variety of purposes such as to opt out of an abusive marriage without the hassle of proving harm, or to claim welfare benefits that they are denied because of their marital status and the specificity of their lived experiences of economic roles and needs.

Contrary to what the opponents of *khul* feared, it is not only rich women who are making use of this new legal right. In fact, my research shows that poor women and those with limited financial means are more likely to resort to *khul* than other kinds of divorce in which they do not need to relinquish their rights to alimony and the dower. This is because these women lack the financial and familial support needed to go through a long litigation process, which is common in cases of divorce on the grounds of harm or abandonment. But it is noteworthy that rather than *khul* being exercised by women as a right that is equivalent to men's right to unilateral repudiation, it is increasingly becoming a guaranteed pathway to what should have been a judicial divorce on the grounds of harm. The question is: is this outcome empowering to women?

Reform approaches and strategies: lessons learned

Recent legal reforms in Egyptian family laws were driven by multiple agendas and actors. Legislators, the judiciary and government officials were keen to get rid of the old court system, which was overloaded and inefficient, and replace it with accessible, affordable and effective legal services. This change required a concise and comprehensive body of procedural laws, and the establishment of a specialized legal system to handle all family law cases. But the government's efforts in reforming family law at the time also need to be understood within the context of competing and sometimes conflicting agendas. On the one hand, the government was constantly striving to assert its religious legitimacy by partaking in dominant religious discourses that regulate family relations and gender roles. On the other hand, the government saw family law reform as a means of modernizing the country, enhancing the development process, and maintaining the support of international organizations that fund the country's various development projects. These conflicting goals translated into an uneven process of reform in family law (Mashhour 2005; Moors 2003; Singerman 2005).

Abu Odeh (2004) points out that since the codification of family laws, apart from the attempt at revolutionary change by President Sadat in 1979, Egyptian legislators adopted a partial and gradual approach to reform in order to accommodate both the advocates for change and gender equality and the religious establishments. As a result, this approach did not seek to change the hierarchical model of marriage that is sanctioned by Egyptian PSLs, in which the husband provides for his wife and in exchange the former is granted more rights. However, Egyptian legislators, Abu Odeh adds, tried to restrict the power that was granted to husbands through a number of reforms such as extending a husband's maintenance duties towards the wife so as to include payment of the wife's medical expenses as well as food, clothes and shelter; granting the wife the right (albeit restricted) to judicial divorce; restricting the husband's right to unilateral divorce and polygamy through imposing financial deterrents such as payment of maintenance to a divorced wife during the waiting period (*idda*) and payment of indemnity (*mut'a*) to a wife divorced against her wishes. Women's rights activists for most of the past three decades had been following a similar approach of cautious and piecemeal reform. To pass the new laws, concessions were made. Contentious articles were camouflaged in procedural codes. One could argue that gradual changes and procedural reforms are not enough to achieve the goal of a new model of marriage and marital roles that upholds gender equality. Yet recent reforms have given women new legal rights and consequently more choices for women.

In the annual convention held in early November 2008, the National Democratic Party, the ruling party in the Egyptian government at the time, announced a new family code initiative. This announcement was the culmination of more than a year's efforts by the party's Women's Committee to review the current personal status codes, identify gaps and gender-biased articles, and propose changes. The party presented its proposed draft law to the Ministry of Justice. In addition to the ruling party, the Legislative Committee of the National Council for Women[4] also drafted a number of amendments to the substantive personal status laws. Government agencies are by no means the only entities who have been working toward reforming personal status laws. Women's rights groups have been very active in advocating for comprehensive legal reforms and have undertaken a number of initiatives to contribute to the process of conceptualizing and drafting a new law. There are a number of key proposals that feature in some way or another in the drafts put together by the government and women's rights organizations, although the exact details of the final drafts are not known. The proposed changes included: raising the minimum marriage age for women from 16 to 18; redefining existing marital roles in terms that are egalitarian and cooperative rather than hierarchical; abolishing a husband's guardianship over his wife and the latter's legal obligation to obey him; restricting the man's right to unilateral repudiation and polygamy; and granting mothers guardianship rights over their children.

Perhaps those proposed changes reflected a shift from a tradition of piecemeal and gradual reform approach to one that was more substantive and sought to address the root causes of gender inequality and injustice that are inherent in the existing laws. But the extent to which the new approach has been fully and effectively adopted remains to be seen. For one thing, reform strategies that were being used by the coalition of reformers were the same – top-down and lacking grassroots societal participation. In other words, the processes of formulating and advocating for new laws were still confined to workshops, seminars, conferences and meetings in which the coalition of reformers mobilize government agencies, members of the religious establishment and some representatives of the media. But many sectors of society were either unaware of or misinformed about the ongoing reform efforts. These sectors included Egyptian women and men at large (many of our interviewees did not have a good knowledge of the purpose and procedures of newly passed laws such as *khul*), more diverse public thinkers, the majority of the media, and religious scholars who are not associated with the government or the religious establishment. It followed then that, regrettably, none of these sectors had been involved in the ongoing reform efforts.

Legal anthropologists and feminist legal scholarship have deconstructed the myth of law as a rational positivist entity that exists separate from social structures and processes (Moore 1978; Shehada 2002). The decentring of law as an objective autonomous body of knowledge or as a bounded and powerful state institution means that we need to be cognizant of the social structures through which legal codes are constructed, interpreted, performed and appropriated. Thus, in 1979, when the late President Sadat decreed a new personal status law that allowed Egyptian married women to file automatically for divorce on the grounds of their husband's taking another wife, and protected working women from the charge of 'disobedience' and loss of spousal financial support, some of the loudest dissenting voices were those of judges – who felt that the new legislation was imposed on them and was in conflict with their (social) understandings of the institution of marriage. The law was revoked by the Higher Supreme Court a few years later on technical grounds. This illustrates the limitations of a top-down reform approach that fails to recognize the social embeddedness of law and does not link the process of law making to multi-layered engagement with different forces and domains in the society, with the aim of creating spaces in which new and just gender roles and relations can be collectively imagined and realized.

We are learning the same lesson from the unfolding story of the recent reforms in the family laws. Law making has to be integrally tied to law acceptance, and this is more likely to be achieved if legal reforms are part of a larger, multi-layered and grassroots-based movement for change. As Khalid Masud says, 'For me, the basic element of a legal system is its acceptability, for this reason, public participation in law making and law reform is inevitable' (2001: 13). And so, like Wang (2004), I contend that if law and legal reform are to play a meaningful role in the empowerment of women, they have to be experienced by the relevant actors (activists and citizens) not as a tool of state power – whether beneficial or detrimental – but as a process in which different actors/stakeholders (civil society, the state, citizens) participate and reach a consensus on a new system of norms and practices that enable the realization of egalitarian gender roles and relations.

Conclusion: towards just family laws

Egyptian substantive personal status laws prescribe and affirm a gendered form of marriage that is unjust to women. In this institutional narrative, wives are subordinate, dependent and sexualized. The realities of Egyptian women, however, demonstrate the contradictions and the limitations of the legal model of marriage. In real life, many Egyptian women are not financially dependent on their husbands. The model of spousal financial support in exchange for wifely obedience does not sustain healthy and happy marriages. And women suffer not only because of the contradictions between the legal construction of marriage and their lived realities, but also because of legal discrimination and marginalization. The changes in Egyptian family law in the past decade and a half have had a mixed impact on the legal empowerment of women. Women's rights to divorce have been expanded. A number of procedural reforms have been introduced to make the legal system in family dispute cases accessible, efficient and effective. But these procedural reforms have not been successful in transforming the gendered and hierarchical model of marriage that continues to be re-enacted through the existing substantive laws.

It is true that the new procedural reforms have created a momentum for change and started a journey towards a new and comprehensive substantive family code. Women's rights activists since 2005 have been seeking a new legal model of marriage that is based on equal rights and responsibilities between husband and wives. But such a marriage may entail a number of things that will affect women differently. For instance, in this kind of marriage, the wife may no longer enjoy the exclusive right to her own financial assets, which she may be obligated to contribute to the family if there is need. Moreover, it may follow that she will not be able to file for divorce on the grounds of lack of maintenance, if she is financially able. Will this model of marriage be just and good to all Egyptian women? On the one hand, the realities of many Egyptian marriages show that women contribute significantly to the financial support of the family. Yet, unlike their husbands, they do not acquire any legal rights from their financial role. But some women may be ambivalent or even opposed to being legally obligated to contribute to the conjugal household and to give up their claim to the financial support of the husband in exchange for equal marital and parental rights. What about women who are not generating income and do not wish to be employed in the labour market? How will their non-monetary labour be credited in the legal discourse?

The momentous events that have been unfolding in Egypt since 2011 may greatly impact on family law reform. The 25 January revolution ushered in a new era of people striving towards social justice, in which women have been visible and important actors. This transitional period has brought about great challenges and opportunities. On the one hand, some sectors of society (such as two organizations led by non-custodial divorced fathers, political actors belonging to or allied with Islamist political groups) have been trying to repeal the reforms introduced in divorce and custody laws. On the other hand, the latest draft constitution, which was put to referendum in January 2014, contains articles that bolster efforts to pass new family laws that are reflective of gender equality. Yet this same draft constitution also contains articles that could well undermine Egyptians' pursuit of a democratic and accountable form of governance and a structure of political processes that safeguard the human rights of citizens.

It remains the case that legal reforms (even the most emancipating ones) are not the end result. These reforms are only meaningful in so far as they actually lead to positive and substantive changes in the lives of those who are targeted by the new laws. This requires adequate and effective mechanisms of implementation and enforcement, on the one hand, and a supportive environment, on the other. The establishment of the latter takes time but it is more possible if the reform process is participatory and takes place at the grassroots level. In other words, reform strategies need to go beyond lobbying the government. What has been lacking in the processes and efforts of reforming Egyptian laws thus far has been the building of support among different sectors of society (religious scholars, Islamic NGOs, legislators, families and communities) through dialogue and awareness raising, and partaking in the process of imparting to new generations enlightened religious knowledge and sensibilities that are appreciative of justice, equality, and acceptance of and respect for others.

In short, those of us who are concerned with women's legal empowerment (whether as activists, policy makers or researchers) need to go beyond understanding and using law as merely a mechanism of granting or withholding rights. We need to heed the ways in which law also functions as a domain where meanings and norms about gender are shaped and contested, and which intersects and interplays with other domains, such as the economic, the social and the religious. And so, in our pursuit towards gender equality and justice, we need to work towards (and better understand) legal reform that is an organic part of a larger, multi-layered and transformative process of positive change.

Acknowledgement

This is an updated version of an article previously published in the *IDS Bulletin*, and we are grateful to Wiley-Blackwell for kind permission to republish it here.

Notes

1 For more on this research, see Al-Sharmani (2009, 2012, 2013).
2 These were religious scholars who are members of the Academy for Islamic Research, which is part of *Al-Azhar*. The Academy is in charge of reviewing draft laws to ensure their compatibility with the principles and injunctions of *Shari'a*.
3 Up until 1967, wives who were found disobedient by the court could be forcibly returned to the conjugal home if their husbands so wished. The practice was then abolished by a ministerial decree.
4 The National Council for Women was established by the government in 2000 to promote policies to strengthen women's rights and enhance their development and to monitor the implementation and impact of policies that pertain to women.

References

Abdel Rahim, A. (1996) 'The Family and Gender Laws in Egypt During the Ottoman Period', in A. Sonbol (ed.), *Women, the Family and Divorce Laws in Islamic History*, Syracuse University Press, Syracuse, NY.

Abu Odeh, L. (2004) 'Modernizing Muslim Family Law: the Case of Egypt', Oxford University Comparative Law Forum 3, http://ouclf. iuscomp.org/articles/abu-odeh.shtml (accessed 18 December 2009).

Al-Sharmani, M. (2009) 'Egyptian Family Courts: Pathway to Women's Empowerment?', Hawwa: *Journal of Women of the Middle East and the Islamic World*, No. 7, pp. 89–119.

—— (2012) 'Egyptian Khul: Legal Reform, Courtroom Practices, and Realities of Women', in R. Mehdi, W. Menski and S. J. Nielsen (eds), *Interpreting Divorce Laws in Islam*, DJOF Publishing, Copenhagen.

—— (2013) 'Qiwana in Egyptian Family Laws: Wifely Obedience between Legal Texts, Court Room Practices and Realities of Marriages', in Z. Mir Hosseini, K. Vogt, L. Larsen and C. Moe (eds), *Gender and Equality in Muslim Family Law: Justice and Ethics in the Islamic Legal Tradition*, IB Tauris, London.

Bibars, I. (2001) *Victims and Heroines*, Zed Books, London.

Boyd, S. (1994) '(Re)placing the State: Family Laws and Oppression', *Canadian Journal of Law and Society*, Vol. 9, No. 1, pp. 39–73.

Fawzy, E. (2004) 'Muslim Personal Status Law in Egypt: The Current

Situation and Possibilities of Reform through Internal Initiatives', in L. Welchman (ed.), *Women's Rights and Islamic Law*, Zed Books, London.

Hallaq, W. (2009) *Shari'a: Theory, Practice and Transformation*, Cambridge University Press, Cambridge.

Kapur, R. and B. Cossman (1994) *Subversive Sites: Feminist Engagements with Law in India*, Sage Publications, New Delhi.

Mackinnon, C. (1987) *Feminism Unmodified: Discourses on Life and Law*, Harvard University Press, Cambridge, MA.

Mashhour, A. (2005) 'Islamic Law and Gender Equality – Could There Be a Common Ground? A Study of Divorce and Polygamy in *Shari'a* Law and Contemporary Legislation in Tunisia and Egypt', *Human Rights Quarterly*, No. 27, pp. 562–96.

Masud, M. K. (2001) 'Muslim Jurists' Quest for the Normative Basis of *Shari'a*', inaugural lecture, ISIM, Leiden.

Mir-Hosseini, Z. (2003) 'The Construction of Gender in Islamic Legal Thought and Strategies for Reform', *Hawwa*, Vol. 1, No. 1, pp. 1–25.

Moore, S. F. (1978) *Law as Process: An Anthropological Approach*, Routledge and Kegan Paul, London.

Moors, A. (2003) 'Public Debates on Family Law Reform: Participants, Positions, and Styles of Argumentation in the 1990s', *Islamic Law and Society*, Vol. 10, No. 1, pp. 1–11.

Mussman, M. J. (1991) 'Feminism and Legal Method: The Difference It Makes', in M. Fineman (ed.), *At the Boundaries of Law*, Routledge, New York, NY.

Sabry, S. (2005) 'The Social Aid and Assistance Program of the Government of Egypt – A Critical Review', *Environment and Urbanization*, No. 17, pp. 27–41.

Shehada, N. (2002) 'Justice without Drama: Enacting Family Law in Gaza City Shari'a Court', PhD thesis, ISS, The Hague.

Singerman, D. (2005) 'Rewriting Divorce in Egypt: Reclaiming Islam, Legal Activism and Coalition Politics', in R. W. Hefner (ed.), *Remaking Muslim Politics: Pluralism, Contestation, and Democratization*, Princeton University Press, Princeton, NJ.

Smart, C. (1989) *Feminism and the Power of Law*, Routledge, London.

Sonbol, A. (2005) 'History of Marriage Contracts in Egypt', *Hawwa*, Vol. 3, No. 2, pp. 159–96.

Thornton, M. (1991) 'Feminism and Contradictions of Law Reform', *International Journal of Sociology of Law*, Vol. 19, No. 4, pp. 453–74.

Tucker, J. (2008) *Women, Family, and Gender in Islamic Law*, Cambridge University Press, Cambridge.

Wang, H. (2004) 'What Can Legal Feminism Do? The Theoretical Reflections on Gender, Law, and Social Transformation', *EurAmerica*, Vol. 34, No. 4, pp. 627–73.

2

Quotas

A Pathway of Political Empowerment

●●

Ana Alice Alcantara Costa

Over the last 25 years women, and especially feminists, have mobilized throughout the world to confront the problem of low levels of female representation in political office. The demand for equality between men and women in every public body has been present in feminist discourse from its beginnings. Feminist movements took shape around arguments for equality as a universal value, framed by the Enlightenment perspective that all human beings have the same rights by virtue of being human. This universalist perspective is the basis supporting the dominant notions of democracy and citizenship in modern societies, under the aegis of the liberal model as a mode of social and political organization that defends the same rights for all individuals based on the equality of these individuals before the law, and on the impartiality of this law in its treatment of all citizens.

Various theorists of democracy have listed the inclusion of women as one of the minimum conditions that define the democratic character of a society. For example Robert Dahl (1993: 29) includes within his minimum conditions for the exercise of democracy the existence of political parties and civil society organizations that promote equal participation of men and women. Anne Phillips (1996) notes that a liberal democracy usually considers that a promise of equality and participation is sufficiently met by legislation for universal suffrage, with an equal possibility for all individuals to take part in elections. However, this ignores prevailing social and economic conditions. As she

49

goes on to note, even in modern societies it is generally women who assume the responsibility of unpaid housework, reproduction and care. These are responsibilities that act as a powerful barrier to women's political participation. In addition, the fact that the cultural construction of politics is fundamentally male contributes to keeping those women at a disadvantage.

With a view to overcoming these obstacles to women's political participation, Anne Phillips (1996: 83) proposes three possible solutions:

1 A different sexual division of labour in production and reproduction, with equal sharing of the entire range of paid and unpaid work.
2 A modification in the work situation of politicians to make possible the participation of individuals with active parental responsibilities.
3 An elimination of the prejudices of the 'gentlemen's club' type among the electorate itself, or among those responsible for selecting candidates within parties, with affirmative action to encourage the election of women.

That feminists in recent years have directed their efforts mainly towards the third solution – affirmative action or quotas – demonstrates, Phillips believes, that they do not see much scope for achieving the first two.

This chapter reflects on the 'quotas for women' experience of Latin America, where their implementation, in a context of affirmative action policies, has figured as a major goal in women's struggles for access to power structures. It asks two main questions: To what extent have quota systems in Latin America served as a pathway of women's political empowerment? And what lessons can be learnt from this experience? In some countries, notably Costa Rica and Argentina, the introduction of quotas has produced changes in the balance of power, with women achieving significant levels of participation in legislative bodies. However, quota systems in many other Latin American countries have produced no such effect. Half a century since they gained the right to vote, Latin American women have come to recognize that, in practice, the right they fought for did not guarantee the right to be elected.

The struggle for suffrage and the democratic deficit

The struggle for women's right to vote in Latin America dates back to the latter half of the nineteenth century, though more concerted feminist mobilization came only in the two first decades of the twentieth century. Ecuador was the first country to give women the vote, in 1929. Brazil and Uruguay followed suit in 1932, and other countries in the 1940s. Paraguay (1961) and Colombia (1964) were among the last. Gaining the right to vote was followed by intensive efforts to enlist women voters, who now represent the majority in the electorates of most Latin American countries.

Until the 1990s the participation of women in formal representative power spheres was occasional, scarce and limited. Women were generally elected because they were the wives, daughters or sisters of well-known male politicians (Veneziani 2006). This is still common practice in many Latin American countries as a means to retain power in a family or social group. Women have played a major role in this game (Costa 1998). Only six women presidents have been elected by popular vote. Four of these were perfect examples of the model of political ascension as family heritage. Violeta Chamorro (1990–7), in Nicaragua, was the widow of Pedro Chamorro, journalist and leader of the non-Sandinista movement who opposed dictator Anastacio Somoza. In Panama, Mireya Moscoso (1999–2004) was elected President when she became the director of the Arnulfista Party on the death of her husband Arnulfo Arias, who was elected President of Panama three times. When Cristina Fernandez was elected President of Argentina in 2007, her candidacy – although she was a lawyer and senator with a political history of her own – represented the continuity of her husband, Nestor Kirchner. Equally, Laura Chinchilla, elected President of Costa Rica in

2010, had a career as an international consultant specializing in judicial reform and made a political career of her own, but also 'represents' a family established in national politics: her father twice served as Costa Rica's comptroller general.

The only two women who depart from this pattern are Michelle Bachelet, President of Chile from 2006 to 2010 and re-elected in 2014 – a doctor and the former Minister of Health and Defence, with a political history of autonomy and independence – and Dilma Rousseff, elected President of Brazil in 2010 after serving as Energy Minister: in her youth she participated in leftist student protests, and came from a family that, although wealthy, was non-establishment.

Table 2.1 Women in the executive

Country	% of participation in ministry offices	Local executive positions
Argentina	25.0	8.5
Bolivia	30.0	4.6
Brazil	14.3	7.5
Chile	36.4	12.1
Colombia	23.1	9.0
Costa Rica	37.5	9.9
Dominican Republic	17.6	11.3
Ecuador	32.0	6.0
El Salvador	15.4	8.0
Guatemala	25.0	2.4
Honduras	25.0	8.1
Mexico	20.0	3.0
Nicaragua	31.2	10.4
Panama	21.4	9.3
Paraguay	10.0	5.7
Peru	26.7	2.8
Uruguay	30.0	n.a.
Venezuela	18.5	7.2

Sources: IDEA (2007) and Llanos and Sample (2008)

Recently there has been an increase in the number of women in national executive roles, principally due to affirmative action. Llanos and Sample (2008, see Table 2.1) show that in Latin America the proportion of positions in the executive occupied by women rose from 8.4 per cent in 1996 to 24 per cent in 2007.

This expansion in the number of women in the executive appears strongest in countries that have developed a specific agenda to incorporate women in this sphere: Costa Rica (37.5 per cent), Chile (36.4 per cent), Ecuador (32 per cent) and Nicaragua (31.2 per cent). The counterpoint is countries like Venezuela (18.5 per cent), Dominican Republic (17.6 per cent), El Salvador (15.4 per cent), Brazil (14.3 per cent) and Paraguay (10 per cent), where the proportion of women ministers is still very low (Llanos and Sample 2008: 18). There is an inverse relationship between the proportion of women and hierarchical position: the higher the position in the hierarchy, the more unlikely it is to find women occupying these positions. In situations where executive power is accessed by elections and there is no quota system or affirmative action policy, there are fewer women still. The data in Table 2.1 clearly show this: even in countries where women's participation in the local executive is higher than 10 per cent – as in Chile, Dominican Republic and Nicaragua – it is still very low.

This low participation of women in formal power structures in Latin American countries does not mean that women have been excluded from political action, or more broadly from political participation. Many studies have shown the intensity and amplitude of women's participation, especially in social movements. Sonia Alvarez (1994) refers to the democratization process in many Latin American countries (like Chile, Brazil, Argentina, Paraguay, Uruguay, Bolivia, Peru) in the 1980s, and emphasizes the importance of women's participation in this process. Alvarez suggests that it was women who led protests against human rights violations, and who thought of creative solutions to community requirements neglected by the state. Women also played important roles in strengthening the trade union movement and in the struggle for land rights. Afro-Brazilian women helped create a growing movement around black consciousness and anti-racism; lesbians joined homosexuals against homophobia; academic women took up arms against the military regime and joined opposing parties. However, all this participation by women did not translate into real opportunities to access political power.

In many Latin American countries, the much-desired democracy that came after decades of military dictatorship left out the majority of voters, the female electorate. The promises of democratic equality weren't fulfilled. In all so-called democratic societies, women have had to struggle hard – as they continue to do – to have access to common rights enjoyed by any male citizen, like equal salaries for equal jobs, promotion opportunities, the right to physical integrity and the right to work.

Quotas in Latin America

Argentina was the first Latin American country to establish a quota system, when it altered its Election Code in 1961. Known as *Ley de Cupos*, this 'quota law' stated that 30 per cent of all candidates on party lists for the national elections should be women. The law was the result of Argentinian women's struggle in a process that started during military dictatorship. The women campaigners known as the Mothers and Grandmothers of the Plaza de Mayo were the first to go public and expose the military dictatorship's atrocities, and also the first to ask for a democratic state. At the same time, a vibrant women's movement developed, connected to movements that resisted military dictatorship. In the late 1980s, there was an intense effort to implement a quota policy, led by feminists with the help of women activists within the political parties.

Initially, taking their example from campaigns in European countries, women tried to negotiate with major parties to introduce quotas on their agendas. As the parties responded negatively, women came up with a new strategy: to influence the national electoral code, with the aim of making it mandatory for parties to include more women on their lists. In 1990, the Political Feminists Network was created, bringing together women in fifteen political parties. Their motto was 'with a few women in politics, women change; with a lot of women in politics, politics changes'. This network became the entity that struggled for the quota law to be approved (Marx *et al.* 2007). In November 1991, the law was passed, and in March 1993 it became a decree that defined more explicitly the mechanism for the quota. By 1994, however, it had become clear that even those parties that were abiding by the law were putting women in positions on the lists where they had no chance of being elected. This gave rise to a change in the *Ley de Cupos*, which established that women must be placed on the lists in positions where there was a real chance of success – one woman to every three positions on the list – and that if this law wasn't followed the party couldn't subscribe its list and would be out of the electoral process. Conflicts emerged as parties persistently placed women in third place, and feminists took out lawsuits to challenge them. As a result, further legislation was passed in 2000 to clarify that: (1) the electoral quota applies to all vacancies for political office; (2) the 30 per cent is a minimum; (3) the quota is only considered fulfilled when applied to all the offices that each party renews in the corresponding election. Despite these difficulties, the quota law in Argentina gave a significant boost to women's presence in the representative system. The percentage of women in politics has risen from 5.9 per cent in 1991 to 38 per cent in 2013.

The Argentinian experience has been an inspirational example for those seeking to implement quotas in other Latin American countries. However, it was the Platform for Action, emerging from the Fourth World Women's Conference in Beijing in 1995, that provided the impetus necessary for national governments to begin to approve affirmative action mechanisms. Less than five years after Beijing, ten countries in Latin America had adopted the quota system. Yet despite the fact that most of them established a 30 per cent quota, and all have in common the active engagement of feminist activists in putting forward proposals, building alliances and persuading political parties, the diversity of experience has been surprising.

Table 2.2 Quotas and electoral systems in Latin America

Country	Year quota established	Percentage of women before quota		Percentage of women 2013	Minimal quota according to the law	Pre-established office on the list	Kind of list
Argentina	1991	Lower House	6.0	37.4	30	Yes	Closed
		Senate	3.0	38.9			
Paraguay	1996	Lower House	3.0	17.5	20	Yes	Closed
		Senate	11.0	20.0			
Mexico	1996	Lower House	17.0	36.8	40	No	Closed
		Senate	15.0	32.8			
Bolivia	1997	Lower House	11.0	25.4	50	Yes	Closed
		Senate	4.0	47.2			
Brazil	1997	Lower House	6.4	8.6	30	No	Open
		Senate	6.3	16.0			
Costa Rica	1997	Unicameral	14.0	38.6	40	Yes	Closed
Dominican Republic	1997	Lower House	12.0	20.8	33	No	Closed
		Senate	–	9.4			
Ecuador	1997	Unicameral	4.0	38.7	50	Yes	Open
Panama	1997	Unicameral	8.0	8.5	50	No	Open
Peru	1997	Unicameral	11.0	21.5	30	No	Open
Venezuela	1997	Unicameral	–	17.0	30	No	Closed

Sources: Veneziani (2006); IDEA (2007); Llanos and Sample (2008); IPU (2013)

In the post-Beijing context, one of the first countries to establish the quota system was Costa Rica. Today it is one of the most successful experiences in Latin America. The struggle to implement the quota system in Costa Rica started in 1984, soon after the ratification by the United Nations of the Convention to Eliminate All Forms of Discrimination against Women (CEDAW). As a result of pressure on the part of women's movements, some parties started to create internal mechanisms to promote and guarantee women's effective participation in political office and in electoral lists. Despite all this mobilization, it was not until November 1996 that the law establishing a quota system was passed. It required parties to guarantee 40 per cent women's participation, not only in the parties' structure, but also in candidacies for public election (Montanho 2007). Like its counterpart in Argentina, the Costa Rican law had to undergo some modifications to incorporate sanctions for parties that did not abide by it, whether by not fulfilling the 40 per cent rule or not positioning women in offices with real possibilities of being elected. In the first election after the law in 1998, it was clear that even parties in compliance with the quotas had put forward women with a scant chance of election. As a result, just two more women were elected compared to the 1994 elections (Perez 2008). In 1999, in response to demands from the Women's National Institute, the Supreme Court established that women should constitute 40 per cent of the candidates lists, in eligible positions, and included mechanisms to guarantee that the law would be respected. Significant amongst these measures were the requirement that public campaign financing guaranteed equal access to party resources for all candidates, and the prerogative given to the electoral tribunal to refuse to register parties who did not comply with the quota law. More recently, in 2007, Costa Rica's national gender equality policy included, among its main issues, the need to enhance women's participation in politics, setting out the goal of equal political participation in all decision-making spheres by 2017 (Montanho 2007). A new law intended to become effective in time for the 2014 election, stipulates a 50 per cent quota for women in the assembly, with strict alternation on the electoral lists (IDEA 2013).

When changes in the numbers of women entering political office as a result of quota systems became evident in Costa Rica and Argentina, Ecuador and Peru began to implement quotas. Although the outcome has been less marked for Peru, both these experiences are important because of the mechanisms used. In 1997, Ecuador established a 20 per cent quota, but initially this did not produce much in the way of results as parties failed to comply with the ranking rules (IDEA 2013). In 2000, under pressure from mobilization by women, the 'Election Law' or 'Political Participation Law' was changed, establishing a 30 per cent quota and a gradual increase of 5 per cent in every election until the balance of 50 per cent is reached. The mobilization was based on Article 102 of Ecuador's constitution, established in June 1998: 'the State will promote and guarantee the equal participation of women and men as candidates in popular election processes, in directional and decision-making spheres of public life, in justice management, public security and political parties' (Government of Ecuador 1998). A new constitution introduced in 2010, together with the Electoral Law of 2009/2012, have provided firmer guarantees of compliance with the electoral quota, lifting women's representation in the assembly to 38.7 per cent.

In Peru, the Congress of the Republic approved the quota law in 1997, establishing a 25 per cent share in municipal elections and in the National Congress. Article 10 of the Municipal Election Law established that the candidates list must be presented in a single document, in which the position of these candidates is made explicit, and in which there is a 25 per cent minimum of men or of women. In December 2000, this minimum quota increased to 30 per cent (Massolo 2007). Alejandra Massolo's study of women's political participation in local spheres in Latin America points out that a fundamental element in Peru's success in the quotas system – despite an open list and the weakness of sanction mechanisms – was the action of four institutions: the Manuela Ramos Movement, the Social Communicators Association (CALANDRIA), the Social Studies and Publishing Centre (CESIP) and the Centre of Studies for Development and Participation (CEDEP) (ibid.). These institutions outlined a women's political promotion programme, PROMUJER, which conducted an intensive conscientization programme to make women aware about politics and to prepare women candidates politically.

Other significant experiences, not so much because of their success but because they exemplify the kinds of problems that can arise, are those of Venezuela and Brazil. In Venezuela in 1997 it was made mandatory that political parties and electorates include a minimum of 30 per cent of women candidates in electoral lists. In 1998, at the time of the first election after this law was implemented, the quotas system was considered unconstitutional by the Electoral National Council, as it was deemed contrary to the equality principles established in the Venezuelan Constitution. Later, the Supreme Court supported this decision. In 1999, the new constitution established for the first time a clear and explicit principle of equality, making clear the difference between formal equality and effective, real equality. The new constitution also gives power to the executive, judiciary and legislative to implement positive actions, whenever they are needed in order to guarantee real and effective equality (Prince 2008). In 2005, after a great deal of struggle on the part of the feminist movement, based on claims using the equality text that is in the Bolivarian Constitution, a new resolution was passed establishing equality and balance in parties' lists. Because this law is still very frail and there is no system that can hold its non-implementation to account, it has done little to expand Venezuelan women's participation in politics.

The Brazilian experience with quotas is the least successful on the continent. Despite gaining political citizenship in 1934 and constituting the majority of Brazil's electorate, Brazilian women haven't managed to be real citizens – exercising an equal right not only to vote, but also to be elected – despite having a female President! Women occupy less than 10 per cent of the electable offices in the country, ranking close to the bottom of the international register (Ballington 2007). Brazil's quota law was passed in 1995. It established that a minimum of 20 per cent of a party's candidates should be women. Applied in the 1996 elections, it wasn't enough to alter the picture of Brazilian women's political exclusion. It was succeeded, in 1997, by a law that made it mandatory to have a minimum of 25 per cent of women candidates in the 1998 elections, and to increase to 30 per cent in the following election. Today the law 'ensures' that

30 per cent of the candidates presented by parties at municipal, state and federal levels should be women. But it is a law that is still to find its declared force.

Before the quota law was passed, Brazil had already experienced a range of other kinds of political quotas. In 1991, the Workers' Party (PT) passed a quota requiring a minimum of 30 per cent of each gender in the directorate of the party. In 1993, the Unified Workers' Central (CUT) did the same thing, demanding no fewer than 30 per cent and no more than 70 per cent of people from each gender. Despite quotas, the increase in women's participation has been minimal. There is no sanction, and so no penalty for parties who don't comply. Transforming this law has been a major challenge for the women's movement. In September 2009 a new electoral law was approved in the National Congress, which represents some small gains for the women's movement. Women had advocated for 30 per cent of the public funds that are given to parties to be spent on the political education of women; the new law proposed 5 per cent, and that each party which did not do this would be obliged to spend an additional 2.5 per cent in the following year – but no specific penalties were defined for those who did not comply. In addition, the law stipulates that at least 10 per cent of the time available to political parties for party political broadcasts on radio and TV should be used to promote women's participation in politics (the original demand of the women's movement was 20 per cent). Finally, the new law maintains the quota of 30 per cent but, while emphasizing that this is an obligation, it does not establish any kind of punishment for parties that do not comply.

The difficulties that women face in prevailing on the National Congress to respond to their demands is a reflection of their political force in this space, where they occupy less than 10 per cent of the seats. Women are absent at the tables where negotiations take place, and experience many constraints on their political effectiveness. Their submersion in a sea of male and party interests makes it difficult to imagine them playing a more active role in modifying or reforming laws. There is an evident paradox between the force of political mobilization of the Brazilian feminist movement and their real representation in the spheres of political implementation and deliberation. Women's absence in power structures in Brazil also determines the opportunities they have for intervention, their capacity for democratic transformation, and their ability to constitute themselves as political actors able to make demands (Costa 2008).

Quotas: a pathway to equality?

A superficial analysis of the outcomes of the adoption of quotas in Latin America can lead to the impression that this experience hasn't been able to alter women's participation in power structures significantly. We can see that, except in a few cases, the indices for women's presence in formal politics are still very low, with only small increases in the wake of the implementation of quota systems. Yet to regard this as evidence that quotas are not pathways to women's political empowerment is to miss the important point that a quota system on its own is not enough to bring about the kind of changes that are needed for women to achieve a greater share of representation in political institutions. Laws by themselves do not ensure greater political representation. As Dahlerup (2003) notes, to work effectively quota systems need to be complemented with programmes that build the capacity of women candidates and women in elected office.

Many studies have also demonstrated that the success or failure of quota systems is directly related to the characteristics of the country's electoral system, to the degree of explicitness in setting out the rules that support measures to increase the representation of women – including elements of design that make it more difficult to relegate women candidates to unelectable positions, to the lowest places on the list, or to positions as surrogates – and to the participation of civil society in monitoring implementation and the application of rules, including sanctions (Veneziani 2006). Some of the countries where quotas have been most successful, amongst them Argentina, use a closed list system, with candidates listed in priority order. The electorate votes for the list in its totality, with no possibility of altering its order. If the quota law defines the position women should occupy in this list, the possibility of success is guaranteed. If the legislation does not mention anything about where women should be placed on the list, parties tend to put them at the end, decreasing their chance of being elected. According to Jones (2000), to make a closed list system effective, the laws that refer to the quota system must include a specific determination of the position to be occupied by women on the list-positioning mandate. The legislation establishes mechanisms to make it mandatory, as well as to make it possible to hold parties to account for non-compliance. This is what happens in Argentina, Bolivia, Ecuador and Paraguay, where the law determines that if the party does not fulfil the quotas, it cannot register its candidates. In Peru, Brazil and Panama, the legislation does not specify the position in which women should be placed on the list, nor does it establish mechanisms to hold parties to account. This kind of quota policy tends to fail in its goal of increasing the presence of women. If there is no express determination to include women in positions on the lists, the whole point of the quota tends to be lost, given that party decisions are generally in men's hands.

Conclusion

The experience of the quota system in Latin America suggests a number of broader lessons for other countries where efforts are being made to expand the numbers of women in political office. The first is that quota systems alone are not sufficient to create the conditions for women to empower themselves politically: quotas are not automatic pathways of political empowerment for women. But when quotas are complemented with public policies to promote equality that can create deeper transformations in the patriarchal structure in society, with a view to expanding democracy, then they can serve as a route to change.

The principal lesson from the experience of quota systems in Latin America is the need for a strong women's movement that can make effective demands. What we see in these diverse experiences is the importance of the pressure that women's movements have brought to bear – their role in developing proposals, establishing alliances and mobilizing the political parties. It is within the political parties that the process of convincing needs to be the most intense. It was only after the activism of feminists within the political parties that the quota system in Argentina and Costa Rica was approved. To have the party as an ally is one of the most indispensable pathways in the process of changing laws. Another lesson emerging from the Latin American experience relates to how the quota system is applied. For quotas to work there needs to be a clear set of rules and procedures, which cover a range of mechanisms for legal punishment and restraints on those who do not comply with the provisions made within the law. Experience shows that an electoral system with closed lists, alternating positions in the list according to sex, and a comprehensive system of incentives and punishment may contribute favourably to the success of the quota system. Ultimately, women's right to equal representation in formal political systems needs to be recognized as a fundamental part of the project of democratization that – in Latin America – remains incomplete as a result of the continued exclusion of women from politics.

In Brazil, the legacy of the military dictatorship has led to resistance to getting involved in party structures, and feminists only have a very limited presence in most political parties. This confines the space they have to negotiate demands. Even in the parties with a significant number of feminist activists – such as the Communist Party or the Workers' Party – there is a tendency among these women to preserve party consensus, or toe the political line defined by the male majority, to the detriment of feminist demands. This positioning became explicit in the vote for political reform in August 2008 in the National Congress, when some deputies – though committed to the demands presented by the women's movement for a closed list, party loyalty, resources for women candidates and so on – voted in plenary according to agreements made with their parties, forgetting totally the agreements they had made with the women's movement. A paradox of feminist activism within political parties is exactly the subordination of women to the authoritarian and patriarchal practices established in the name of party discipline. We know that quotas by themselves are not sufficient to change the patriarchal structures of society. There has been a trend in the majority of countries where quotas have been implemented towards significantly favouring the election of women with links to the hegemonic sectors. In general, women are elected who are linked to the dominant political groups with more conservative agendas, thus making use of the prerogatives of the quota system. This has been the case in Costa Rica particularly. It is important to recognize that an increase in the number of women within representative structures does not signify the empowering of women as a collective subject, or even the existence of a critical consciousness regarding their condition of subalternity or the guarantee of a mechanism for confronting dominant patriarchal structures. However, these are not grounds for invalidating the use of quota systems as an important mechanism for expanding the access of women to formal power, nor for seeking to maintain women's exclusion from power. Guaranteeing equal participation for women in the structures of power is a question of democracy, of guaranteeing democratic rights. Women *have the right* to occupy these spaces under equal conditions to those of men.

Acknowledgement

A version of this chapter was previously published in the *IDS Bulletin*, and we are grateful to Wiley-Blackwell for their kind permission to republish it here.

References

Alvarez, S. (1994) 'La (Trans)formación del (los) Feminismo(s) y la Política de Género en la Democratización del Brasil' (The Transformation of

Feminisms and the Politics of Gender in the Democratization of Brazil), in M. Leon (ed.) *Mujeres y Participación Politica*. *Avances y Desafios en América Latina* (Women and Political Participation: Advances and Challenges in Latin America), Tercer Mundo, Bogota.

Ballington, J. (2007) 'Implementando Medidas Especiais: Tendências Globais' (Implementing Special Measures: Global Trends), Seminário Trilhas do Poder das Mulheres. Experiencias Internacionais em Ações Afirmativas (Seminar on Women's Pathways of Power: International Experiences in Affirmative Action), Congresso Nacional, Brasilia.

Costa, A. A. A. (1998) *As Donas no Poder: Mulher e Política na Bahia* (Mistresses of Power: Women and Politics in Bahia), Assembléia Legislativa da Bahia/NEIM-UFBa Coleção Bahianas, Salvador.

—— (2008) 'Construindo um Novo Contrato: o Feminismo e a Democracia Paritária no Contexto da Reforma Política de 2007' (Constructing a New Contract: Women and Party Political Democracy in the Context of the Political Reform of 2007), paper presented at the II Seminário Internacional Enfoques Feministas e o Século XXI: Feminismo e Universidade na América Latina (2nd International Seminar Focusing on Feminists in the 21st Century: Feminism and the University in Latin America), Universidade Federal de Minas Gerais, Belo Horizonte.

Dahl, R. (1993) *La Democracia y sus Críticos*, Paidós, Barcelona.

Dahlerup, D. (2003) 'Quotas are Changing the History of Women', paper presented at the conference 'The Implementation of Quotas: African Experiences', Pretoria, 11–13 November.

Government of Ecuador (1998) 'Constitution of the Republic of Ecuador', approved 5 June 1998, http://www.ecuanex.net.ec/constitucion/ (accessed 2 January 2009).

IDEA (2007) *Political and Electoral Reform in Latin America 1978–2007*, International Institute for Democracy and Electoral Assistance, Stockholm.

—— (2013) 'Quota Project: Global Database of Quotas for Women', http://www.quotaproject.org, International Institute for Democracy and Electoral Assistance (accessed 7 August 2013).

IPU (2013) 'Women in National Parliaments', http://www.ipu.org/wmn-e/classif.htm, 1 July, International Parliamentary Union (accessed 7 August 2013).

Jones, M. P. (2000) 'El Sistema de Cuotas y la Elección de las Mujeres en América Latina: el Papel Fundamental del Sistema Electoral' (The System of Quotas in the Election of Women in Latin America: The Fundamental Role of the Electoral System), in *Impacto de los Sistemas Electorales en La Representaciòn Política de las Mujeres* (The Impact of Electoral Systems on the Political Representation of Women), http://www.celem.org/prog_europeos/demo_paritaria2000/pdfs/capitulo01.pdf (accessed 17 December 2009).

Llanos, B. and K. Sample (2008) *30 Anos de Democracia: En la Cresta de la Ola Participación Política de La Mujer en América Latina* (30 Years of Democracy: Riding the Wave? Women's Political Participation in Latin America), International Institute for Democracy and Electoral Assistance (IDEA), Stockholm.

Marx, J., J. Borner and M. Caminotti (2007) 'Cuotas de Género y Acceso Femenino al Parlamento: los Casos de Argentina y Brasil en Perspectiva Comparada' (Gender Quotas and Women's Access to Parliament: The Cases of Argentina and Brazil in Comparative Perspective), http://pnud.mediagroup.com.ar/boletines/2007/42/Notas/IMG/Cuotas_de_genero_en_Argentina_y_Brasil.pdf (accessed 2 January 2009).

Massolo, A. (2007) *Participación Política de las Mujeres em el en el Ámbito Local en América Latina* (The Political Participation of Women at the Local Level in Latin America), Instituto Internacional de Investigaciones y Capacitación de las Naciones Unidas para la Promoción de la Mujer, Santo Domingo, Dominican Republic.

Montanho, S. (2007) 'A Contribuição das Mulheres para a Igualdade na América Latina e no Caribe' (The Contribution of Women to Equality in Latin America and the Caribbean), paper presented at the 10th Regional Conference on Women in Latin America and the Caribbean, 6–9 August, Quito, Ecuador.

Perez, N. (2008) 'La Cuota Mínima del 40% de Participación Política de las Mujeres en Costa Rica: a Diez Años de su Implementación' (The Minimum Quota of 40% of Women's Political Participation in Costa Rica: Its Implementation over Ten Years), presentation at Seminario Internacional una Década de Cuota Femenina en America Latina: Balance y Perspectivas para la Participacion Politica de la Mujer (International Seminar of a Decade of the Women's Quota in Latin America: Balance and Perspectives for the Political Representation of Women), 13–15 October, Santo Domingo, Dominican Republic.

Phillips, A. (1996) 'Deben las Feministas Abandonar la Democracia Liberal?' (Should Feminists Abandon Liberal Democracy?), in C. Castells (ed.), *Perspectivas Feministas en Teoría Política* (Feminist Perspectives on Political Theory), Paidós, Barcelona.

Prince, E. G. (2008) 'Analisis de La Situación de la Participación Política de las Mujeres en Venezuela' (Situation Analysis of Women's Political Participation in Venezuela), paper presented at Seminario Violencia, Salud y Derechos Políticos con Perspectiva de Género, 31 July, Friedrich Ebert Foundation, Caracas.

Veneziani, M. (2006) *Experiencias Latinoamericanas: Mecanismos de Cuotas a Favor de la Participación Política de las Mujeres* (Latin American Experiences: Quota Mechanisms in Favour of the Political Participation of Women), UN International Research and Training Institute for the Advancement of Women (INSTRAW), Dominican Republic.

3

Advancing Women's Empowerment or Rolling Back the Gains?

Peace Building in Post-Conflict Sierra Leone

● ●

Hussaina J. Abdullah

When the Sierra Leone civil war was declared over in January 2002, the concept of women's empowerment was firmly entrenched in development discourse and practice. Engaging with the aftermath of the brutalities of rape, gang rape, sexual slavery, forced pregnancy and abduction – among other atrocities to which women and children, especially girls, were subjected during Sierra Leone's eleven years of civil war – was firmly on the post-war agenda. There was a groundswell of protest from women's NGOs and activists demanding the protection and promotion of women's rights as part of peace negotiations, post-conflict reconstruction and peace consolidation processes. As the Government of Sierra Leone (GoSL) noted in its medium-term economic framework, the Poverty Reduction Strategy (PRS) 2005–7:

> The economic, social, cultural and political status of women in society has been identified as a major determinant of the poverty status of a country. Recognition of their role and empowering them is critical to poverty reduction at household level and overall na-tional development. (GoSL 2005: 104)

Sierra Leone's reconstruction and peace consolidation policies and programmes are pursued within the post-conflict peace-building framework (UN 1992). Within this framework, women and gender issues have been articulated through a series of UN Security Council resolutions, such as 1325 (in 2000),

1820 (in 2008), 1888 and 1889 (in 2009), 1960 (in 2010) and 2106 and 2122 (in 2013). These resolutions specifically address women's rights in post-conflict societies, their participation in reconstruction processes, their protection from violence, and the strengthening of justice systems. For instance, resolution 1325, the premier declaration on Women, Peace and Security, clearly links sexual violence as a weapon of war with the pursuit of peace and security, and outlines a legal structure for addressing these concerns at various levels.

Hence, it focuses on 'the responsibility of all states to put an end to impunity and to prosecute those responsible for genocide, crimes against humanity, and war crimes including those relating to sexual and other violence against women and girls, and in this regard, stresses the need to exclude these crimes, where feasible, from amnesty provisions'. Furthermore, the resolution calls for 'all parties to armed conflict to fully respect international law applicable to the rights and protection of women and girls ... and to bear in mind the relevant provisions of the Rome Statute of the International Criminal Court'. It states further that the protection of and respect for the human rights of women and girls should be included in all peace negotiations and implementing agreements.

To further consolidate the Women, Peace and Security agenda, the UN released two reports – 'Report of the Secretary-General on Women, Peace and Security' and 'Report of the Secretary-General on Women's Participation in Peacebuilding' – on the tenth anniversary of the adoption of resolution 1325. The outstanding element in the latter report, which looked at women's needs and participation in post-conflict reconstruction and transformation and peace-building processes, was the stipulation that 15 per cent of all UN-managed post-conflict financing funds should support projects that 'address women's specific needs, advance gender equality or empower women' (UN 2010). While this framework has a transformatory edge, it does not go far enough to ensure women's empowerment. Its application in post-conflict Sierra Leone is disjointed and full of loopholes that can be used to roll back whatever gains women have achieved. This chapter explores and reflects on this outcome.

Women's empowerment in a post-conflict context: two different entry points

The Association of African Women for Research and Development (AAWORD) and Development Alternatives for Women in a New Era (DAWN) were pioneers of the empowerment approach to development in the late 1980s. Srilatha Batliwala, one of the leading scholars advocating an empowerment approach, declared that:

> The goals of women's empowerment are to challenge patriarchal ideology, to transform the structures and institutions that reinforce and perpetuate gender discrimination and social inequality, and to enable poor women to gain access to, and control over, both material and informational resources. (1994: 130)

The empowerment approach advocated by feminists and their organizations gives primary importance to women's demand for political change along with the political will of state actors to bring about change. Feminists put individual and group empowerment (including that of poor women) at the centre of their discourse. They see empowerment as the basis for social transformation. Measures for creating the change are political mobilization, legal changes, consciousness raising and popular education.

The UNDP's flagship publication on development, the *Human Development Report*, on the other hand, sees empowerment as 'people's participation in and benefit from development' (UNDP 1995: 1). A five-point agenda on how women can be empowered is given: (1) legal reforms; (2) better employment opportunities for women; (3) a minimum of 30 per cent of women in politics and public decision-making spaces; (4) universal female education, improved reproductive health care and increased credit facilities; and (5) increased international and national support for programmes that will create more economic and political opportunities for women (*ibid.*).

While these two approaches see the process of women's empowerment as a multi-dimensional project, their focus and solutions differ greatly. Feminists emphasize group mobilization and engagement with the status quo; the UNDP/UN family approach stresses a conducive environment and giving opportunities to individual women to enable their access to the system. Both these discourses inform the meaning and practice of women's empowerment in post-war Sierra Leone by the GoSL and the UN system. In spite of their differences, the two conflicting methods have a point of convergence as a result of women's activism at the global level. Women and gender issues have been placed at the centre of the international peace and security agenda in an attempt to ensure women's safety and security in situations of conflicts and during post-war reconstruction and peace-building activities at both national and local levels.

As a result, Truth and Reconciliation Commissions (TRCs) have been established, legal reforms and constitutional review processes have been instituted to tackle the structural causes of inequality in post-war societies, and national action plans for the implementation of resolution 1325 have been developed. For example, the TRC in Sierra Leone noted that women were targeted systematically during the war, and suffered some of the worst atrocities, which the Commission notes were based on pre-existing notions of gender relations and women's marginalized position in society (GoSL 2004). As a result, the TRC recommended the repeal of all discriminatory laws and practices in both statutory and customary laws, and the enactment of laws to promote gender equality and women's empowerment. Also, the Sierra Leone National Action Plan (SiLNAP) on resolutions 1325 and 1820 was adopted and added to the country's policy framework on gender equality to 'engender' the country's reconstruction and peace-building programme, and a Constitution Review Process was undertaken in 2007.

Operationalizing women's empowerment in post-conflict Sierra Leone

The operational guidelines and functions of the Ministry of Social Welfare, Gender and Children's Affairs (MSWGCA), the government's focal point and coordinating agency for gender issues in the country, does not include the empowerment of women (GoSL 2007). In 2000, however, the Parliament of Sierra Leone passed two gender policies, namely the National Policy for the Advancement of Women and the Policy on Gender Mainstreaming (GoSL 2000a, 2000b). These two policies contained broad statements of the government's agenda on women and gender issues. The National Policy for the Advancement of Women seeks to improve women's status by eliminating discrimination against women in society. In particular, the policy states that the government will 'provide a conducive environment, which will allow women to improve their status and participation, to empower them and enhance their capacities as agents of change and beneficiaries of political and economic development, thus ensuring the full use of human resources for national development' (GoSL 2000a: i). The gender mainstreaming policy outlines the government's commitment to a gender-sensitive approach in its development objectives and programmes. The gender equality policy framework was strengthened with the adoption in 2010 of the National Gender Strategic Plan (2010–13) and the SiLNAP. These two frameworks are closely aligned to the government's PRSP 2, 'The Agenda for Change'(GoSL 2008).

The GoSL spells out broad policy commitments in its Poverty Reduction Strategy Papers (PRSPs) 1 and 2, the National Gender Strategic Plan 2010–13 and, more recently, in PRSP 3, the Agenda for Prosperity for the 2013–18 national development cycle. In PRSP 1, the GoSL identified four issues as obstacles to Sierra Leonean women's empowerment: (1) gender-based violence; (2) barriers to economic empowerment (access to markets, training, finance, technology, education, counselling, and entrepreneurship development to build social capital); (3) exploitative or hazardous forms of livelihood of poor unskilled women and girls, especially commercial sex workers; and (4) the need for sensitization and education on gender and development issues (GoSL 2005: 104). A series of Acts were to follow. The Local Government Act of 2004 stipulated a minimum of 50 per cent female representation in the Ward Committees; the Child Trafficking and the Anti-Human Trafficking Acts were passed in 2005; Parliament also adopted the gender acts on the Registration of Customary Marriages and Divorce, Devolution of Estate, and Domestic Violence in 2007; and the government presented a periodic report (covering the first five stages) on the implementation of the Convention on the Elimination of All Forms of Discrimination against Women (CEDAW) to the CEDAW Committee in New York in May 2007.

In PRSP 2, or the 'Agenda for Change' (2008–12), the GoSL notes that its goal for gender equality and women's empowerment is in line with the third Millennium Development Goal (MDG 3) to 'eliminate gender disparity at all levels with a special focus on secondary education for girls, sexual and reproductive health and rights; time-saving infrastructure; effective property and inheritance rights; formal employment and equal employment opportunities; participation and representation of women in politics and public administration; and ending violence against women' (GoSL 2008: 94). The GoSL then rolled out the nine programme activities it intends to pursue to achieve women's empowerment, including:

- Launch a temporary affirmative action plan that stipulates a 30 per cent quota for women in elective and appointed positions;
- Set up an Independent Gender Commission to promote gender equitable development, and undertake focused, evidence-based, action-oriented research and advocacy;
- Domesticate CEDAW into Sierra Leonean law;
- Increase micro-credit facilities for women, and provide training in budgetary and implementation matters;
- Build the capacity of women through education, training and access to capital (GoSL 2008: 95).

Regrettably, none of these initiatives was implemented during the four years of the Agenda for Change, though it must be noted that the Chieftaincy Act (2009) (giving women the right to contest at the highest level of local government[1]) and the Sexual Offences Act (2012) were enacted. And following women's renewed activism just before the November 2012 presidential, parliamentary and local government elections (questioning the government's gender equality agenda), the government re-committed itself – in PRSP 3, the Agenda for Prosperity (A4P) for the 2013–18 development cycle – to focusing support and resources on accelerating the achievement of gender equality and women's empowerment. Toward this end, a presidential Gender Adviser was appointed to liaise between executive, legislature and civil society, and gender equality was designated both as a cross-cutting issue to be mainstreamed across all seven pillars of the A4P and as a stand-alone pillar to move the state's agenda forward. In addition to the usual outlining of its programmes for women's empowerment, the GoSL has committed itself to enacting gender equality legislation based on the principles of affirmative action, establishing a Women's Commission and em-barking on a coordinated 'gender awareness and action' initiative across and among ministries, departments and agencies (MDA) (GoSL 2013: xvi).

There is little if anything here that relates to the kind of meanings that feminists have associated with the term 'empowerment', such as political mobilization and consciousness-raising activities, legal reforms, access and control to economic and livelihood resources and the political will by the powers-that-be to ensure transformational change.

The UN's intervention in post-conflict Sierra Leone has metamorphosed in line with the institution's international peace-building framework. The original mandate of ·the United Nations Assistance Mission in Sierra Leone (UNAMSIL) – the UN's peacekeeping force during 1999–2005 – did not include women and gender issues, but subsequent revisions in 2000–3 took note of issues of sexual violence and other violations of women's and children's rights (Date-Bah 2006: 16). The United Nation's Development Assistance Framework (UNDAF) (2004–7) and its revised version (2006–7) were the UN system's first consolidated programme engagement in Sierra Leone's post-war efforts. The original UNDAF focus was on recovery and humanitarian assistance, while that of the revised version was on 'peace consolidation and development, the achievement of the MDGs and aligning its priorities to the country's PRS' (UNDAF 2006: 2). UNDAF, it is said, reflects 'a rights-based strategic and result-driven approach' (UNDAF 2006: 2). This shift reflects the UN–GoSL view of the country's move from recovery and humanitarian assistance to peace consolidation and longer-term development.

This resulted in the creation of the United Nations Integrated Office in Sierra Leone (UNIOSIL). UNIOSIL's mandate was to 'enhance political and economic governance, build national capacity for conflict prevention, and prepare for elections in 2007' (UNDAF 2006: 2). Women and gender issues were marginal to it and were mentioned only once: assistance to the government is to include 'developing initiatives for the protection and well-being of youth, women and children' (UN 2005: quoted in Date-Bah 2006: 32).

The revised UNDAF was built around the following five outcomes reflecting the GoSL's PRS pillars:

- Transparent, accountable and democratic governance advanced at national and local levels;
- Increased production, availability, accessibility and utilization of food with improved employment opportunities for youth;
- Improved health for all citizens, especially women of child-bearing age and children under five years of age;
- Intensified response for HIV and AIDS prevention, care and support;
- Strengthened capacity of key national and local institutions for reconciliation, security, improved governance and respect for human rights. (Date-Bah 2006: 3)

These outcomes included gender equality as a cross-cutting issue, alongside capacity building and youth employment. Some of the possible outputs for women were enhanced knowledge and information on democratic processes, poverty reduction issues and MDGs; increased nutrition for pregnant women; knowledge, skills and positive attitudes towards business, entrepreneurial development and self-employment; and reduced morbidity from malaria. In 2008 UNIOSIL was replaced by the United Nations Integrated Peacebuilding Office in Sierra Leone (UNIPSIL), whose stated aim is to 'provide support to the GoSL in identifying and resolving tensions and threats of potential conflict, monitoring and promoting human rights and consolidating good governance reforms' (UN 2008b). UNIPSIL's gender mandate is to recognize the role of women as outlined in resolutions 1325 and 1820, to integrate gender perspectives in programming activities, and to work with the GoSL in this regard (UN 2008b). To further this mandate, UNIPSIL and the UN Country Team (UNCT) initiated a new consolidated intervention strategy to incorporate the latter's political mandate and the UN agencies' development agendas. This effort resulted in the Joint Vision Document (JVD) for the 2009–12 development cycle. Although gender equality is still a cross-cutting issue to be applied across all programme areas, the JVD states how the UNCT intends to intervene to promote this goal:

> The UN Family through its various programmes will promote the rights of women through the accelerated implementation of CEDAW, Resolution 1325 and 1820 as well as Sierra Leone's National Gender Strategic Plan. (UN 2009a: 5)

This new intervention strategy is being implemented under Programme 17, entitled 'Gender Equality and Women's Rights', and managed by UN Women (UNW), formerly the United Nations Development Fund for Women (UNIFEM), in collaboration with the UNCT's Gender Theme Group and other development partners. At the initial phase, UNW's intervention focused on implementing the Peacebuilding Fund

(PBF) initiative in collaboration with the MSWGCA, NGOs and community-based organizations (CBOs). This initiative aims to promote and protect women's rights and guarantee their safety by popularizing the Gender Bills that were adopted by Parliament in 2007 in two of the country's administrative regions, the Northern and Southern provinces. Other women-focused, PBF-funded projects include strengthening the integration of gender and women's issues in security sector reform processes at the local level; the construction of safe houses for the protection of gender-based violence (GBV) survivors in two provinces; and support for a commission of enquiry to investigate allegations of sexual abuse and violence after a political fracas between the two main political parties in Freetown in April 2009.

The meaning of women's empowerment being bandied about by the GoSL and the UN system in Sierra Leone is the mainstream approach: it lacks the political mobilization and consciousness raising for structural change that feminists have demanded as the bottom line in the empowerment process. While the GoSL is formulating public policies to empower women, the UN's mandate to engage in the country has tended to marginalize women in their policy framework. This difference in their policy construction, even while working within the same framework, highlights the complexities involved in empowering women in a non-emancipatory structure. The difference between international- and national-level discourses does not augur well for the future of the women's empowerment project, because of the current dominance of the mainstream agenda.

The practice of women's empowerment in post-war Sierra Leone

The practice of women's empowerment by the GoSL and the UN system in Sierra Leone is directly related to their understanding of the concept. The GoSL, since the end of the 11-year civil strife, has initiated a wide-ranging set of reforms as part of its women's empowerment project. While the government's effort is indeed extraordinary in a society in which gender discrimination, abuse and violence are ingrained in everyday practices, it still has to be noted that its legal reforms on inheritance, bodily integrity and marital relations are being promoted within a discriminatory framework. The 1991 Constitution, which is the basis of governance in Sierra Leone, includes a Bill of Rights guaranteeing the human rights and freedom of all citizens, and outlaws discrimination on the basis of sex, religion and political views – but it also has a provision in Section 27 (4) (d) that nullifies the above:

> Subsection (1) shall not apply to any law so far as that law makes provision: 'With respect to adoption, marriage, divorce, burial, devolution of property in death or other interests of personal law'. (GoSL 1991)

This caveat (which is yet to be repealed) puts Sierra Leonean women in a limbo of having rights they cannot exercise because of the contradictory provisions contained in the constitution. Another contradiction in the government's women's empowerment project relates to the issue of affirmative action and gender quotas for women seeking political office. While the Constitution Review Committee (CRC) objected strongly to women's demands for a 30 per cent quota, the government promised in PRSP 2 to introduce a temporary policy in women's favour. The government has failed to say how it intends to marry this promise with the CRC's objection, and why the policy will be temporary rather than permanent. A third shortfall in the government's agenda for women lies in its inability to confront the hard economic issue of land tenure reform in order to grant women rights to inherit lands from their fathers and husbands. The post-war economy – in which men have been killed or refused to return home, 70 per cent or more of the people live in rural areas, and women account for over 50 per cent of the country's population – makes a mockery of the inheritance bill, as there are no corresponding land reform bills acknowledging women's independent land rights.

In response to the international agenda on Women, Peace and Security, the MSWGCA has taken various initiatives. It celebrates the annual 16 Days of Activism as an advocacy project on gender violence to raise awareness and increase support from stakeholders in addressing the issue. It has established the Family Support Unit (FSU) within the Sierra Leone Police to respond to cases of domestic violence and all forms of child abuse. It has formed the National Committee on Gender-Based Violence (NaC-GBV), and developed both a National Referral Protocol for child victims/survivors of SGBV (Sexual and Gender-Based Violence) and a referral pathway for all categories of SGBV in the country. In addition, both the police and the military have adopted a gender equality policy to protect women against sexual harassment and ensure equality in promotion and recruitment processes. The Special Court's sentencing of senior members of the three main factions in the country's civil war for rape and other acts of sexual violence against women acted as a signal that impunity for sexual crimes will not be tolerated. And in 2011 the Saturday Courts were established to expedite the trial of SGBV cases.

While the GoSL can be said to be 'talking the talk' and making the right noises about women's empowerment, it is failing to put its money where its mouth is. Resource allocation for gender programmes has been meagre. For example, the MSWGCA's annual budgetary allocation between 2005 and 2010 has hovered between 1.1 and 2.7 per cent[2] of the sectoral allocation, and between 0.2 and 0.7 per cent of the national budget (AfDB 2011: 11). Hampered by its poor financial and technical capacities, and in spite of its inter-ministerial mandate, the MSWGCA is one of the weakest and least influential ministries on the national political scene (*ibid.*).

Like the GoSL, the UN system's practice of women's empowerment in the Sierra Leone field office does not reflect its global gender agenda. As already noted, UNAMSIL's original mandate did not include any substantive gender provision. This oversight was rectified with the appointment of a presidential Gender Adviser (GA) in 2000. With its expanded mandate, UNAMSIL provided capacity-building training for government agencies, NGOs and civil society groups on gender and sexual violence; organized public debates on UNAMSIL's radio on domestic violence, gender equality and CEDAW; trained local women in voting and the electoral process in the 2002 general election and the 2004 local elections; offered technical support to the Truth and Reconciliation Commission and the Law Reform Commission; and promoted knowledge and observance of international instruments, particularly in reporting to the CEDAW Committee and in popularizing resolution 1325 (Date-Bah 2006: 16). These achievements were attributed to the commitment of the Special Representative of the Secretary-General (SRSG), Ambassador Daudi Mwakawogo, who gained a reputation for being 'more committed to gender mainstreaming than his predecessor' (*ibid.*: 20).

However, the job description, staffing conditions and the location of the GA within the mission's structure have been subjected to intense scrutiny. The GA's position, from its creation, was peripheral in the mission's structure unit until 2005, a year to its drawdown, when it was moved to the office of the SRSG. This move was significant as it raised the profile of gender within UNAMSIL, the Sierra Leonean population, and the entire development community in the country. However, the unit was grossly understaffed: one person had to undertake the enormous task of gender mainstreaming and sensitization of over 17,000 UNAMSIL personnel, liaise between the mission and the GoSL, on one hand, and engage with a wide range of development actors within the country on the other (*ibid.*).

The drawdown of UNAMSIL and the creation of UNIOSIL was seen as an opportunity to carry forward the former's gender and peace-building activities. This did not happen, as UNAMSIL's exit strategy lacked a strong gender input and the transitional plan did not include 'a sex breakdown of most of the outcomes and progress indicators' (*ibid.*: 32). UNIOSIL's staff structure, like UNAMSIL's, did not include the post of a GA. However, a GA was appointed in 2007 and the office was downgraded to its original location, the human rights division. Despite these shortcomings, UNIOSIL noted that it encouraged the appointment of a Commission for the Implementation of Resolution 1325 and the establishment of gender theme groups in governance and leadership with a view to empowering women to participate in decision-making bodies; it also collaborated with NGOs to monitor and evaluate government commitment to promoting women's political participation through legislation and enforcement, and to the economic empowerment of women (WIPSEN 2008).

UNIPSIL's holistic political and development mandate gives it a more robust standing to push through the UN's international gender and peace-building agenda in its field operations in Sierra Leone, because of the existence of resolutions 1325 and 1820. Unfortunately, instead of a boost, we are experiencing a further marginalization of gender issues in the UN's field operations in post-conflict Sierra Leone. For example, UNIPSIL does not have a GA within its structures. The post of a GA is currently being manned by the National Professional Civil Affairs Officer, who acts as a gender focal person in the Political Affairs and Peace Consolidation Section. She doubles up her civil affairs portfolio with being UNIPSIL's gender focal point (see Date-Bah 2006 for a detailed discussion of this on UNAMSIL). Her position is weaker than that of the GAs who served UNAMSIL (before it was upgraded into the SRGS's office) and UNIOSIL: she is a national programme officer and, in the structure of the UN system, has absolutely no decision-making power. Furthermore, UNW, the lead agency for women's empowerment, is grossly understaffed. The Sierra Leone field office currently has two programme staff, a National Programme Officer and a Programme Officer. The post of Country Programme Manager has been vacant for almost two years.

Even though UNIPSIL's mandate is political, and gender issues are political concerns, they are marginalized in the allocation of resources. Of the expected US$345 million for the 2009–12 funding cycle, only US$7 million (or 2 per cent of the budget) has been allocated to women's empowerment projects. While it can be argued that because gender is a cross-cutting issue in the UNCT's programming framework it will be mainstreamed across all projects, our analysis of PBF-funded projects proves the contrary. Apart from the UNW and MSWGCA women-focused projects, all the other projects that included both women and men did not include a sex breakdown in their outcomes and outputs.

The UNCT, like the GoSL, has incorporated new issues into their work that reflect responses to the international agenda, the GoSL's policy and development programme, and women's civil society demands. For example, under the auspices of UNIPSIL, the All Political Party Women's Association (APPWA)[3] was established in response to President Koroma's pledge of honouring women's demand for a minimum 30 per cent quota in politics and public affairs. Through this initiative, political party women for the first time in the history of the country started working together and strategizing to push forward their issues within their various political parties. Consequently, all the major political parties developed gender policies to negotiate with if the 30 per cent quota were to be instituted. UNW funded a Campaign School for female political party aspirants to strengthen their bids in party nomination processes, and the Women's Situation Room to ensure a violence-free election and women's safety and security during the 2012 electoral process. The UNDP's support provided training of competitive female contestants for the 2012 elections process. UNICEF provided assistance to the MSWGCA to develop both the National Action Plan on GBV in 2012 and the National Referral Protocol on GBV to complement the Sexual Offences bill.

Since the government has recommitted itself to execute a more gender-responsive agenda in its third legislative and development cycle since the end of the civil war, it has reconstituted a new CRC to ensure that all discriminatory clauses in the constitution and laws are repealed and/or amended. UNW supported both the MSWGCA and the Ministry of Finance and Economic Development with a consultant who assisted with making the A4P gender-sensitive, and has promised to provide support during the implementation and monitoring phases of the programme to make sure that gender equality issues are incorporated all through the process. In the same vein, UNW will provide a consultant to assist in the upcoming UNDAF process. In the legislative arena, UNW has supported the MSWCGA with a consultant, who will review the constitution and all laws to identify the various gender discriminatory clauses for presentation by the MSWGCA to the CRC.

Women's lives in post-war Sierra Leone

In spite of progress in the legal and policy arenas and the establishment of institutions to promote and protect women's rights and their empowerment, traditional gender roles, customs and social norms still prevail in the country. Women continue to face structural discriminations in all spheres of life due to various legal loopholes within the country's legal structure, weak institutional and human capacities to implement the new laws, and their own lack of knowledge of the existence of the new laws. As a result, poverty, illiteracy, early and forced marriages, and social and physical insecurity characterize women's everyday lives. Finally, neither the GoSL nor UNCT have adhered to the UN's call on budgetary allocation in funding gender equality and women's empowerment programmes.

While the country has moved from its unenviable position at the bottom of the UNDP's Human Development Index (HDI), its Gender Inequality Index (GII) value of 0.643 ranks Sierra Leone 139th out of 148 countries in the 2012 rankings (UN 2013c).[4] In the Social Institutions and Gender Index (SIGI) of non-members of the Organisation for Economic Co-operation and Development (OECD), Sierra Leone ranks 66th out of 88 countries. SIGI's ranking, based on five criteria (SIGI 2012),[5] notes that the establishment of new laws and institutions has not brought qualitative changes in women's everyday existence. Not only are rape and physical violence commonplace, but the conviction rate is low and the culture of silence condoned by society breeds impunity. A very worrying feature of sexual violence in post-war Sierra Leone is the very young age of both the victims and perpetrators, which means no one is safe. At the political level, the number of women representatives, positioned to advocate for the strengthening of legal instruments and the promotion of women's rights, has shrunk in every electoral cycle since the end of the election – from 14.5 per cent in 2002 to 13.5 per cent in 2007, and then to 12.9 per cent in 2012.

Conclusion

While it can be argued that considerable progress has been made in the gender equality arena, a lot of challenges remain. This is because the meaning of women's empowerment being used by the GoSL and UNCT in Sierra Leone is the mainstream version or what Cornwall has termed 'empowerment lite':

> It sounds like the real thing, borrowing words from the feminist lexicon, although often in combinations that deprive them of their bite. And it seems to be doing just what feminists have been doing and demanding for decades: from organizing women into groups to providing training, resources and rules that get more women into work and politics. (Cornwall 2007)

In relation to practice, women's empowerment in post-civil-strife Sierra Leone is beset with a myriad of problems – from inadequate resource allocation to the piecemeal application of women's empowerment, the barriers presented by the legal system, and the marginalization of gender issues in the political and development discourses in the country. The question to ask is why is it so difficult to translate the international gender and peace-building agenda (gender standards and policies) at the national and/or grassroots levels? In other words, why is there such a huge gap between theory and praxis at the international and national/local levels? This is due to the fact that the gender components (resolutions 1325 and 1820) of the peace-building agenda, which were a product of feminists and women's advocacy and activism, but have been added onto the liberal peace framework and its 'main components' – democratization, the rule of law, human rights, free and globalized markets, and neo-liberal development (Richmond 2006: 292) – are now the subject of intense scrutiny from various perspectives. Liberal peace theory is being criticized primarily for its focus on governance reform and the non-inclusion of issues such as character, agency and the needs of civil society in its proposals. If feminist activists, scholars and policy makers want to make the international peace-building agenda and women's empowerment project emancipatory, they need to reclaim the discourse from the neo-liberal establishment and chart the way forward.

Acknowledgements

This is an expanded version of an earlier paper by Hussaina Abdullah and Aisha Fofana-Ibrahim entitled 'The Meaning and Practice of Women's Empowerment in Post-Conflict Sierra Leone' published in *Development*, Vol. 53, No. 2 (June 2010).

Notes

1 However, two women were not allowed to contest for the Paramount Chieftaincy in their chiefdoms in 2010, because subsection (1)(b) of Section 8 of the Act includes the proviso 'where tradition so specifies'.
2 The Gender Directorate's share of the Ministry's sectoral budgetary allocation is between 0.75 and 1.35 per cent.
3 Membership of APPWA included female political party executives, MPs and local government councillors.
4 The index reflects gender-based inequalities in three areas: reproductive health, empowerment and economic activities.
5 Family code, physical integrity, son preference, civil liberties, and property rights.

References

AfDB (African Development Bank) (2011) *A Multi-Sectoral Country Gender Profile of Sierra Leone*, ADB, Tunis.

Batliwala, S. (1994) 'The Meaning of Women's Empowerment: New Concepts from Action', in G. Sen, A. Germain and L. C. Chen (eds), *Population Policies Reconsidered: Health, Empowerment and Rights*, Harvard University Press, Boston, MA.

Cornwall, A. (2007) 'Pathways of Women's Empowerment', http://www.opendemocracy.net/article/pathways_of_women's_empowerment (accessed 8 June 2013).

Date-Bah, E. (2006) 'Evaluation of Gender Mainstreaming Work and the Impact of United Nations Assistance Mission in Sierra Leone (UNAMSIL)', UN Department of Peacekeeping Operations, New York, NY.

Government of Sierra Leone (1991) 'Constitution of the Republic of Sierra Leone', http://www.sierra-leone.org/laws/constitution1991.pdf (accessed 3 June 2013).

Government of Sierra Leone (2000a) 'Policy on Gender Mainstreaming', Ministry of Social Welfare, Gender and Children's Affairs, Freetown.

Government of Sierra Leone (2000b) 'National Policy on the Advancement of Women', Ministry of Social Welfare, Gender and Children's Affairs, Freetown.

Government of Sierra Leone (2004) 'Witness to Truth: Report of the Sierra Leone Truth and Reconciliation Commission', Freetown.

Government of Sierra Leone (2005) 'Poverty Reduction Strategy Paper (SL-PRSP)', Government Printer, Freetown.

Government of Sierra Leone (2007) 'Ministry of Social Welfare, Gender and Children's Affairs', http://www.daco-sl.org/encyclopedia/1_gov/1_2mswg.htm (accessed 8 March 2013).

Government of Sierra Leone (2008) 'The Agenda for Change – Second Poverty Reduction Strategy Paper', Government Printer, Freetown.

Government of Sierra Leone (2013) 'An Agenda for Prosperity', Ministry of Finance and Economic Development, Freetown.

Richmond, O. P. (2006) 'The Problem of Peace: Understanding the "Liberal Peace"', *Conflict, Security and Development*, Vol. 6, No. 3, pp. 291–314.

SIGI (2012) http://genderindex.org/country/sierra-leone (accessed 5 July 2013).

United Nations (1992) 'An Agenda for Peace', http://www.un.org/document/ga/res/47/a47r120.htm (accessed 6 February 2013).

United Nations (2000) 'Security Council Resolution 1325 on Women,

Peace and Security', http://www.peacewomen.org/un/sc/1325.html (accessed 15 February 2013).

United Nations (2008a) 'Security Council 1820', http://www.IFUW.org/advocacy/docs/UN_SC_Resolution1820.pdf (accessed 31 January 2013).

United Nations (2008b) 'UN Resolution 1829', http://www.security councilreport.org/atf/cf/%7B65BFCF9B-6027-4E9c-8CD3-CF64 FF9%7D/SL/%20RES1829.pdf (accessed 3 February 2013).

United Nations (2009a) 'Joint Vision for Sierra Leone of the United Nation's Family', United Nations Integrated Peacebuilding Office, Freetown, Sierra Leone.

United Nations (2009b) 'UN Resolution 1888', http://www.peacewomen. org/assets/file/BasicWPSDocs/scr1888.pdf (accessed 5 February 2013).

United Nations (2009c) 'UN Resolution 1889', http://www.womenpeace security.org/media/pdf-scr1889.pdf (accessed 5 February 2013).

United Nations (2010) http://www.securitycouncilreport.org/atf/ cf/%7B65BFCF9B-6D27-4E9C-8CD3-CF6E4FF96FF9%7D/ WPS%20SRES%201960.pdf (accessed 3 July 2013).

United Nations (2013a) UN Resolution 2106, http://peacemaker. un.org/sites/peacemaker.un.org/files/SC_ResolutionWomen_ SRES2016(2013)(english).pdf (accessed 19 January 2014).

United Nations (2013b) Resolution 2122: Women and Peace and Security, http://unscr.com/en/resolutions/2122 (accessed 19 January 2014).

United Nations (2013c) http://hdrstats.undp.org/images/explanations/ SLE.pdf (accessed 10 July 2013).

UNDAF (2006) 'Sierra Leone UNDAF Revised', http://www.undg.org/ index.cfm?P=234&f=S (accessed 10 February 2013).

UNDP (1995) *Human Development Report*, http://hdr.undp.org/en/ reports/global/hdr1995/ (accessed 10 June 2013).

WIPSEN (2008) 'Expert Consultative Meeting: Towards a Region Specific Manual for Mainstreaming Gender and Women's Issues in Multidimensional Peace Support Operations in West Africa', http://www.wipsen-africa.org/wipsen/publications/file_2:en.us.pdf (accessed 27 May 2013).

4
Education
Pathway to Empowerment for Ghanaian Women?

● ●

Akosua K. Darkwah

Education has long been seen as an important means by which the lives of individuals, particularly women, can be improved. Indeed, the importance of girls' education is such a well-entrenched view that universal primary education is one of the Millennium Development Goals. Girls' education, research shows, delivers a whole host of advantages. It has been linked with improved child health, lower rates of infant mortality, and lower rates of fertility (King and Hill 1993). The extent to which this is true is rarely interrogated. In this chapter, we take the arguments of scholars such as Stromquist (2002) and Grown et al. (2005) as a starting point and ask to what extent education has made a difference in the lives of three generations of Ghanaian women. To assess differences in the lives of women, we look specifically at the correlation between levels of education and paid work in the public sector of the economy, which has the most decent of working conditions as identified by the International Labour Organization.

This chapter begins with a discussion of the Ghanaian context and how traditionally access to educational institutions has been configured in a manner that limits women's opportunities for educational attainment, with consequences for their access to formal sector employment. It then provides an account of the research methods used to derive the data upon which the argument is based. The argument that follows begins with a discussion of the current level of women's educational attainment, its implications for their job opportunities in the various sectors of the economy, and a survey of earned incomes over the course of three generations.

The national context: gender, education and formal sector employment in Ghana

Formal education was introduced to Ghana in the eighteenth century by missionaries and extended in the late nineteenth century by the British colonial administration. From its inception, formal education in Ghana was gender-biased. Boys were favoured over girls from both an institutional and family perspective. The state was only interested in equipping girls with an education that would make them 'better wives [for] the rising crop of educated clerks, teachers, catechists and few professional men' (Graham 1971: 72). Families were also convinced that educating a woman was a waste of family resources because the benefits of a woman's education would accrue to her future husband. In 1890, when the British began to pay attention to formal education in Ghana, the gender ratio in primary school enrolment was 11 girls for every 100 boys (Fant 2008: 18).

This disparity persisted throughout the twentieth century and is very clearly reflected in the educational attainment of the adult population. The most recent demographic and health survey conducted in Ghana in 2003 shows that 28.2 per cent of women compared with 17.6 per cent of men have never been to school; that 6 per cent of women compared with 10.5 per cent of men completed primary school; and that 5.2 per cent of women compared with 9.7 per cent of men completed secondary school. These numbers are most striking in terms of gender disparities in tertiary education. The number of Ghanaian men who have post-secondary education is almost three times the number of Ghanaian women – 6.3 per cent of Ghanaian men compared with 2.6 per cent of women have post-secondary education. Ghanaian girls born in the twenty-first century will not be disadvantaged so far as the attainment of primary education is concerned.

Gender parity in primary school enrolment was finally achieved in 2006 (Ghana Statistical Service 2007: 30). In secondary school, however, the inequalities persist. While for boys the enrolment rate in secondary schools during the 2005/6 academic year stood at 45 per cent, the rate for girls was 42 per cent (*ibid.*: 33). The gender gap in tertiary enrolment has also narrowed considerably over the last two decades, although it still remains. At the University of Ghana, for example, female enrolment at the undergraduate level was just under 40 per cent of the total in 2008 (University of Ghana 2008).

A second bias in the provision of education in Ghana is geographical. Bening (1990) notes that there was a systematic attempt at limiting the number of government and mission schools in the northern part of Ghana to ensure that a pool of unskilled labour was available to work in the mines and plantations in the southern part of the territory. Thus the first northern schools, both primary and secondary, were set up over a century later than the first southern schools. Ghana's first President, Kwame Nkrumah, attempted to remedy the situation by providing Ghanaians from the north with free education during his term of office. This and other efforts by successive governments have failed to change the educational disparity between the north and the south. In the rural Savannah, for example, net enrolment rates at primary level are below 70 per cent, even though the average in all other localities is approximately 85 per cent (Ghana Statistical Service 2007: 30). Ghanaian women who come from the northern part of the country are therefore doubly disadvantaged regarding access to education.

Women's general lack of access to education is reflected in labour force participation rates. While women dominate in the informal economy, their presence is poorly felt in the formal sector of the economy, where incomes are generally higher and more secure. According to the Fifth Round of the Ghana Living Standards Survey (Ghana Statistical Service 2008), while 27 per cent of all males between 15 and 64 were in waged employment, the figure for females was 8.9 per cent. In addition to their low numbers in the formal sector, women are over-represented at the lower levels of the occupational hierarchy. Data from the Women in Public Life Project conducted in 1995 showed that 95 per cent of the secretaries and all the receptionists in the civil service were women. Meanwhile, there was no female Chief Director as at 1995 and only 10.9 per cent of the directors were female (Awumbila 2000: 53). By 2003, the situation had improved only marginally; two out of the 11 chief directors of ministries in the country were women (Ministry of Women and Children's Affairs 2004: 35).

Methodology

The discussion draws primarily on a survey of 600 adult women in both rural and urban communities in three regions of Ghana: Northern, Ashanti and Greater Accra. The survey was conducted in two districts (one rural, one urban) in each of the three regions. The communities selected in the urban areas represented different income groups. Women were selected randomly from three age groups: 18–29, 30–49, and 50 and over. The number of women sampled in each of these three age groups was in-keeping with the fact that the Ghanaian population is a relatively young population. Thus the 18–29-year-olds constituted 40.3 per cent of the sample, the 30–49-year-olds constituted 39.5 per cent and those over 50 constituted 20.2 per cent.

Since it was impossible to use a survey to track the trajectories of particular women in their attainment of an empowered status in various aspects of their lives, in-depth interviews were conducted with three generations of women (grandmother, mother and daughter). A total of 12 sets – four from each region – were conducted. The in-depth interviews were to illuminate change processes and nuances and to foreground issues such as national context and local specificities, which could not be addressed with survey questions. This chapter draws largely on the findings of the survey and buttresses these findings with interview material where possible.

Statistics and life experiences across regions and generations

The first thing to note about the literacy levels of the women in our sample is the unsurprising fact that levels of illiteracy are high among Ghanaian women. Two-fifths of the sample had not received any form of education at all. In this sample, a quarter of the women, once they were provided with the opportunity to go to school, acquired what is considered to be a basic-level education (six years of primary and three years of middle school). More women dropped out of school with only primary education (11.7 per cent) than those who spent extra years acquiring secondary education (8.6 per cent). Less than 1 per cent of the women in this sample have a tertiary degree, although almost 4 per cent of the women in the sample have acquired some post-secondary training, such as a computer skills course.

A woman's access to education also depended on when she was born. Table 4.1 shows that there is a negative correlation between age and access to education. Indeed, the percentage of women above the age of 50 who had not acquired any education

Table 4.1 Educational levels of respondents (%)

Educational level	18–29 years	30–49 years	50+ years	Total
None	23.5	40.5	69.4	44.5
Informal	2.1	4.2	1.7	2.6
Primary	15.7	13.5	5.8	11.7
Middle/junior secondary	32.6	24.5	13.2	23.4
Secondary	18.1	8.0	0	8.6
Vocational/ technical	2.0	3.4	5.8	3.7
Apprenticeship	1.6	0.4	0	0.7
Tertiary	1.2	0.9	0	0.7
Other tertiary	2.9	4.6	4.1	3.9

Source: Fieldwork, 2008

at all was three times higher than that for women aged between 18 and 29. The percentage of women who had acquired the various levels of education was lowest among those aged above 50 and highest among those aged between 18 and 29. The only exception was with vocational/technical education. Here, the scenario was reversed. The percentage of women among the youngest cohort who had this level of education was far lower than those among the oldest. Another important point to note is the fact that apprenticeship training, although limited, is confined to the women under the age of 50, particularly those between the ages of 18 and 29. Apprenticeship training is seen as a way out if general education fails. Many mothers and daughters we interviewed had learned one of the female-dominated trades, such as hairdressing and dressmaking. However, a number were not practising their trades and were instead involved in petty trading and farming. In several cases, they said they had no capital to buy the equipment with which to ply their trade. To become an artisan, training was not sufficient. A sponsor was also needed to get the vocation started. In the case of one woman who had trained as a baker in the Ashanti Region, her teacher had to provide her with flour and sugar on credit for several years, and her own mother had provided the money for the oven she used for baking.

There are two important points to note about the statistics on education. First, although three-quarters of the women aged between 18 and 29 had been to school, it is important to keep in mind that a quarter of the same cohort were unable to attend because of the prevailing socio-economic circumstances during the period when they were of school-going age. Those in our sample aged between 18 and 29 grew up during the height of the implementation of the structural adjustment programme in the 1980s, when the lack of subsidies restricted educational provision. Our interviews in rural Accra highlight what such arrangements for schooling meant for young rural girls. Adikuor is a 23-year-old mother of one who grew up in a village about an hour's drive east of the capital city of Ghana. Adikuor's parents put her in school when she was six and, although neither of them had completed their schooling (her father dropped out in his first year of secondary school, while her mother dropped out in her fifth year of primary school), they had high hopes for Adikuor. She would be the first female in the family to earn, at the very least, secondary education. All was well until Adikuor turned nine. That year her father died and her mother, who was a food crop farmer, was incapable of single-handedly putting her two children through school. She, like many other African parents who faced the dilemma of choosing between a daughter's and a son's education, decided to keep Adikuor's brother in school. Adikuor was sent off to her paternal aunt as a foster child. Fostering is an old practice in Ghana. Indeed, anecdotal evidence suggests that many Ghanaians are raised by relatives and, although recent material on the incidence of fostering is hard to come by, earlier studies such as that conducted by Aryee (1975) of 1,337 households in Accra found that 63.1 per cent of the fathers and 44.9 per cent of the mothers had at least one child living elsewhere.

In interviews, we came across several women in the mother's generation who had also grown up as foster children. The stories of these women suggest that fostering does not augur well for girls. In one case in northern Ghana, the grandmother sent each of her three daughters to extended family members, who failed to put them in school, while she put two of her own sons through school. The story of Adikuor also highlights the disadvantages of fostering as far as girls' educational attainment is concerned. When Adikuor was sent off to her aunt, there was a tacit agreement between her mother and her aunt that her aunt would take good care of her, including sending her to school. Instead, Adikuor's aunt put her to work as her shop assistant to help to raise the monies with which her male cousins could be schooled. Adikuor worked diligently in the hope that eventually her turn would come.

After a decade of waiting in vain, she returned to Ghana with nothing to show for her years abroad. Adikuor is now married with a four-year-old daughter, and her career prospects are limited. She spends her days helping her mother-in-law, who makes doughnuts for a living, and now hopes that her husband will be able to find the resources to finance the apprenticeship training programme in hairdressing on which she has set her sights. Not being able to read, however, means that Adikuor will not be able to write the National Vocational Technical Institute's qualifying examination, which is necessary if she intends to work in the formal sector as a hairdresser. To be able to earn a reasonable living in the informal economy as a self-employed hairdresser, Adikuor would have to purchase the basic equipment needed to run a hair salon, which in her current circumstances seems impossible. As matters stand, her best option would be to work in the private informal economy for sub-subsistence wages and without job security. Like her mother, the food crop farmer, and her grandmother, the priestess, Adikuor will have to eke out a living for herself and her family.

A second important theme arising from the statistics is that the most significant change across three generations is the increasing number of women with education. Only a few grandmothers, but many more mothers and daughters had gone to school. This finding was replicated in our intergenerational interviews across the country, but was most striking in the Northern Region. There, three out of four mothers and all four grandmothers had no formal education. Yet in northern Ghana, in particular, education is seen as crucial for improving one's life. This social perception is related to the fewer economic options available there when compared with the Ashanti and Greater Accra regions. In our interviews at Damongo, Azara – a mother who had had the benefit of tertiary education and ended up in formal-sector work, partly through her active engagement in the Catholic Church – was a good example of the value of education for intergenerational class mobility: we return to her story below. Northern Ghanaian women in the second generation were acutely aware of the ways in which their lack of education had affected their life chances. These mothers had therefore been instrumental in ensuring that their daughters received the education they had been denied. Sakina, a 51-year-old mother in Tamale, noted the importance of education for her children, daughters included.

Even though I didn't get the opportunity to go to school, I entreat my kids to take their education seriously. Even though I did not go to school, all my kids (two boys and five girls) have had the opportunity to go to school.

Muni, also from the Northern Region, describes her mother's instrumental role in ensuring that her children went to school:

My father didn't want us to go to school because especially for the boys he wanted them to help him on the farm, but there was a lot of discussion in the community about the importance of education – that was when my mother said she wanted us to go to school, so through my mother's efforts, we went.

These mothers went to great lengths to ensure that nothing stood in the way of their daughters' educational success. Two of the three daughters whose mothers had not gone to school were exempted from house chores to ensure that they had all the time they needed to study. In our discussions of employment however, it will become clear that the significance of education for employment has changed over the years, for the worse.

The relationship between education and employment

We will now explore the relationship between education, generation and terms of employment to assess the extent to which the educational levels of women translate into economic empowerment as suggested in the literature, measured here as access to decent work as defined by the International Labour Organization and provided in the Ghanaian context by work in the public formal sector.

Table 4.2 affirms the importance of education for employment. It shows clearly that access to formal salaried employment is a function of whether or not one has acquired an education. While

Table 4.2 The importance of education for employment

Terms of employment	None		Primary–high school		Total	
	Freq.	(%)	Freq.	(%)	Freq.	(%)
Formal sector employees	3	1.7	54	21.1	57	13.2
Self-employed with employees	25	14.3	40	15.6	65	15.1
Self-employed without employees	130	74.3	134	52.3	264	61.3
Apprentices	4	2.3	16	6.3	20	4.6
Agricultural day labour	4	2.3	1	0.4	5	1.2
Unpaid work on family farm/ enterprise	3	1.7	3	1.2	6	1.4
Other	6	3.4	8	3.1	14	3.2
Total	175	100	256	100	431	100

Source: Fieldwork, 2008

21 per cent of those with some amount of education worked in the formal economy, the same was true for less than 2 per cent of uneducated women. With regard to agricultural labour, an uneducated woman was five times more likely to work on a farm as an educated woman, although the numbers were not high enough to make conclusive findings. In assessing the relationship between education and entry into 'decent' work, which we defined as public formal employment, it was quite clear that education allowed entry into this type of work. Twenty-one per cent of women with some education as opposed to 2 per cent of women with no education were involved in work that satisfied some of the indicators of decent work. However, for workers in the informal economy, the relationship between education and decent work was not so clear-cut; 52 per cent of women with

some level of education as opposed to 74 per cent without any education were self-employed without employees.

Age also makes a difference to whether or not a woman is likely to work as a salaried employee in the formal economy, with all the benefits that accrue to workers in such jobs. As evident in Table 4.3, the percentage of women aged 18–29 who were salaried employees was three times higher than that of

Table 4.3 Generational differences in terms of employment

Terms of employment	18–29 years		30–49 years		50+ years		Total	
	Freq.	(%)	Freq.	(%)	Freq.	(%)	Freq.	(%)
Agricultural day labour	1	0.7	4	2.0	0	0.0	5	1.2
Non-agricultural day labour	0	0.0	1	0.5	0	0.0	1	0.2
Worker (contractual wage-based)	1	0.7	0	0.0	1	1.3	2	0.5
Salaried employee (permanent/ regular)	22	15.0	22	10.7	4	5.0	48	11.1
Salaried employee (irregular)	5	3.4	2	1.0	2	2.5	9	2.1
Self-employed (employer)	17	11.6	34	16.5	14	17.7	65	15.0
Self-employed (no employees)	70	47.6	136	66.0	58	73.4	264	60.9
Unpaid work on family farm	3	2.0	3	1.5	0	0.0	6	1.4
Unpaid work in family enterprise/ business	8	5.4	3	1.5	1	1.3	12	2.8
Apprenticeship (salaried/non-salaried)	19	13.0	1	0.5	1	1.3	21	4.8
Total	146	100	206	100	81	100	433	100

Source: Fieldwork, 2008

women aged 50 and above. Conversely, 73 per cent of women over 50 were in self-employment without employees, as opposed to 66 per cent between 30 and 49, and 48 per cent between 18 and 29. The patterns were similar for self-employment with employees, with women over 50 having the highest percentages and women 18–29 having the lowest figures. Not surprisingly, apprenticeships were largely the reserve of women aged between 18 and 29, as was unpaid work. More than half of the women who worked for no pay in our sample were aged between 18 and 29. Agricultural labour was largely the preserve of the middle generation, with 83 per cent of the women in agricultural labour aged between 30 and 49.

Table 4.4 Generational differences in kinds of salaried employee positions

	18–29 years		30–49 years		50+ years		Total	
	Freq.	(%)	Freq.	(%)	Freq.	(%)	Freq.	(%)
Government	8	27.6	14	60.9	5	100	27	47.4
Private formal	8	27.6	2	8.7	0	0.0	10	17.5
Private informal	13	44.8	7	30.4	0	0.0	20	35.1
Total	29	100	23	100	5	100	57	100

Source: Fieldwork, 2008

To explore further the significance of our findings that younger women were more likely to be employed in the formal economy than older women, we examined differences in the kinds of employer that the employees in the sample had. As shown in Table 4.4, all the women above the age of 50 were employed by state institutions. None of them were employed in the private formal or informal sectors. For the women aged between 30 and 49, 60 per cent were employed in state institutions and 30 per cent in the private informal sector, with only 9 per cent employed in the private formal sector. For women aged between 18 and 29, only 28 per cent were employed by the government, another 28 per cent by the private formal sector, and 45 per cent by the private informal sector. These figures are due to the shrinkage in public sector employment since the economic liberalization policies of the 1980s. This has implications for acquiring decent work, suggesting that, for younger women, educational levels on their own were no guarantee of securing this, as Table 4.5 demonstrates. All three people who earn 500 Ghana cedis and above are government employees, while 19 people earning 200 Ghana cedis and above are in government (16) or private formal (3) employment. Conversely, of the 16 whose monthly earnings are below the government-stipulated minimum wage, 10 have employers in the private informal sector. All of the 15 employees with employers in the private informal sector earned less than 200 Ghana cedis. These findings are supported by the literature on the informalization of work and informal labour markets in Ghana, which argues that employees in the informal economy are in some of the most insecure and poorly remunerated jobs (Heintz 2005; Tsikata 2008).

Table 4.5 Employer and income (Ghana cedis)

	<58	59– 100	101– 149	150– 199	200– 299	300– 399	400– 499	>500
Government	2	3	2	4	9	3	1	3
Private formal	4	3	0	0	2	1	0	0
Private informal	10	4	0	1	0	0	0	0
Total	16	10	2	5	11	4	1	3

Source: Fieldwork, 2008

Tables 4.2–4.5, taken together, tell an important story about the changing significance of the value of education. While clearly many more of the women aged 18–29 have had formal education as compared with those aged above 50, the impact of this education on women's ability to enjoy the benefits of decent work has not been similar. The women aged 18–29 are far more likely to work in the private formal and informal sectors of the economy as compared with the educated women aged 50 and above, all of whom worked in the public formal sector. Yet workers in the private sector are not remunerated as well as workers in the public sector.

This story is also clearly reflected in the lives of Azara and her daughter, Alima, one of the four families we interviewed in the Northern Region of Ghana. Azara, the mother, is 49, a staunch Catholic and married. She grew up in the capital city of one of districts in the Northern Region. Neither of her parents ever attended school; her father was a farmer and she describes her mother as a housewife. Her mother was one of four wives with whom the father had a total of 26 children (7 male and 19 female). Only four girls out of the 19 ever attended school and Azara is the most highly educated of these. She started her career as a typist at the Ministry of Health in 1980 and one year ago earned a diploma in secretarial studies and management, after which she was promoted to her current position as an executive officer.

Azara was educated through perseverance on her part. Her father had many children and could not afford to educate them all. Azara, however, was very determined to go to school, even though she was growing up at a time when many thought that girls did not need to go to school. She recalls periods when she had to stay away from school but her insistence on going was critical to ensuring that resources were found to enable her to resume her education. At one point, even though her father had put her in school, he gave her in marriage to an older man; she fought against this and the proposed marriage did not take place. Her father then decided not to maintain her in school any longer, and her mother agreed to take up responsibility for her education. Azara for her part helped her mother by collecting and selling firewood and making *garri*. All that hard work paid off. Azara's steady source of income from her work in the public sector has enabled her to care for her children, to acquire land and to build a house. She also believes that her ability to work has played a major role in the success of her marriage to her husband with whom she has five children, two sons and three daughters.

The oldest of her daughters is 29-year-old Alima. Alima was brought up in the capital city of a largely rural district, but she has also spent some years in the capital of the Northern Region as well as in southern Ghana because of her education. Although she would have liked to go on to university after her secondary school, she did not do well enough in the qualifying examination. She therefore proceeded to a series of secretarial schools, where she earned a National Vocational and Technical Institute (NVTI) certificate in secretarial studies, a diploma in business and secretarial studies, and a Higher National Diploma in secretarial and management studies. Alima, it seems, is all set to follow in her mother's footsteps. However, although she is starting her working life with the qualifications her mother only recently earned, the chances of Alima working her way up the professional track like her mother are doubtful.

Currently, in spite of the fact that she has more educational qualifications than her mother did at the start of her career, Alima is unemployed and looking for work that would allow her to use the skills she has acquired through training. She is unlikely to find an opening in the near future, although thanks to their connections in the church something may turn up. The public sector, as we have already shown, provides the most secure of jobs and better income, but Alima cannot look in that direction because public sector employment has been shrinking over the years. The district capital in which she lives does not offer many options for secretarial work in the private formal or informal sectors, either, and even if she had these options they would not guarantee her the security that her mother has after working for almost 30 years in the public sector. Not having found the kind of work that she is looking for, Alima has chosen to acquire more education in the hope that it will improve her job prospects, preferably in the public sector.

Conclusion

This study affirms the importance of education for determining whether a woman works in the public sector or is able to run a business that employs others in the Ghanaian context. While 94.5 per cent of the women who worked in the public sector were educated, this was true of 62 per cent of those who were self-employed and had employees. While we therefore acknowledge that the education of girls is a key ingredient in producing empowered women, this study also suggests that conventional empowerment initiatives, which assume that providing education for girls is all it takes to produce empowered women, are problematic.

Context is the key in determining whether or not an educated girl will grow up to become an empowered woman. As clearly shown in this study, the provision of universal primary education without concomitant attention to the provision of jobs that satisfy the conditions of decent work as stipulated by the International Labour Organization hinders educated women's efforts at gaining control over financial resources. Two decades after empowerment entered development discourse as a guiding principle or goal of development work, this study shows that we need a multi-pronged approach to empowering women around the world. Education in and of itself is not good enough. It needs to be matched with better access to public sector jobs or laws that ensure that private formal and informal sector jobs provide decent work as defined by the International Labour Organization.

Acknowledgement

This chapter was previously published as an article in the *IDS Bulletin* and we are grateful to Wiley-Blackwell for their kind permission to republish it here.

References

Aryee, A. (1975) 'A Study of Parent-Child Separation in Accra', *Legon Family Research Papers*, No. 4, pp. 85–91.

Awumbila, M. (2000) 'Women and Gender Equality in Ghana: A Situational Analysis', in D. Tsikata (ed.), *Gender Training in Ghana: Politics, Issues and Tools*, Woeli Publishing Services, Accra.

Bening, R. (1990) *A History of Education in Northern Ghana 1909–1976*, Ghana Universities Press, Accra.

Fant, E. (2008) 'Education and Girl Child Empowerment: The Case of Bunkpurugu/Yunyoo District in Northern Ghana', MPhil thesis, Faculty of Social Studies, University of Tromsø, Norway.

Ghana Statistical Service (2007) *Pattern and Trends of Poverty in Ghana*, Ghana Statistical Service, Accra.

—— (2008) *Ghana Living Standards Survey 5*, Ghana Statistical Service, Accra.

Graham, C. (1971) *The History of Education in Ghana: From the Earliest Times to the Declaration of Independence*, Ghana Publishing Corporation, Accra.

Grown, C., R. Gupta and A. Kes (2005) *Taking Action: Achieving Gender Equality and Empowering Women*, UN Millennium Project (Task Force on Education and Gender Equality) and Earthscan, London and Sterling, VA, Sakinatp://www.unmilleniumproject.org/documents/Gender-complete.pdf (accessed 5 February 2009).

Heintz, J. (2005) 'Gender, Employment and Poverty in Ghana', background paper prepared for the 2005 Progress of the World's Women, UNIFEM, New York, NY.

King, E. and M. Hill (eds) (1993) *Women's Education in Developing Countries: Barriers, Benefits and Policies*, Johns Hopkins University Press for the World Bank, Baltimore, MD.

Ministry of Women and Children's Affairs (MOWAC) (2004) *Ghana's Second Progress Report on the Implementation of the African and Beijing Platform of Action and Review Report for Beijing+10*, MOWAC, Accra.

Stromquist, N. (2002) 'Education as a Means for Empowering Women', in J. Parpart, S. Raj and K. Staudt (eds), *Rethinking Empowerment: Gender and Development in a Global/Local World*, Routledge, London.

Tsikata, D. (2008) 'Informalisation, the Informal Economy and Urban Women's Livelihoods in Sub-Saharan African since the 1990s', in S. Razavi (ed.), *The Gendered Impacts of Liberalisation: Towards Embedded Liberalism*, Routledge, New York, NY.

University of Ghana (2008) *Basic Statistics, 2008*, University of Ghana, Legon.

5

Paid Work as a Pathway of Empowerment
Pakistan's Lady Health Worker Programme
••

Ayesha Khan

Increased decision making and status in the home have been shown to be positive outcomes of women's paid work (Kabeer *et al.* 2012). If the work is valued by society and improves women's self-perception, it can have an even stronger positive impact. Other benefits include a decrease in gender discrimination against sending girls to school and an improvement in autonomy indicators (Khan 2010). This chapter explores the contributions that paid work can make to creating pathways of empowerment for women in Pakistan. It draws on the case of Pakistan's government-run Lady Health Workers Programme (LHWP), which employs almost 100,000 women across Pakistan as community health workers who act as a vital link between communities and primary health care (Douthwaite and Ward 2005). The chapter focuses on the experiences of Lady Health Workers (LHWs), exploring the impact of paid work on their lives and communities, and the processes enabling their empowerment as women.

The LHWP was established in 1993. It recruits single or married women with a minimum of eight years of education to become LHWs; they undergo training from a qualified doctor at the closest government Basic Health Unit (BHU) over a fifteen-month period, followed by regular refresher courses and skill enhancement training. An LHW works from home, where she sees community members, holds meetings, maintains her household register, and stores contraceptives, medicines and communication material. She registers all the population in her catchment area in order to identify their needs for health and family-planning services; organizes local health committees to raise maternal care awareness; serves as a health and hygiene information resource; provides essential drugs and contraception; and administers polio drops to children during regular government-sponsored polio drives. LHWs work an average of 30 hours a week, and are paid less than the national minimum wage of US$70 a month.

This chapter draws on qualitative fieldwork conducted in 2007 in four districts: rural Jhang and peri-urban Faisalabad in the province of Punjab, and rural Tando Jam and peri-urban Karachi in the province of Sindh. Qualitative research tools were used to interview LHWs and key informants, and to hold community-based group discussions with men and women in selected sites. First-round interviews with 27 LHWs explored how and why they became LHWs, their marriage and childbearing history, decision-making and mobility patterns, sources of support and opposition to their work, training and duties, and impact on gender relations. Twelve of these LHWs were interviewed again to explore these topics further, with additional questions relating to their responsibilities within and outside the home, job satisfaction, personal development and changes in social relations. Similar themes were explored with key informants, household members and community groups.

This fieldwork focused on the subjective experience of the health workers in terms of the positive impact of their work on various dimensions of their lives. Kabeer (2001) places women's enhanced access to *resources* and their increased *agency,* or ability to exercise these choices, at the heart of processes leading to their empowerment. The particularities of context and circumstance, as in the case of LHWs, need to be elucidated further to understand how these processes develop in women's lives. For this reason, the interview material was analysed first to draw out common themes among women's experiences, and then to trace out how certain circumstances shaped particular or different trajectories of change in the context of individual women's stories.

These trajectories form the basic structure of this chapter, which draws on a series of stories that provide illustrative material to explore the pathways of empowerment pursued by LHWs. The first story follows what emerged as a standard work and empowerment experience among LHWs. The second story features another possible trajectory – empowerment and enterprise – and illustrates how basic changes can be built upon if a woman lives in an environment that offers more opportunities for growth, and if she also enjoys a strong social network that facilitates her work. The final story follows a trajectory of repeated personal crises, illustrating how circumstance can almost nullify the potential and growth of a woman.

Work and empowerment

Rabia lives in a village of 550 households in the central and agriculturally rich area of Punjab Province. The major livelihood sources for men are agricultural work, government jobs, the brick-kiln industry and overseas work in the Gulf. Women's paid work opportunities are limited, with the greatest number employed in brick kilns, and a few working as teachers, midwives and LHWs. Residential areas are organized along caste lines; most homes belong to the dominant land-owning caste G, the rest to the lower-caste Kammis and Mussalis who work in the brick kilns. The Rural Health Centre is five kilometres away, and there are four local doctors and one *dai* (traditional birth attendant) in the village, along with the LHWs. There are no community-based organizations, but both men and women have informal savings committees. Basic services in the village also include electricity and telephone connections. A few houses have television, but there is no cable connection.

> Rabia is a friendly 34-year-old. She completed class ten and married her first cousin at 21. Her husband, who has eight years of schooling, has never brought in any consistent income. She has one young daughter, and lives in an extended household with her brother-in-law and his family.

When the LHW vacancy was announced Rabia's husband convinced her to apply. She started work after the initial training conducted at a BHU nearby. At first, villagers were suspicious about the medicines she would offer them. One tactic she used to win them over was to offer cheap rates for sewing. She also secretly helped younger women to use contraceptives. Her supervisor visited homes to reinforce her messages. Over the last four years she has managed to deliver health services as required, always emphasizing related religious teachings, and says that with the passage of time people's fears subsided.

When she first ventured out as an LHW she didn't know many people, being from another village herself and having only ever visited homes of members of her own caste and relatives. Now she knows everybody, and on the days when she helps out with the polio vaccinations she even goes into the fields where women and children can be found with their livestock. Because of the respect she has claimed among villagers, even the higher-caste women are permitted to visit her. When Rabia has to attend a group meeting, her husband will take and fetch her on his motorbike. He also fetches her supply of medicines from the BHU once a month. Rabia can only leave the house – without first asking permission from him or his brother – to make duty calls, or to go to the market, the fields, the BHU, or funerals.

Her husband's family, and her own parents, are pleased that Rabia works. They say her husband should have made her do so before, since she is educated and doing such useful work. Now they seek her advice and guidance because she is earning. Earlier her father-in-law used to take all the decisions. After he died her brother-in-law took over, and now she feels she too has an essential decision-making role in the extended home, particularly regarding the children's education or market purchases. She says her husband is more accommodating about sharing his earnings with her, probably because he knows that he might have to ask her for money himself some time! She says her husband thinks she knows best, even waiting for her agreement before starting construction in the house.

The main family income sources are her earnings as an LHW, her intermittent stitching, her husband's occasional wages, and her brother-in-law's teaching salary and army pension. Six people live off US$82 per month. While she is out of the house on duty, her sister-in-law has to do all the household chores, including cooking, cleaning, caring for the livestock, and washing dishes and clothes. Her own young daughter avoids pitching in, preferring to be in school. Rabia would like her daughter to study and become a religious instructor by going on to an Islamic school after completing class five.

It is important for women to work and earn their own money, says Rabia. This way they can contribute to their daughter's dowry, since fathers often cannot afford to give much, and continue to help support a daughter even after marriage. Through paid work, a woman can change her situation and provide for her own home and children. Now there are village men who will allow women to work, because they have seen how Rabia has improved her life. But there are still women who are not allowed out of the house, such as the wife and daughters of the *imam* at the mosque. Still, girls of her caste are now allowed to go to school. Now the problem for those women and girls who are educated is that other than a handful of job options they are stuck tending livestock, or stitching clothes.

Rabia's story illustrates a kind of empowerment trajectory that other LHWs have followed. This trajectory has distinct landmarks. For one, she had a headstart by being educated. She built upon this advantage when poverty drove her to take up this job opportunity, but only with the strong support of male family members. This led to her enhanced education through training and work experience; this added to her knowledge but also turned her into a resource for the community. This in turn is linked with her increased decision-making power within the family and mobility within her community. Finally, her enhanced status at home and in her community has affirmed the possibility of breaking down some caste, class and gender barriers.

Although LHWs are privileged compared to other women in their communities by virtue of their education, this does not necessarily indicate that they are financially more secure or that they will marry into families with relatively better income-earning strategies. Rabia's husband is as educated as she is but has never earned enough to support them both, and has never spent his earnings on their household regularly. The pressure this puts on other family members, who live in the same compound although they have independent kitchens, drove them to support her entry into paid work and to minimize any social barriers in the way of this move. In fact, Rabia speaks for many others when she says that, if not for her earnings, her daughter might have died and her marriage might not have survived under the pressure.

Her story demonstrates that income generated from the public sector, in the form of pension, salary or her own 'stipend', is a vital source of predictable income underpinning livelihood strategies.[1] Her sewing also brings in a few hundred rupees more per month despite the ban on LHWs earning through other means, and their income is sometimes supplemented by Rabia's husband's occasional wages. Support for her work within the family is, therefore, fairly strong because the benefits are so obvious. Rabia's mother-in-law was no longer bringing in income as a traditional birth attendant, and Rabia's own parents encouraged her to apply for the job, possibly out of concern that they might have to support her themselves if she did not generate some income in her marital home.

No LHW interviewed had initiated her job application of her own accord, although not all had to be pushed into it like Rabia. It was the pressure and continuous support of a male family member or parents-in-law that made the difference in facilitating the work of LHWs in both Sindh and Punjab. One unmarried LHW in rural Sindh was deeply grateful to her father, first for educating her and then for insisting she take up the job opportunity despite opposition from her mother and community members. This indicates how necessary the support of influential family members is for the boundaries of gender norms within the home to be extended.

Another reason Rabia became an LHW is that she liked the idea of the work involved. This is a major factor in making her work a success and skilfully managing initial dissent within the community. Other LHWs are more effusive, and have said with surprising regularity that they particularly enjoy the job because it is *bhalai ka kam* (pious work) and they feel they are helping the poor. Some LHWs harboured dreams of becoming doctors or trained midwives, and see their work as a partial fulfilment of this wish. The nature of the work, the opportunities for socializing, the obvious gratitude from the community, and the improved status of the LHW in her home and village all contribute to a high level of job satisfaction. This is in contrast to some of the other work opportunities available to women, such as brick-kiln or factory work, where earnings may be higher but the work is mainly performed by low-caste poor women and is associated with extreme drudgery.

One of the most profound changes for an LHW is that her mobility norms and patterns are immediately expanded. Rabia became acquainted with other villagers from outside her family and caste for the first time as an LHW, through going out to register them. Mobility norms in villages in the Punjab and Sindh are linked with the concept of *purdah*, or segregation of the sexes, and *izzat* (honour), believed to be located in women but owned by men. In rural settings women usually need to gain the permission of a male family member in order to leave the house alone, and need to be accompanied by a group of women or male relatives in order to visit homes outside their extended family and caste. In urban settings, women may find that their mobility is even more restricted to limit their encounters with people outside their kinship group and caste who may be living in close proximity. In all cases *purdah* and mobility practices are subject to much variation dependent on caste, class and poverty levels.

In both settings, an LHW triggers some re-casting of gendered space because of her unusual job description and because her target population is determined by the state independent of social hierarchy norms. She is required to step into spaces that were previously out of bounds and to provide services on the basis of population and not blood ties. Because she is of the community and lives within it, people have to accommodate themselves to her presence and expand their definition of what is possible and acceptable for women. Her increased mobility as a matter of routine, which starts with three months of daily training outside the village at a local BHU, becomes justifiable in the context of her duty and contribution to the community.

There are two changes in Rabia's decision-making power that are noteworthy and shared with other LHWs. The first is an increase in the quantity of decisions Rabia can have a significant role in, pertaining to the family and private sphere. The second is a qualitative change. For example, she has control over her earnings and decides how to spend her money; she also engages with issues pertaining to house construction and repairs, which would have been unlikely before she became an independent earner. The type of family-related decisions, such as contraceptive matters, that she can now participate in has also expanded because her husband believes she knows best. Other LHWs interviewed also experienced more regular and also more consequential decision-making power as their status in the family increased, even though almost all of the decisions that they cited pertained to the private, domestic sphere.

Enterprise and change

The village of RP in rural Sindh is the only place in the district where people from the S caste live. They own most of the agricultural land, and those caste members without landholdings work as their tenants. Those outside S caste work as casual labour in the landlords' fruit orchards or on farms outside the village. The village has basic utilities, transport, one clinic and one boys' school. The only woman engaged in regular paid work in the form of a job is the LHW. The village elders maintain strict *purdah* norms with women in their own families. Women are not allowed contact with people outside their caste and there is almost no contact with Kohli (low-caste Hindu) women, who observe extreme *purdah* even from men in their own caste and live on the edge of the village.

Fatima, aged 35 and a mother of five, became an LHW eight years ago and has since grown into a community leader. She lives with her uneducated husband, an agricultural labourer, in a village in Tando Jam, a district in Sindh province. Her house consists of two rooms opening onto a small courtyard, with walls made of brick and mud.

She used to make *charpai* beds, *rillis* (quilts) and men's caps. Her children were born at home with the help of a *dai*. Fatima didn't know about family planning and spacing of children until she became an LHW. She had no medical care either before or after her pregnancies.

At first her husband did not approve when a doctor recruited her for the programme, but Fatima convinced him. 'If he earned then he would never let me go. I am educated – that is why I got the job, otherwise we would have died of hunger.' The doctor told her whatever she wanted to learn she must learn now – there would be no such opportunity again.

She believes she learned everything she knows once she left the house. Now her husband is impressed that she works for the government and never stops her from leaving the house, even to visit a woman in labour at night. Before working she rarely left her own house and could not go anywhere alone. She believes her *izzat* is in her own hands and once people saw she was not arrogant, they ceased their gossip. Now villagers, including the landlord's family, know about contraceptives and spacing their children, and Fatima organizes trips to the city to get tubal ligations. Women approach her for advice on conflict resolution and other matters, for which she has even taken them to the landlord for help.

The landlord has asked her to do duty at the polling booths twice during local elections. If she needs something from the women who sit on the local councils she can ask him to forward her request. Fatima has also used her influence with the women in the landlord's house who want to make some money of their own. She helps them to give some cash to the poorest in the village to invest in a buffalo. Out of their earnings they pay back the loan. When they sell the buffalo the profit is split between all the women involved.

There are two government-run micro-credit schemes in the village. They offer loans to groups of villagers to buy animals or seeds for crops. Fatima sells milk from a buffalo she has purchased through such a loan, and has recently bought another. She also rounded up women in the village to get them registered for loans, by travelling to the city to have their photographs taken and their identity cards copied. The women gave surety for one another, and so far two groups of 22 have got loans on the basis of assets such as livestock. Women return their money on schedule, and have been able to set up small shops using micro-credit.

Most villagers, including the landlord, are members of Fatima's caste. There is no primary school for girls in the village, but twenty girls from Fatima's caste are enrolled in the boys' school. Fatima says she reaches out to the Kohlis, but Kohli women respondents disagree. They say she only visits them for polio day vaccinations, not for mother-and-child health care, and they knew nothing about the micro-finance schemes in the village.

Because of her enhanced status in the village, Fatima believes her husband does not make decisions without her. She is sure she will be consulted when it is time to arrange her children's marriages, in contrast to the experience of other women. She does the budgeting for the house and her husband's livestock, because she is educated and he is not. People say he has learned everything he knows from his wife. Now that her husband is earning, Fatima keeps her own salary. She enjoys full control over her assets, including livestock, and even provides loans to relatives.

Fatima's oldest daughter left school to shoulder the burden of housework. 'I am sad that because I am so busy my daughter is not able to go to school. I have explained to her that I will bring books for her so that she can take tests privately.' Despite this, Fatima will continue as an LHW. 'It helps people. The poor pray for me. My household needs it.'

Given the right conditions and high personal motivation, Fatima has shown how an LHW can seize and build upon the gains of her social network and education, and position herself as a leader. Before she became an LHW she had already explored as many paid work ventures as she could within the confines of her village – such as presenting her husband with an income-generating activity in the form of a goat. Poverty, and the need to compensate for a husband who could not support his family, primarily drove Fatima to take up this job; now she has used her new status to develop even more income-generating activities, not just for herself but for other women as well. This demonstrates her creativity and ability to use her advantage to cross class barriers and generate business. It is no surprise that two micro-credit finance organizations have used her to launch their schemes.

Caste and class have worked in different ways to the advantage of Fatima. As an LHW it is her duty to serve the entire population assigned to her, irrespective of existing social hierarchies. Since she is a member of the S caste, which represents most of the community, her house visits were not a major challenge to existing mobility norms. Better yet, the landlord and most powerful person in the community is an S, too. As an LHW she is required to engage with his household and thereby cross the class barrier that previously would have denied her such direct access. However, her protestations that she does not discriminate against lower-caste households as a LHW (or as an entrepreneur) may not be accurate if the Kohli women are to be believed. In other communities studied, marginalization on the basis of caste status similarly reduced people's access to services and opportunities. From Fatima's perspective, and that of other LHWs interviewed, the fact that they access any such households at all is considered enough of an accomplishment. But the deeper reality of caste-based marginalization is also played out in access to education; only girls from the S caste can be found in the boys' primary school.

Interviews suggest that LHWs do not want to engage in any explicit confrontation with structures of male control and domination, even though this may be taking place in an implicit manner. For example, Fatima's story provides insight into how LHWs are changing the discourse of *purdah* to accommodate their work. She faced hostility in the community because her increased mobility within her village was an encroachment on public, or male-dominated space, and also because she made these forays alone. The segregation of spaces is customarily justified by the argument that a woman represents the honour of her family and to venture out of the private sphere is to invite male attention, which brings dishonour to a woman and her male relatives. Fatima uses the tactic of re-conceptualizing *purdah* by arguing that her honour lies within her, under her own control, and unless she deliberately invites unwelcome attention from men, this honour is not in jeopardy. This is a tactic adopted by most LHWs to justify their enhanced mobility, and it works well because they are delivering a service that is appreciated more as time goes by.

All LHWs interviewed have negotiated some expanded version of the traditional gendered space. In one case, two LHWs covered their combined target households together, thus minimizing the risk of gossip and male attention while enjoying the comfort of each other's company. Another LHW had already crossed into the public sphere when her father pushed her to pursue secondary education and college outside her village, and she quoted many instances when she had tackled unwelcome taunts from boys on buses with indignation, safe in the knowledge that her father was on her side.

The paid work of an LHW brings with it advantages that women who do piece-rate work, or labour in factories and brick kilns, cannot enjoy. The fact that it is a government job impresses Fatima's husband and the broader community, once they begin to understand the purpose of her work. The service she offers is an important resource – providing health care to others by giving injections, referring cases to hospital, and personally making regular house visits. This earns her the title of 'lady doctor', which is indicative of how vital she is in a community that has few other medical care options.

A cautionary note may be added here. Despite the positive changes in the lives of LHWs, this is not associated with the overall gendered roles in their homes. While an LHW's status has improved, another woman or girl has stepped in to fill the space she left behind in the house. Other LHWs' daughters, like Fatima's, deeply resent the fact that their education has been curtailed to allow their mothers to work, and mothers do acknowledge their sacrifice. There is clear attachment to the job itself, and particularly given its usefulness to the community, which makes it hard to give up despite its strains.

Personal survival and crisis management

GG is a settlement of about 200 households adjacent to other densely populated areas on the outer limits of Karachi. It is not clear where one neighbourhood ends and another starts, but each is distinguished by ethnic mix and political affiliation. What little infrastructure exists is more the result of private efforts than of any state intervention.

There are more work and training opportunities here for girls than would be possible in a village. A few educated girls are employed as teachers, and others do domestic work or have jobs in nearby factories. Many women who have moved here from rural areas are competent in sewing and embroidery, but they say they lack market control due to a dominant middleman and because they avoid using public transport. Men work in nearby industries or the university, or else as casual or skilled labour.

Women are constrained by their lack of education and restricted mobility, because in an urban setting they are not given permission to mingle with people of different castes and ethnicity without good reason. Women wear the *burqa* (full veil) when they leave their homes, usually in groups, although they would not necessarily do so in their villages. In cases of dispute among residents, or between castes, the elected local council head intervenes. The current head is Aasia's brother, which has facilitated her acceptance as an LHW.

> Aasia, 22, was born in a Sindhi village. Now she lives with her husband, four children (ages five and under), and his extended family, in a two-room compound that is home to 17 people. Her husband, who completed high school, is her first cousin and was betrothed to her in an exchange marriage because his sister was married to Aasia's brother. After losing his last job selling snacks at the university, he spends most of his time smoking marijuana and drinking.

Her brother's wife, an LHW herself, persuaded Aasia to apply for the job. Her husband allowed her to work because most neighbours are fellow Sindhis and he is not earning himself. When she was eight months pregnant with her third child, she was called for training. The child was born, back at her parents' home in the village, with a cleft palate that needed multiple surgery. She resumed work when he was 40 days old, leaving the children in the care of her mother in-law. Without the benefit of spacing brought by breastfeeding, she soon had a fourth baby. The timing of this birth meant that she missed out on the next scheduled free operation on the third child. She plans to start contraception soon, but has not yet done so.

It took her a year to earn the trust of community members, particularly the ethnic Pathans, who were reluctant even to allow her to register their households and refused her medicines at first. At one stage she told her supervisor that she could not continue because she was too disheartened and overwhelmed – but her down-to-earth words persuaded Aasia to persevere: 'Everyone has small children, don't lose heart, your husband is unemployed.'

Her salary is gone within a few days of receiving it, spent on food and medicines. She insists her husband does not take much money from her. When he does, she says it is better to keep her self-respect than to fight over money. Her sister-in-law complains that Aasia is manipulated into supporting his drug habit. When they run out of money she borrows from her brothers.

She looks back fondly on her own childhood, during which she felt greatly loved by her parents and brothers. 'I had the confidence then, and I would tell my parents I am going to become something.' Now she has those dreams for her own daughter instead, who at age five attends a government school. The LHW job has given her a sense of stability and pride because she can look after her own children. At some stage, when her children become older, she would like to find a way to earn more money.

Aasia does not feel that her status among her husband's family has changed much since she started to earn money. She says her husband has always let her take decisions and they only fight when she tries to convince him to get a job. She does feel all her husband's family command authority over her, but adds that they have treated her well, too.

Once a woman is launched into the role of a paid worker and a community resource, her opportunities for empowerment and the constraints she faces will differ according to her context and unfolding life circumstances. Aasia's story illustrates this, in contrast to the stories of Rabia and Fatima, who each managed to maximize the opportunities that opened up to them after becoming LHWs. Despite the advantages she enjoys, which put her in a position to qualify for the job, the particulars of her personal circumstances have not allowed her to build further on her auspicious start.

The possibilities of expanded mobility and improved status that are opened up by being an LHW are not the same in peri-urban and rural communities. In Karachi and its peri-urban sites, there is an ethnic mix of population that is seen as a threat by migrants from the rural areas, and is used to restrict women's mobility even more than in their villages. Aasia says it was only because she had lived so long in this predominantly Sindhi community that her brothers and husband felt they could justify her expanded mobility.

It is difficult to assess if and how Aasia's status in the community has changed, because in this peri-urban site there is no cohesive community. For example, in lanes adjacent to hers there were residents who had never heard of her, either because their homes did not fall into her catchment area or because they were not Sindhi and she may never have visited their homes. However, access to Pathans in her area remained problematic and Aasia was not yet able to break through these cultural and linguistic barriers. It is clear that this particular urban setting curbed her potential as a community resource.

Aasia acknowledges some positive changes within herself now that she is working, but they are offset by her challenging circumstances. For example, she says that this job has given her a sense of stability and expanded her horizons; she is now more comfortable meeting new people and finds her work is received more favourably in the community. But she also says that she had more confidence in her childhood, and no longer entertains the dreams she used to have. She has developed a sense of sisterhood in suffering with other women, but it has not translated into an urge to act and become more assertive with her husband. In fact, she falls back on another interpretation of the concept of honour, by arguing that by not fighting with him she is maintaining her self-respect. Although she distributes contraceptives, she has not yet begun to use any method herself.

Aasia's example illustrates how it remains possible to work as an LHW, yet experience little change in status. Aasia has not been able to push her husband into earning a steady living, as Fatima did, and is resigned to the state of her marriage for the moment. Her decision-making power in her marriage remains constant, probably by default, because her husband is not interested in taking an active role in their household. She has achieved some greater freedom in physical mobility, but her emotional life is circumscribed by the tension between her brothers' family and her in-laws, death, and the stress of a drug-addicted husband.

In this context, her supervisor has played a supportive role, encouraging her to continue work when she was ready to give up in the face of her personal problems and negative input from the community. Aasia's forbearance in the face of repeated set-backs, at only 22, suggests that she has the strength to build her life and achieve some of the stability she craves. That she even manages to perform as an LHW is an achievement in itself, and the responsibility and interaction involved in her work may also be a source of strength to her.

Paid work as a catalyst of positive change

The above analysis of selected LHW stories illustrates how paid work combines with circumstance and context to effect positive change at the personal and community levels. Caste and class, for example, are major forces of social organization – and we have seen that an LHW, backed by state sanction, is equipped to cross these barriers to perform her duties. Her success depends on many other factors, too, such as supportive family members who permit her expanded mobility, and how meaningful the work becomes to her on a personal level. This programme is timely because rapid urbanization, increased exposure to television, and the increasing acceptance of female education are having an effect on communities in both Sindh and Punjab. Women are demanding more paid work opportunities. Girls appear to be increasingly resentful if they are excluded from studies and contact with the wider world. Such tensions remind us that among women there is often a price to pay as expansion of opportunity for one woman may mean restriction for another, and this must be taken into account when assessing women's empowerment.

Within the private sphere and her own family, the LHW is redressing gender imbalances without directly confronting this most patriarchal of institutions. We have seen how her work has earned her increased agency. She enjoys increased decision making over her own reproductive health, the schooling and marriage decisions of children, and the management of her own and family finances. Even though life circumstances do not always permit women to follow a linear trajectory of empowerment, as illustrated in the story of Aasia above, we should view the training of an LHW, which converts her into an intellectual and community resource, as we do education itself – once given it cannot be taken away, no matter what contingencies surround and impede her. The full potential of her enhanced agency will only be known over the full course of her life, and time-bound research can only glimpse this potential.

The role of television and government-run advertisements in support of the LHW Programme have helped the LHW to gain credibility as a working woman. The public domain, through this medium, has inserted itself into the private sphere of the home, at the same time providing sanction to a specific type of increased mobility and income generation for women. This observation can be further appreciated by the fact that men often forbid women to watch television, perceiving this exposure as somehow violating segregation norms. Purdah norms are not static across Pakistan's diverse communities, and they even vary according to the stage in a woman's life cycle. Mumtaz and Salway (2007) found that women have greater restrictions on their mobility during pregnancy, yet as a woman ages her status within the household grows and changes, so that her empowerment cannot be assessed only in terms of indicators such as changes in her marital relationship or increased mobility (Das Gupta 1995). But it is while women are in their childbearing years, and most in need of reproductive health services, that they experience their greatest disadvantage, due to their low status in a joint family household and limited mobility. The LHW Programme breaks through this barrier of disadvantage by bringing vital services directly into the home to provide access to resources that would otherwise be denied to community women during their reproductive years.

What makes the programme so interesting is that the state is so vital to a process that can have such a transformative effect on women's lives. Development initiatives can build upon the LHW as a resource and community actor, as evidenced by Fatima's success with the micro-credit project. The LHWP must also continue to provide strong backing and support to LHWs in the form of media spots and even refresher trainings – which strengthen their position as a resource and emphasize state support for the programme. It is not possible to predict a general trajectory of empowerment that employment may trigger among women, as this study has shown. But if social policy is shaped alongside current social changes, then processes that support empowerment will surely be strengthened.

Note

1   Even though an LHW's earnings have only grown from a mere US$23 per month at the start of the programme to just US$60 per month today.

References

Das Gupta, M. (1995) 'Life Course Perspectives on Women's Autonomy and Health Outcomes', *American Anthropologist*, Vol. 97, No. 3, pp. 481–91.

Douthwaite, M. and P. Ward (2005) 'Increasing Contraceptive Use in Rural Pakistan: An Evaluation of the Lady Health Worker Programme', *Health Policy and Planning*, Vol. 20, No. 2, pp. 117–23.

Kabeer, N. (2001) *Resources, Agency, Achievements: Reflections on the Measurement of Women's Empowerment*. Sida Studies No. 3, SIDA, Stockholm.

N. Kabeer with R. Assaad, A. Darkwah, S. Mahmud, H. Sholkamy, S. Tasneem and D. Tsikata (2012) *Paid Work, Women's Empowerment and Inclusive Growth: Transforming the Structures of Constraint*, UN Women, New York, NY.

Khan, A. (2010) 'Women's Paid Work and Empowerment in Pakistan', in F. Azim and M. Sultan (eds), *Mapping Women's Empowerment: Experiences from Bangladesh, India and Pakistan*, University Press Limited, Dhaka.

Mumtaz, Z. and S. M. Salway (2007) 'Gender, Pregnancy and the Uptake of Antenatal Care Services in Pakistan', *Sociology of Health and Illness*, Vol. 29, No. 1, pp. 1–26.

6
Steady Money, State Support and Respect Can Equal Women's Empowerment in Egypt

Hania Sholkamy

Social protection programmes aimed at reducing vulnerability and promoting resilience to the shocks and risks of poverty and exclusion are spreading quickly all over the world. Cash transfers, public works programmes, pro-poor insurance schemes and subsidies are reaching millions in hundreds of countries (Holmes and Jones 2013; Hanlon *et al.* 2010; McCord 2009; Churchill and McCord 2012; Kabeer and Cook 2010). These interventions necessitate the redistribution of resources, assets or jobs, and can go beyond remedial measures to establish structural changes in the political economy of countries that adopt them on a large enough scale. They can also establish new rights. For example, the Mahatma Gandhi National Rural Employment Guarantee Scheme, started in India in 2006, provides a legal guarantee of 100 days' employment each year to anyone who requests it. If the guarantee is not met, the state must provide an unemployment allowance at a quarter of the wage due for each day that employment is not given (Holmes and Jones 2013).

This chapter examines the development of a pilot conditional cash transfer (CCT) programme carried out in the Cairo neighbourhood of Ain el Sira during 2008–12 by the Egyptian Ministry of Social Solidarity and its partners, with technical and research support provided by the American University in Cairo and the Pathways of Women's Empowerment programme. The aim was to test the programme in one urban setting in Cairo as a learning model for future national-level implementation. CCTs are seen to be efficient, effective, popular and even progressive because they divert resources to women. This programme sought to be even more progressive in that it contested the gender dynamics usually associated with CCTs: typically, these validate women's roles as mothers and ignore their productive roles and agency.

In the following sections the importance of social protection for women will be outlined before exploring some of the critiques of CCTs and their impact on women's empowerment. The Egyptian pilot study will then be discussed, showing how this attempted to be different and more 'feminist' in design. The conclusion will examine the impact the programme had on the residents of Ain el-Sira. It is the contention of this chapter that social protection programmes not only need a gender lens to be more effective in their primary role of mitigating poverty and vulnerability, but can also be the levers for a political transformation enabling poor women to escape the narrative of victimhood and gain recognition as citizens with rights.

Why women are a priority for social protection

There are four reasons why women should be the primary beneficiaries of social protection interventions/entitlements. These are the same reasons why social protection should be informed by feminist principles and practices. The first is that poverty has been feminized. While the concept that women are economically poorer than men worldwide has been refuted (Chant 2006), the 'feminization of poverty' theory with regard to control of resources, choice, equity and relations within the family unit is still valid in looking at gender inequity. Chant terms this type of poverty burden on women 'the feminization of responsibility and obligation'. While women increasingly work outside the home, their contribution is seen as a supplement to their husband's income and they are still expected to perform all the household tasks. Women are also primarily responsible for dealing with poverty within the home. And, while the burden of development is increasingly feminized, there is no corresponding increase in women's rights and rewards (Chant 2006: 182).

The second reason for feminizing social protection is that women have limited access to work, particularly formal work that brings benefits of social protection, security, access to networks, rights and power. In Egypt, the four million jobs that have been added to the labour market in the past decade have been informal ones that women, specifically rural ones, have entered. Informalization of labour markets is a growing phenomenon that is not abating as the cost of providing 'decent work' continues to challenge private and public sectors. Women in Egypt favour this work as it is easy to find and easy to leave. They accept poor working conditions with little or no rights so as to make up for shortfalls in household income. Men work informally, too, but they have an advantage when negotiating work and rights as the strictures of social norms value men over women. Young girls, on the other hand – employed on fruit farms, in informal workshops and factories, or in domestic work – cannot form alliances to negotiate their working conditions or rights. The most that these women can do is leave work – to their own detriment, as their need for income makes them accept other informal jobs.

The third reason why women need to be targeted with social protection is the lack of recognition for care work that lingers in public policy. The work that women do for their family does not enter public accounts. This work is a labour of love, but that does not mean it has no value. It should at least be recognized, if not rewarded. Developed economies and societies facilitate the care work of women by availing them of training; services that support their work such as pre-schools, home carers for the elderly or the sick, and after-school clubs for older children; and benefits that enable them to buy these services.

Less-developed economies do not provide these services. For example, in Egypt it is estimated that only 15 per cent of the under-fives go to nurseries or to pre-school. All day care is privately run and may be affordable to poor women if run by a charity, particularly a religious one, but these facilities are few and are beyond the means of most, and not available to rural women. Women who work in formal markets are the lucky few as they may get maternity leave, shorter working hours, benefits, access to day care and to health insurance for themselves and their families. Women who are self-employed, active in informal markets, or have no work outside the home have to fend for themselves.

The fourth reason for feminist social protection is that women may only be recognized as citizens through state benefits and programmes that target them, and have the creation of citizenship rights as an objective. Women who are poor and not formally employed have no access to recognition as citizens, as families and communities mediate their civic identity. Although these women are 'free' citizens, they are contingent ones. For example in Egypt, and during the now discredited parliamentary elections, a survey found that women living in conservative upper Egypt, and specifically those working at home and not for wages, were consistent voters – much more so than professional women in urban settings. The practice of block voting explains these findings, whereby women have voting cards but they are told who to vote for in accordance with the collective decision of the family – and in some cases block votes are sold by family elders. The voting practices of these women, and of male members of the clan who are young and less powerful, are counterfactuals that illustrate the contingency of citizenship on family, and underlie the complexities that riddle the relationship between women, their families and the state.

A decade ago women's rights advocates drew attention to the fact that most poor women do not have identity cards, thus making them unable to own or register property, access police stations, judicial processes and state benefits – or register their children in schools. This important finding led to a surge in projects that seek to register and formalize women's citizenship so as to give women access to their rights.

Critiques of conditional cash transfers

Champions of women's empowerment have been both triumphant about and troubled by the rise and spread of conditional cash transfers (CCTs). The triumph is that these programmes put resources directly into the hands of poor women, on condition that they access health and education and other services that they need for their families. These innovations have learned from decades of experiments and analysis of poverty, gender and service delivery that the burden of accessing health and education services can be onerous for poor households, and that women have often been at the front line, negotiating for resources for health care or education. Transferring cash is undeniably an efficient start; but small amounts of cash alone do not necessarily deliver enough to enable women to secure the services they and their families need.

The feminist critique, however, focused on the rewarding of motherhood to the exclusion of other bases for female entitlement and the individualization of women that dissembles their abilities for collective action. Some argue (Molyneux 2008; Chant 2006) that this focus on women's role in child care and women's responsibility for children will only further entrench them in a reproductive capacity, fortifying the traditional status quo rather than empowering women to make a difference in their lives, and in their 'bargaining position' within the family. While CCT programmes are built to be gender-aware, there are questions as to whether CCTs work towards empowerment or whether in effect they may be strengthening the traditional social constructs that confine gender equity. CCT programmes worldwide, though, champion the practice of giving the female family head cash transfers directly. It is argued, throughout the literature, that this is included in design to ensure that money will be spent on the home and the children, which is more likely to happen if the mother receives the cash transfer directly (Adato *et al.* 2000).

Studies of the Progresa/Opportunidades CCT programme

of Mexico show that it requires women to take their children to health clinics, meet with support groups, attend workshops, do community service, and obtain their transfers from a central location. These actions, it is argued, are empowering because women get out of the house. However, it is also argued that women, who are increasingly working outside the home, in addition to being solely responsible for all domestic tasks, are incredibly burdened and constrained (Molyneux 2008; Chant 2006). Requiring them to volunteer this time to fulfil programme conditions without offering any rights or rewards in return does not work towards increased gender equity. It is inherently unjust, as Chant points out, to require women to carry the burden of development and responsibility while not requiring anything of the men. Including the men in this dynamic is necessary, as their exclusion can encourage them to 'limit women's rights and to avoid assuming responsibilities for their children's upkeep' (Chant 2006: 185).

Criticism levelled at CCTs has not dented the appetite of countries for introducing them. But there are valid concerns about the merits of giving cash to people who need it. There are concerns about the promotion of dependency on these payments, and the associated impact this could have on the desire of adults to find work. Key to the concept of CCTs is the size of the transfer. It needs to be large enough to cover the costs of the family and provide incentive for the human development investments that are asked by way of the conditions, while at the same time small enough not to create dependency. But will giving 'small' cash transfers, others object, make it impossible for the family to fulfil the conditions or make life changes – leading to disposal of the cash in directions other than those intended?

Another problem that arises with CCTs is lack of control in the supply of public services offered to people who are required to use them to comply with cash transfer conditions (Hall 2008; Soares 2004; Soares and Britto 2007). Government expenditure on public goods such as health and schooling must rise in quality and quantity to meet the increased demand. Requiring families to get poor health care is simply counter-productive. As Soares points out, 'it is necessary to improve the quality of social services so that the promises of a break in the intergenerational cycle of poverty can be fulfilled' (Soares 2004).

Social assistance in the form of regular cash can be designed either to retain traditional gender roles or to question them. Critics of cash transfers have highlighted the role of cash in keeping women back and foisting on them traditional cares and responsibilities. The pilot CCT programme in Egypt tried to advance the second – critical – objective. This was a programme that recognized women's needs and rights as individuals and promoted cash as a way to relieve women from 'bad' work and enable them to have money to spend on the things that are important to them, while not discouraging them from work.

Design features that enable cash to honour and empower: the Ain-el-Sira experiment

The Ain-el-Sira CCT pilot scheme based in a Cairo slum benefited from feminist activism, scholarship and practice throughout its four stages of development. The pilot was inspired by a woman politician's visit to Chile's Solidario CCT programme. She enlisted the support of a feminist social policy expert to help propose a CCT at the ruling party's conference in 2006. Backed by the Egyptian Human Development Report 2005, which argued for a CCT programme for Egypt, and framed it as an anti-poverty programme with great potential for popular political support, the proposal won powerful allies within the ruling party, and funds were earmarked for it within the budget.

At first the policy space this carved out looked set to be filled by ideas generated by the World Bank, working with top officials. The social policy expert who had helped prepare the original proposal was positioned to advise the minister informally, and proposed instead an experiment to contextualize the programme for Egypt. Participatory research in the pilot site uncovered a range of issues that had not been expected: women's informal economic activity was an important – but unrecognized – element of household economies, while schools were corrupt and failing: poor households were spending – on average – an exorbitant 164 Egyptian pounds (164 EGP = $30) monthly on compulsory private tuition from school teachers. The design of the programme took these findings into account, focusing on developing recognition of women's informal work and facilitating civil society organizations to provide after-school activities.

Molyneux (2008) has warned against any association between cash and women's empowerment. Despite decades of interventions that seek to empower women economically and have become a foundation of gender and development, it is not the cash *per se* that empowers. All of the interventions that seek to boost women's incomes – skills training, support for paid work, and (the most ubiquitous of all programmes) micro-credit and access to finance schemes – work best if they go beyond income. Independent incomes seemingly enable women to do things, make choices, resist pressures, have voice and protect themselves, but income alone cannot challenge hierarchy, nor transform relationships. Key to the potential of income to empower are the implications of this income on agency, personhood, status and rights. The key question is not how much women make but rather what income makes them. It is the contention of this chapter that conditional cash transfers can empower poor women if the transfers are made as recognition of women's unpaid care work, and if they structure a basis of entitlement that recognizes the value of women's work.

Designing programmes that address social life from a woman's perspective is a feminist approach to programming and policy making. The Egypt programme began by interviewing women individually and collectively and asking them to describe what they experienced as their burdens, challenges, and desires or aspirations. Women expressed a need for cash to make up for shortfalls in spouses' incomes, a desire to ensure that their children go to, stay in, and excel at school, a wish to know more about programmes, services and opportunities in their community, and a thirst for decent work and viable shelter. This information became the basis of the Egyptian CCT programme, and led to a number of design features. Unlike previous social policy interventions, it was clearly announced as one that targets women in families, not only women heads of families, and requires them to sign a contract of mutual obligations with the state, thus honouring women's responsibilities as mothers and as citizens. Women had complained that they were mistreated by service providers, whether teachers, health-care officials or social workers. The programme therefore stressed the role of social workers in supporting women to access existing services and to become more demanding consumers of these public goods and services.

The programme was clearly advertised and implemented as one that did not require proof of unemployment, and as one that would continue to support families of working women even if their income improved, but would reassess family needs after a two-year period. This gave families the security they needed for long-term planning of home improvements or of stable employment. It enabled participating women to engage in work on better terms as they felt that they had some money coming in that was not conditional on the employer's favour .

Co-responsibilities, previously known as conditions, empower women and enable them to make decisions at the household level in ways that they are not able to do in the absence of such terms. In cases where men have privileged rights to decision making, especially concerning household expenditure, childhood education and savings, the conditions enable women to 'guard' the money from transfers and ensure that it is spent on education, nutrition, health and home improvements. These conditions also enable women to receive social workers that visit once a month to track progress, and to go to meetings at school or to seek health care so as to abide by these conditions.

Co-responsibilities are frowned upon as either unnecessary – families want to educate their children and care for them anyway, so why bother – or as undignified: parents know what they need to spend their money on, so there is no need for the state to tell them what to do. Both these claims ignore the unequal distribution of power within the household. Women in Egypt had said that by and large they have to make the daily decisions on household expenditures. They also said that they tend to keep their own income from work. However, both of these norms are often frustrated or decimated in times of crisis, whether economic, social or intimate. The conditions provide succour to women when they disagree with spouses or older women on how money should be spent. They are then able to decide to support or ignore competing demands on their cash.

The conditions are also a vehicle that identifies care work as labour that is worthy of compensation. Women are paid to care for and spend cash on their children. The programme in Egypt was clear in stating that the cash compensates women for their time in attending programme meetings and social worker visits, as well as acting as a partial support for women's income needs. In this way the cash became an entitlement for work done and time spent.

Poor women have few ways of protecting their income or saving their money. The Egypt programme followed other programmes such as Brazil's 'Bolsa Familia' and 'bankerized' the payments, thus enabling women to access their transfers through a bank card. Not only did no women report losing their cards, but all were able to use ATM machines and to regulate their expenditures based on their need. Most women in the urban slum where the pilot took place still wanted to withdraw all their cash at the beginning of the month just to make sure it was all there, but some did save, while others just liked the privacy afforded by a bank account. The bank cards gave women a sense of security and protection. To be issued with the cards women had to have identity cards and to go to the bank to register. The bank refused to let these poor women in, and the manager explained that having 'their sort' on the bank floor would drive away regular customers. 'Women like this do not enter banks!' the manager exclaimed. The bank sent employees to the programme offices to register the women and issue their cards. This incident made the cards into objects of status and entitlement. This is far from a trivial detail or story. Women need not only services, but good ones that enable them to catch up with the rest of the world. Protecting the money meant that women did not have cash on them, so could not be forced into paying or giving up their transfers, but also had a 'modern' and safe way of saving and guarding this money.

One of the objectives of the programme in Egypt was to ensure that women's citizenship and their social and political rights were supported and enhanced. The social worker is instrumental in this regard. The experiment took mutual accountability between women and officials seriously. The social workers tasked with delivering the services – themselves mainly low-income women – were trained to support the programme design process. This helped to raise their low official status and encouraged a strong sense of programme ownership. Social workers visited women to monitor the conditions but also to provide information and clarifications. The most important of these was that, beyond the contractual conditions, women are neither obliged nor indebted to anyone. The monthly sessions organized by social workers for groups of 30 women at a time were also devoted to rights awareness and covered topics such as independent voting, micro-credit and indebtedness, housing rights, and reproductive or general health concerns. Women cannot become more powerful by money alone, but the confluence of cash, service-provider support and co-responsibilities builds a force sufficient to address power disparities. The social worker provides support, information, clarifications, and a connection with the state.

Safeguards were inserted against social worker corruption or control. Bankerized payments ensured that bribes became impossible. A self-monitoring tool was given to each woman, so she could follow her own performance *vis-à-vis* the conditions, and thus have evidence to argue against injustice. A contract was signed between the women and the state with clear terms and entitlements so that there was transparency in all aspects of the programme. This contract was given to families so that it became a point of reference for grievances. The model of social work was also addressed, with training for social workers that promoted values of rights and gender justice. Social workers were encouraged to share information, to guard confidentiality, and to rotate their supervision of families so that no family was stuck with one social worker all the time. The programme did not tell women what to do but rather supported their own choices with information, administrative/service provider support, respect and cash. The objective was to create a channel between women and state-supplied goods and services, and a relationship that was not mediated by family or kin.

A programme that works towards enabling, and maybe in the long run empowering poor women in families should also be one that supports them by recognizing their own choices and obligations while instilling a relationship between them and a progressive state that is equitable in its policies. This relationship must bypass old and new kin and community structures that entrench principles of bias against women and impose unfair burdens on them. A deeper engagement of social workers who are committed to a progressive form of social work and who are state agents can make a big difference in the impact of the programme. The difference between state and civil society in this respect is the difference between projects and policies. Civil society can monitor programmes, can organize social audits, can provide auxiliary benefits and projects, can even take on the responsibility of providing work opportunities or better markets so that families will find exits from poverty. But the state is the duty bearer in the case of social protection and, for these transfers to work, they must be entitlements not handouts.

Conditions or co-responsibilities can enable women to fund decisions that would otherwise require a male or older person's authority and approval. In Egypt, most women spent the money on children's education, clothing, nutrition and on home improvements. They did use the cash to be 'better mothers', but in doing so had used a bank card, accessed information on rights and resources, attended a few collective meetings, and financed their own enterprises or looked for work opportunities. Micro-credit was the option that both state and civil society took as a social protection intervention. During fieldwork in the Cairo slum where the programme began, most men who were asked had refused to take micro-credit because of the 'high interest rate and repayment schedule', adding that it is for women not for men. They preferred the small loans made available by mosques and some social banks, which give the borrower enough of a grace period to be able to pay back the sum with reasonable interest rates. Women in this slum not only take micro-credit but are embroiled in cycles of debt with money borrowed from neighbours, relatives, NGOs and local loan sharks. If anything, the programme helped these women manage their debts and extract themselves from situations in which they had to pay very high interest rates.

The predictability of the transfers enabled women to plan household expenditures over a longer cycle and so save for times when expenditures were high, while splurging in the summer when there is no tuition to pay. This was the time of home improvements, fixing drains, doors, buying simple furniture, fixing leaking roofs and spending on clothes for the children and some outings. The programme confirmed the entitlements and opportunities of the young and recognized the roles and rights of women in family survival and support.

A reality check on women's lives in Egypt

In Egypt, women's security in the present and future used to be guaranteed by the mutual obligation created by marriage and motherhood ties. A succession of economic and social transformations has dissolved these ties and left women without a predictable or sufficient source of protection. Citizenship rights and entitlements are still predicated on a specific and no longer universally valid model of the family. This model assumes that conventional gender roles are intact and that women are still performing familial duties as men undertake to provide for their families through work. The model has retained its moral and ideological authority, but it no longer informs the practical decisions and experiences of men and women. The state is obliged to reformulate the entitlements of citizenship so as to provide women with the right to social protection, whether they are single or in families.

Pathways researchers interviewed Nagah at the offices of the CCT pilot programme in Ain el-Sira. Nagah's story is typical of the complex lives of urban women living in poverty in Egypt. She has been married and divorced twice. She has two daughters from her first husband and Mohamed, her son, is from her second marriage. Both marriages ended badly and she receives no money from either man in terms of maintenance or child support. The first husband has a disabled child and cannot afford to give her any support. The second husband threatened to take the child away if she demanded money. Nagah does not want to enter a legal battle for fear that her husband would contest her support of the child, even though she knows she has the right to maintenance. Like millions of others she has no recourse to security or protection save that of family or husband support. She is the victim of the enduring myth of the male breadwinner.

Nagah learned welding from her father and fixes gasoline stoves and small appliances for people in the community. She only works a few days a month, and charges one or two EGP, but sometimes she gets bigger projects. To expand the business she needs more supplies, but she has a young son so she prefers to use the money for his education and other basic needs.

When Nagah was asked what she did with the money from the CCT, she said she bought special treats for her family, using her bank card to withdraw the monthly transfer. This month she purchased two kilos of oranges, *koshari* (an Egyptian ready-cooked food made from pasta, rice and lentils) and milk for her son. This month she paid 17 EGP on a family outing. She also paid to renew her ration card, which cost 40 EGP. Over the past year she used some of the transfer to make improvements to her home, such as fixing the leaking toilet and buying a new fan and refrigerator, 'of course in instalments'.

When Nagah needs money she takes out a loan from a local organization. Recently, she took out 500 EGP from an NGO, which was to be paid back at 57.50 EGP per month for ten months. She gave this money to her daughter who is getting married so that she would be able to buy a stove with an oven. She has already paid back the money. She has also borrowed 4,000 EGP [400 GBP] from a 'kind woman' who wanted to help her and her daughter out. But she does not think she can pay this money back. For Nagah and many other women, the monthly transfer is her only source of stable income and the only income upon which she can rely.

Conclusion

The CCT pilot programme in Ain el Sira was terminated in 2012 by the then minister on the grounds that it was illegal and wrongly targeted because it gave support to women. The revolution and subsequent upheavals had already stalled the payments for many of the families and prevented a second wave of applications, despite the large number of almost destitute women who applied. All women who had been clients of the programme were interviewed at the end of the second year of payments. Despite the difficult circumstances[1] in which these interviews were taking place and the relatively small number of families who had been beneficiaries, there were some noteworthy findings.

There was a remarkable decrease in reported domestic violence. A third of women who had said they were abused reported that this abuse had stopped. 'There is less to fight about,' one said. The explanations were as follows. The cash had relieved the whole household of much stress. Women did not have to pressure men for urgent money, and that made for a more peaceful home environment. When asked if the payment had made them stop work the answer was overwhelmingly negative. They still worked but did so on the basis of choice, not desperation. They managed their work by making the most of the security offered by knowing that they were getting a monthly transfer. Women who worked in markets could buy better-quality goods to sell without feeling they were depriving their children of food or education. Those who used to sweep or wash floors could hold out and look for less demeaning work. Women who used to keep their children from school so that they helped them out in their chores stopped doing so, as the programme required children to attend school.

Managing work with less pressure was a contributing factor to the drop in domestic violence. Women were also happy to report that their children had achieved better school results than in the preceding years. They were able to afford tutorials but also able to pressure their children to attend school so as not to forfeit their transfers. The schools were still as bad as ever but the children were keen on attending, and on resisting the factors that push them out of school such as classroom violence.

A feminist approach to social protection is one that defines, targets and alleviates poverty as the women who are living in deprivation define it. As a feminist social protection intervention, the cash transfer programme in Ain el Sira sought to redress gender imbalances by restoring the accountability of the state to poor women and their families. It sought to do this by enhancing women's identities as citizens, and by enabling women to assume the roles that they want to assume and fulfil the obligations that they value. Any social intervention can be good or bad for women. An approach framed by feminist principles made the Egyptian experience into a social intervention that could empower women because it recognizes their roles, aspirations and choices.

Social interventions that are intended as poverty alleviation or mitigation programmes can create new gendered hierarchies. Micro-credit, for example, may have increased incomes but it has also created a credit market in which women bear the burden of high interest rates and low returns on the investments that they do make. Initially micro-credit was intended as an empowering vehicle that delivered women from dire poverty through a system of lending that encouraged collective action and solidarity. These are feminist ideals and principles, which somehow got lost when micro-credit became an international success story.

Conditional cash transfers have been criticized for the burdens they place on women and are not in themselves empowering to women. This chapter has illustrated how they can be made to serve the needs of very poor women when these programmes are designed with this intent in mind. The Egyptian experience recognized the necessity of women's recognition, respect and support as key elements of social protection and poverty alleviation. Although the monitoring and evaluation of the programme were incomplete, since it was prematurely terminated in 2012, the experience still shows the possibility of conceptualizing a women's empowerment strategy that is grounded in the rights to work and to social protection. Just as women must have rights equal to those that men enjoy, they must also have the right to be recognized as caregivers and breadwinners, and to ensure that the state recognizes all of these rights. The programme described in this chapter was framed as an intervention that sought to realize and confirm these rights.

Note

1 Interviews were conducted in April 2012, when most husbands and partners had lost their work and the transfers were the only source of income for many families. Moreover, there were gang wars going on in the area and over 80 people were killed or severely injured in the week preceding the interviews.

References

Adato, M., B. de la Brière, D. Mindek and A. Quisumbing (2000) *The Impact of Progresa on Women's Status and Intrahousehold Relations*, International Food Policy Research Institute, Washington DC.

Chant, S. (2006) 'The "Feminization of Poverty" and the "Feminization" of Anti-Poverty Programmes: Room for Revision?', *Journal of Development Studies*, Vol. 44, No. 2, pp. 165–97.

Churchill, C. and M. J. McCord (2012) 'Current Trends in Micro-insurance', in C. Churchill and M. Matul (eds), *Protecting the Poor: A Microinsurance Compendium Vol. II*, ILO, Geneva.

Hall, A. (2008) 'Brazil's Bolsa Familia: A Double-edged Sword?', *Development and Change*, Vol. 39, No. 5, pp. 799–822.

Hanlon, J., A. Barrientos and D. Hulme (2010) *Just Give Money to the Poor: The Development Revolution from the Global South*, Kumarian Press, Sterling, VA.

Holmes, R. and N. Jones (2013) *Gender and Social Protection in the Developing World: Beyond Mothers and Safety Nets*, Zed Books, London and New York, NY.

Kabeer, N. and S. Cook (2010) 'Introduction: Overcoming Barriers to the Extension of Social Protection – Lessons from the Asia Region', *IDS Bulletin*, Vol. 41, No. 4, pp. 1–11.

McCord, A. (2009) 'Cash Transfers: Affordability and Sustainability', ODI Project Briefings 30, Overseas Development Institute, London.

Molyneux, M. (2008) 'Conditional Cash Transfers: A "Pathway to Women's Empowerment"?', Pathways Working Paper 5, Pathways of Women's Empowerment Programme, Brighton.

Soares, F. (2004) 'Conditional Cash Transfers: A Vaccine Against Poverty and Inequality?', IPC-IG Collection of One Pagers, p. 3, International Policy Centre for Inclusive Growth, Brasilia.

Soares, F. V. and T. Britto (2007) '"Growing Pains": Key Challenges for New Conditional Cash Transfer Programmes in Latin America', Working Paper No. 38 (November), International Poverty Centre, Brasilia.

7

Changing Representations of Women in Ghanaian Popular Music

• •

Akosua Adomako Ampofo and Awo Mana Asiedu

Music does not come to mind immediately as a site for development work or advocacy. However, it is an important conduit for the transmission of society's cultural values, beliefs and norms, including notions of womanhood and women's place in society, and for the formulation and contestation of black identity (Collins 2004). Across Africa, music is constantly heard booming from shops, restaurants, taxis, buses, lorries and other public sites, and it plays a significant part in the everyday lives of people – across boundaries of age, class, religion, ethnicity and social occasion. Events such as marriages, naming ceremonies and funerals – or public and state functions such as lectures and the commissioning of projects – are deemed incomplete without music. People draw inspirational, educational and emotional messages from music, and the lyrics are repeated in daily conversations. Musicians frequently become powerful public figures capable of conveying ideas that enter the weave of popular culture through their lyrical and verbal pronouncements. In this way, the whole society is exposed to songs and their messages.

While there are several studies on the role of music in political activism (Asante-Darko and van der Geest 1983; Kong 1995; Vambe 2000), work on gendered images in popular music and their potential to (dis)empower women is rarer. Music, like other art forms, often relies on stereotypes to create and convey its messages. Stereotypes may serve as sites where models of behaviour (representation) become models for behaviour (warnings, advice), making narratives available for practical application to listeners' experiences (Barber 1997; Newell 2000). Women in a variety of cultures have been represented either as decorative, fetishistic, manipulative, fragile, or in need of rescuing (or 'protective' domination) in contemporary popular music lyrics, music videos, music concerts and movie soundtracks (Hobson and Bartlow 2008).

Among the major musical genres that enjoy tremendous popularity in Ghana today are highlife, hip-life, hip-hop and gospel.[1] Highlife, together with its more recent offshoot, hip-life, lends its voice to the issues of the day, as well as values and belief systems in Ghanaian society, be they gender conventions or more general notions about human nature (Collins 1994). Entering the Ghanaian music scene in the early 1990s, hip-life – a hybrid musical genre with its roots in highlife and heavily influenced by hip-hop and reggae rhythms – has since become the dominant musical form in youth pop culture. Rapped in local Ghanaian dialects,[2] pidgin and English, hip-life has been dubbed 'the voice of a generation' (Asante 2004). Collins (2000) claims that the lyrics of contemporary Ghanaian highlife focus almost solely on romantic love and sexual innuendo; in the case of hip-life there is a definite macho flavour to the lyrics and a tendency to objectify women in the songs and videos of the genre.

In this chapter we take as given the notion of gendered interpretation, the prevailing sexual stereotypes of women within Ghanaian popular music, the role that popular music has played and will play in shaping and reflecting society, and the need to take a comprehensive approach to women's empowerment. We consider the possibility that while popular music may be a significant contemporary site for women's disempowerment through gender stereotyping, popular music can also be used as a vehicle for the empowerment of women through innovative and transformative approaches. Echoing Simone, we ask: 'if urban culture is a mirroring process through which residents understand something about their collective life, as well as a vehicle through which implicit forms of social collaboration are put to work'

(2008: 76), how do images in popular music reproduce or subvert particular constructions of women and gender relations?

In what follows we draw on a project that explored the gendered stereotypes of women in popular music, and sought to contribute to reflection on, and creation of, alternative (empowering) narratives about women through song. The project involved an extensive analysis of the lyrics of music produced by Ghanaian popular artistes since the 1930s,[3] using emerging themes as an entry point for workshops[4] with musicians. Focus groups and workshops with those involved in the music industry as producers and consumers of popular music in Ghana contributed to a process that brought scholar-activists, music producers and music consumers together in a conversation that culminated in a competition to generate 'empowering songs'. This chapter reflects on representations of women in Ghanaian popular music culture, and the challenge of change.

Popular music and sexuality: women as objects or subjects?

Human sexuality is an important part of life and so it is not surprising that it should form such an important pivot for popular cultural products. The question of *how* this is represented is, however, paramount. Clearly sexuality can be presented in ways that may be creative or destructive. When does the representation of sexuality in popular music cease to be creative and become destructive and demeaning of women? Are women presented merely as objects of sex with a focus on their bodies, or are both men and women presented as respectful mutual partners? Cole challenges African gender scholarship to interrogate 'the rift between theories of how gender is constructed and the actual on-the-ground practices of how gender is performed and enacted' (2007: 272). Popular culture provides vivid on-the-ground enactments of gender that must be confronted. A cursory examination of the representations of women in contemporary popular media suggests a conflicting, ambivalent at best, relationship to women's bodies and sexuality. Music videos herald a dress culture where less and tighter is better. At the same time, public rhetoric is saturated with the notion of women's 'indecent dress'.[5] The danger that a male-dominated production of popular culture will continue to replicate gender stereotypes and misrepresentations is very real; Collins (2000) argues that the majority of Ghanaian rap singers tend to objectify women in their songs and videos.

Representations of women's bodies and sexualities in the media have a bearing on women's actual and potential pathways of empowerment for, in addition to configuring representations of sexuality, popular media such as music also organize and express *norms* around women's sexualities. In view of this we theorize our work within the larger body of work on sexual politics – representations, identities and power (Collins 2004). Pereira notes that sexuality is 'articulated with the ways in which gendered human beings become defined within particular, singular *identities* and the *cultural* frameworks that give meaning to such constructions at given historical moments' (2003).

The literature on women's empowerment has pointed to several areas where this 'empowerment' should occur, and is or is not occurring – domestic decision making, access to resources, control over resources, equal rights and freedom from discrimination, the sexual division of labour, and participation in public office, to name a few. Sexuality usually enters the discourse via the concept of 'bodily integrity'. Here one is talking about women's 'control' over their fertility and reproductive behaviour; access to reproductive health-care information and services; care and nurture of the body; restrictions on physical mobility; policing of appearance; and exposure to violence. Thus, the process of empowerment is expected to increase women's capacities to make choices that will enhance 'bodily integrity' – increase the ability to take care of one's body and enhance the level of personal (bodily) security.

Although the literature examines the misrepresentation of African female sexuality and the complex intersecting dimensions of gender, race, religion and culture, as well as same-sex relationships, some African feminist scholars and activists have suggested that a strong silence remains regarding the question of female sexuality within African women's and gender studies, particularly in relation to pleasure (Adomako Ampofo *et al.* 2004; McFadden 2003; Mama 1996). An interesting debate ensues between McFadden and Pereira in a 2003 issue of *Feminist Africa*. McFadden argues that sexual pleasure is intrinsic to feminist empowerment and that the silences around the subject reflect a lack of feminist agency and determination:

> For the majority of black women, the connection between power and pleasure is often not recognised, and remains a largely un-embraced and undefined heritage.... In often obscure or hidden ways, it lies at the heart of female freedom and power; and when it is harnessed and 'deployed', it has the capacity to infuse every woman's personal experience of living and being with a liberating political force. (McFadden 2003: 50)

Pereira's response is not simply to consign women's bodily integrity to constructions of practical (versus strategic) needs, such as protection from HIV infection, but to legitimize these so-called silences from a historical perspective, 'given the historical conditions of imperial expansion and racist fascination with the hypersexuality projected onto Africans by Europeans'. She advocates that it would be more productive to map sexualities 'with a view to their future exploration and understanding' (2003: 62). Collins articulates the ways in which the representation of (black) bodies reinforces gender and racial stereotypes: 'Because of its authority to shape perceptions of the world, global mass media circulates images of Black femininity and Black masculinity and, in doing so, ideologies of race, gender, sexuality, and class' (2004: 122).

As with its American precursor, Ghanaian hip-life music provides no easy distinction between representations of sexually liberated women and those who are sexual objects, 'their bodies on sale for male enjoyment' (Collins, 2004: 126). However, as Anyidoho argued in our textual analysis workshop, more important than what and how musicians self-identify is how these messages are read by the music's consumers. Thus, the creators and consumers of music may share (and not always unequally) in the power to provide meaning to the lyrics.

Identity and power are associated with the language and practice of development. When it comes to the question of development practice, Armas (2007) claims that sexuality has actually been sidelined by development. Associated more with disease, risk and danger than with pleasure or love, sex has been treated by development agencies as something to be controlled and contained; thus African people are often presented by others as over-sexed, and policies are geared to controlling their sexuality (Arnfred and Adomako Ampofo 2010; Ezumah 2009). In contrast to the 'development discourse' of the 1970s and 1980s, issues affecting women today are frequently discussed within the framework of 'rights'. Since the 1990s the rights-based approach has become a critical element in development discourse, policy and practice. The AIDS epidemic has broken old taboos and silences, and begun to open up space for the recognition of how central sexual rights are to well-being. However, efforts need to be made beyond the confines of narrow, problem-focused thinking. Feminist scholars argue that sexuality is a vital aspect of development, and that sexual rights are a precondition for reproductive rights and for gender equality (Armas 2007; McFadden 2003).

Armas further advocates the use of rights as an entry point to talk about sexuality in relation to development. We agree that there is value in promoting sexuality beyond the narrow confines of disease, and recognizing the importance of pleasure; however, as we have mentioned, we feel that it is extremely important to examine how 'pleasure' is represented. This is particularly important given the connections between sexual representations and society's differing moral prescriptions for women and men. Rights-based approaches that take on questions of sexual rights could be a part of the process of creating positive representations of women as gendered bodies, and this could be articulated through song.

In a lot of ways, therefore, popular music can be politicized. Emphasizing the accessibility of the popular music medium, with particular reference to (Ghanaian) highlife, Asante-Darko and van der Geest (1983) promote the potential for political – overt or subtle – messages to be expressed within Ghana. Beyond Ghana, studies have explored the use of popular songs for a variety of ends: to reinforce an ideology and legitimize a ruling elite; to act as a rallying call to others so as to establish and reinforce group identity; and to voice dissatisfaction with society, including social norms and political conditions (Kong 1995). Kong further notes how political dissatisfaction is captured, for example, in American 'protest songs', while opposition to social norms has been expressed in rock 'n' roll. She notes that slave songs, for example, provided African-Americans with a way of expressing and communicating under conditions of great oppression, and freedom songs associated with the civil rights movement provide an illustration of how songs help mobilize protest and create group solidarity in specific situations. In Zimbabwe the tradition of song as social commentary has been well established (Vambe 2000). In the US, educators have harnessed the power of popular music through the rewriting of rap lyrics to help in the fostering of children's self-esteem and the countering of negative images of women in the media.

According to Carla E. Stokes, the founder of HOTGIRLS (Helping Our Teen Girls In Real Life Situations) rewriting song lyrics helps girls 'critically analyse the messages they encounter in the media and in their daily lives', moreover 'girls are *using* hip hop as a vehicle to reach their peers and raise awareness about issues that affect their lives' (cited in Kieya 2007). Teens have taken to the recording studio to create their versions of popular songs, such as 'Let Me Tell You How You Talk to Me', a reworked version of Justin Timberlake's song 'Sexy Back'. Thus popular music can become a powerful vehicle for cultural and political expression and prompt the politicization of personal spaces (the home, street, music shop or club, for instance) as it provides 'portable politics' over which individuals may exert some control (Allen 2004: 4).

The combination of entertainment and education is seen in contemporary practice as an innovative approach to achieving social change (Singhal and Rogers 1999). The process of deliberately designing media messages to both entertain and educate in order to increase knowledge about an issue, create favourable attitudes and change overt behaviour has been coined 'enter-education' (Singhal and Rogers 1999). Our study sought to harness this potential of popular music. In the next section we report on what we learned about the potency of popular music, and on our efforts to challenge popular musicians to be more reflexive and critical in their representations of women.

Changing the representations of women in popular music

Reflection workshops and conversations with music consumers threw up several popular themes about women in songs. On the positive side they are seen as the keepers of tradition, they are dependable, a source of joy, virtuous angels (usually as wives and mothers); they are (appropriately) submissive, never angry, caring, kind and welcoming of a man's relatives. Songs evoked praise for women's intelligence and spirituality as well as their reproductive/mothering roles and their being faithful lovers (even when their men went astray). Participants in the first workshop also noted that the theme of beauty was common in songs and not always in an objectifying sense. However, in both reflection workshops and the conversations with students and taxi drivers, participants felt that on balance the images were more negative, or at least not empowering. On the negative side participants agreed that women are objectified sexually, with a focus on (big) breasts/butt and other motifs that go beyond appreciating the body and desire, to mere lust.

Other portrayals included women as exploitative, unfaithful, unreliable, enchantresses, witches, jealous, competitive (typically with other women over men), unstable, weak-minded, fickle, greedy/materialistic, exploitative, ungrateful and lazy. Some notions could be described as neutral or merely factual descriptions, such as women being described as subordinate to men or ready to defer to men, and women being 'weaker' than men (their role does not include the use of the gun, and men defend women/children). Not surprisingly, in both workshops the older musicians felt that it was principally the younger ones who provided women's bodies as fodder for the male imagination. In the 2010 workshop, Nana Ampadu, a veteran from the 1970s and 1980s, insisted that love songs of his generation were not imbued with 'pornography'.

Participants in the two reflection workshops suggested several reasons for the negative representations of women, including tradition, religion, capitalism and generational tensions. Argued one:

> I see people refer to religion as a reason for women to submit ... religion makes it taboo to say certain things ... it is wrong for a woman to say [the same things as men] because of religion even though she feels so inside ... and on the capitalism side ... sex sells, it's commercially viable, musicians doing good work are not respected ... they want to see women shaking their buttocks. (Kubolor the WunLuv, musician)

Thus, while tradition controls women, the capitalist market provides opportunities to sell them. Collins (1994) argues that when traditional expectations of women's roles come into conflict with some aspects of urban lifestyles and Westernization, they combine to threaten 'traditional' male authority, which helps to explain why popular texts so often dwell on the subject of sexual tension, marriage treachery, prostitution, witchcraft accusations and the duplicity of city women.

Participants in both workshops and group discussions stressed that music is influential. In the second reflection workshop, Carlos Sakyi, music producer, noted simply that 'music can influence the way people think and act'. A taxi driver who had ceased listening to a particular musician because of his negative portrayal of sex, which he felt would influence him, now listens only to gospel music and says, 'the words in the [gospel] songs touch my heart that is why I listen to them'. Another driver noted, 'I strongly believe that songs have a great influence on people.' In the conversation snippets below, a taxi driver not only identifies the power of songs, but calls for advocacy around music:

> *Taxi driver:* When we were young, during the olden days our grandparents used to tell us stories through songs and the words would make you have change of mind about a lot of things. The words made you respectful ... and they made you responsible.

> *Discussion leader:* Do you really believe that songs can change a man's way of thinking or have great impact on people?

> *Taxi driver:* I strongly believe that songs have a great influence on people. There are certain songs when being played; you feel the words cannot help you positively. There are others too when played, everybody joins in singing because the words are encouraging. For this reason, there is the need to have leaders who would frankly come out to say the words in a particular song are bad and would influence the youth negatively.
>
> Something like '*adepa hye adepa mu*';[6] if you are a mature person you realize the song can harm children. If I hear such songs I switch my radio off. If there is a passenger in the car and the song is being played, you the driver feel guilty.
>
> When you listen to Fiifi Banson's[7] programme ... when you have passengers in the car you would be forced to switch off the radio. Because I wouldn't like the passenger to listen to such a song ... either I switch it off or tune it to a different station. And most passengers do not complain.

The students were even more convinced of the power of lyrics. One female student said, 'I weigh the contents of the music before I listen to it.' And another explained, 'Some make you depressed, some make you emotional. Some of these songs create some perceptions like, I don't want to be in a relationship.' A male student noted:

> When I look at the lyrics of this particular song, I think it is full of sexual elements and it will really trigger relationships. As young people if you should be alone with your girlfriend and you play such songs no matter who you are something will happen.

Particularly influential is the fact that today the music is heard over and over again; as one female student explained, 'When something is said over and over again it affects your thinking. It's the lyrics that affect you when listened to over and over again'.

The conversations with the students and taxi drivers also provided support for the view that songs negatively stereotype and/or sexualize women. Not surprisingly, women students were more critical of the representations of women in song than the men were, and they complained strongly about the sexual objectification of women in songs and how this made them feel. They also hinted at what this might mean for their own relations with men. One woman student said:

> I don't like the way they portray women in their clips. I think it's so shameful and degrading. You see them wearing all sorts of clothes. They are exposing their body parts. It's bad, very bad and I feel so shameful [sic] because I feel like it makes me so transparent around guys and I don't like it.

Others noted:

> There is this song recently and it talks about girls. It goes like, 'you be *yawa* girl'. I don't know what the girl did and it's like the guys are really on the girl telling the girl she is *yawa* [posturing]. Maybe they asked for something from her and she didn't give it out − I don't know what it is, maybe sex or anything. It's like most guys if they should ask you and you don't give it to them, they tell you, you are *yawa*. I think that song is very bad. (Female student)

> What I feel is some of these songs portray women as sex objects. It's like they see us as something they can play with. (Female student)

Some men, especially the taxi drivers, also acknowledged that popular urban music, especially in its video version, objectifies women sexually:

> Well we can say that most of our songs do not say anything good about women. They most often talk about ladies' style of dressing and their body parts. It's not nice. I have not heard them using men in their songs. (Taxi driver)

The all-pervading power of music makes messages about

women part of people's realities in subtle ways. Some participants insisted that song lyrics could influence one's behaviour for good or ill, and men acknowledged that they would themselves use songs to manipulate or control women:

> I have also personally used the words in a song to insult a woman who proved stubborn when I wanted to propose to her. I used those words until she agreed.... If this song had not come out, I don't think it would even have occurred to me to use those words. (Taxi driver)

This driver was certainly convinced that he had successfully employed the lyrics of a popular song to overcome the 'stubbornness' of a woman he was interested in, and who had been playing hard to get.

The songs also reinscribe gendered power relations and underscore the importance of women being 'good' girls in order to 'win' (their) husbands. While men can play with sexualized women in the songs, and can have multiple partners, in order to become someone's wife, or to sustain this position, a woman must be humble, submissive and not sexually available. This mixed bag of messages must surely continue to be confusing for young people seeking to make sense of gender politics. Some women students felt that music helped them figure men out and how to please them. A female student complained about this stereotyping:

> Nobody sings that for a man to get a good wife he has to be this, he has to be that. It's always the women – we have to be this, we have to [be] humble. I think it's not good. It makes us like we are their subordinates, which is not good. We are supposed to be equal.

The litany of negative images notwithstanding, the first reflection workshop gave us reason to believe that taking our research to town, so to speak, was a project with potential for the transformation of representations of women we sought to engender. The musicians referred to themselves as activists, and claimed the power to reflect, condone or challenge contemporary practices. One said, 'When the musician is given the gift of music you have to reflect society.' Another described himself as an 'activist', and Diana Hopeson, the president of MUSIGA, conferred on musicians the role of 'lyrical prophets'. Although the media representatives were less sanguine about the prospects of musicians as social prophets (given the commercial nature of the industry), they agreed that musicians are powerful and have a social responsibility not only to entertain, but also to educate. Musicians, media persons and researchers agreed that musicians can and should be part of a larger cultural project of social transformation that would include changing the representations of women in song texts.

The three winners of the song competition were: first place, Kwabena Quaicoo, for 'As Long As You Are a Woman'; second place, Osei Korankye, for 'Mmma Moo' ('Women Kudos'); and third place, Born African for 'Equal Rights'. The judges subsequently worked with the winners to enhance the 'empowerment' appeal and diversity of representations of women. Ultimately the popular appeal and lyrics of the winning song identified many prominent historic and contemporary female figures that the song celebrates; for example Ellen Johnson Sirleaf, the current President of Liberia; Miriam Makeba, an influential anti-apartheid musician; and Efua Sutherland, a playwright. The chorus goes:

> As long as you are a woman/If I were a woman, you/I would control the universe
> If I were a girl/As long as you are a girl, I/you would rule the world
> For the strength of the world lies in a woman
> Women have the power to change the world.

The lyrics and the imagery in the song's video address women's sexualization and gender-based violence, as well as highlighting women's decision-making power – many of the questions addressed in development issues.

Since the launch the winning song and video have been played on radio and TV on occasions such as Valentine's and Mothers' Day, and at activist events. In 2011 the song was nominated for a national music award. The launch and ensuing media advocacy provide some direction for the larger question of linking research and advocacy. During each radio or TV appearance, sometimes with other guests, on occasion with our first- and second-place winners, we would make reference to actual song lyrics, and suggest the negative effects of stereotyping and sexualizing women (and men, for that matter). Because we incorporated the views and voices of consumers of music, and used the media to reach a wide audience, the musical impact and the collective conversations have had an impact beyond the analysis of song texts, which was where we began. While we recognize that the music industry is a formidable one to enter or influence, we found radio DJs, TV presenters and even some musicians really interested in working further with us. In 'taking our research to town', a discussion of popular forms of expression (including other forms of popular culture such as proverbs) has been generated. Soon after the winning song's launch a TV presenter remarked, 'I have never thought of music in such terms. This launch will make me more aware when I listen to music.'

Conclusion

Much development literature defines African women as the most vulnerable and disenfranchised segment of contemporary African society. In many ways today's Ghanaian woman enjoys greater opportunities and freedoms than her sister of the 1930s, the era where the songs in our musical collection start. At the same time, feminist scholars and activists struggle to contend with and address the many new ways in which women have become tradable goods in the new markets created in the most private of spaces thanks to music videos and porn (both soft and hard) that is merely a mouse click away. Some argue that while the language of gender has become almost mainstream, the political project of gender and development has been reduced to a technical fix

> by powerful institutions that understand the importance of controlling discourse well.... There has been a separation of political and economic empowerment and a return of instrumentalism

that privileges a meaning of empowerment associated with formal institutions and individual autonomy. Emphasis is more on the economic actor contributing to growth and less on issues of body autonomy and the power within. (Armas 2007: 14)

Armas goes on to argue that donors do not understand women's empowerment as changing patriarchal structures but rather as meeting women's practical gender needs. If this is indeed so, then 'empowerment' can easily be interpreted as something that takes place at the individual level without any real changes to existing oppressive structures. According to Dogbe (2002), women's empowerment is an oft-stated mission in Ghana's development and cultural policy documents; however, she questions what it means to harness culture for development – which culture and whose culture? How, she asks, can cultural development become 'empowering' for women when aspects of these same cultures – including representations of women in music – are used to oppress them?

Ghana's cultural policy over the past decade has focused on culture's restorative, therapeutic, protective and creative potential to transform the national development processes. However, Dogbe suggests that even if these intended roles for culture are interpreted progressively, current development policy-making and implementation processes have been formed on the basis of implicit assumptions that empowering women and other marginal groups can be achieved without fundamental changes to the status quo.

In the light of our work, questions of women's 'sexual empowerment' become all the more pressing, given their continuing objectification and infantilization – and the pervasiveness of highly sexualized representations of women within widely available popular music songs and videos. Can things be done differently? Can music serve as a pathway for women's empowerment? Can lyrics that challenge negative stereotypes of women through their empowering subject matter be written, sung and, perhaps more pertinently, popularized? Our project has shown that there is a place for popular music beyond its role as a mere accessory to contemporary urban life – that it can contribute to the empowerment of women through linking research to action that resonates with people's daily lives. Our work has also shown that feminist scholars can join forces with popular musicians, members of the media and consumers of music to propose a variety of potential pathways to alternative, more diverse and empowering representations of women – and that working together is a powerful tool for transformation.

Acknowledgements

A version of this chapter was previously published in *Current Sociology,* and we are grateful to Sage Publications for kind permission to republish it here. We would like to acknowledge the work of Anne-Marie Bourgeois, CEGENSA intern in 2009, who worked extensively on much of the literature review for this chapter. The research on which this chapter is based was carried out as a project of the Pathways of Women's Empowerment Programme, funded by UKAid from the Department for International Development.

Notes

1 Gospel is a very popular genre that, like its variants around the world, invokes Christian themes and scripture to convey messages of hope, comfort and redemption, as well as moral instruction (Adinkrah 2008: 300).
2 Akan is one of the most widely spoken Ghanaian languages and is used extensively in social interaction and popular music.
3 The 1930s were chosen as the starting period to capture the genesis of recorded popular music. John Collins permitted access to some songs from his substantial archive (Bapmaf Foundation) and our research assistant, Nana Dansowaa, collected the rest of the selected songs from CD vendors, the Ghana Broadcasting Corporation (GBC) library and also from the Audio Visual Archive of the International Centre for African Music and Dance (ICAMD) at the University of Ghana.
4 Pathways of Women's Empowerment researchers, including two from Nigeria and two from Egypt, also joined us for the workshop.
5 Any debate on the University of Ghana campus about sexual harassment and abuse will invariably boil down to commentary on women's

'indecent dress'.
6 Literally, a good thing is found inside a good thing.
7 Name of radio DJ.

References

Adinkrah, M. (2008) 'Witchcraft Themes in Popular Ghanaian Music', *Popular Music and Society*, Vol. 31, No. 3, pp. 299–311.

Adomako Ampofo, A., J. Beoku-Betts, W. Ngaruiya Njambi and M. Osirim (2004) 'Women's and Gender Studies in English Speaking Sub-Saharan Africa: A Review of Research in the Social Sciences', *Gender and Society*, Vol. 18, No. 6, pp. 685–714.

Allen, L. (2004) 'Music and Politics in Africa', *Social Dynamics*, Vol. 30, No. 2, pp. 1–19.

Armas, H. (2007) 'Whose Sexualities Count? Poverty, Participation and Sexual Rights', IDS Working Paper 294, Institute of Development Studies, Brighton.

Arnfred, S. and A. Adomako Ampofo (2010) 'Introduction: Feminist Politics of Knowledge', in A. Adomako Ampofo and S. Arnfred (eds), *African Feminist Research and Activism – Tensions, Challenges and Possibilities*, Nordic Africa Institute, Uppsala.

Asante, S. (2004) 'Africa on your Street. Ghanaian Hip Life', www.ghana music.com/artman/publish/article_557.shtml (accessed 25 July 2008).

Asante-Darko, N. and S. van der Geest (1983) 'Male Chauvinism: Men and Women in Ghanaian Highlife Songs', in C. Oppong (ed.), *Male and Female in West Africa*, Allen and Unwin, London.

Barber, K. (1997) 'Preliminary Notes on Audiences in Africa', *Africa*, Vol. 67, No. 3, pp. 347–62.

Cole, C. (2007) 'Give Her a Slap to Warm Her Up': Post-Gender Theory and Ghana's Popular Culture', in C. Cole, T. Manuh and S. F. Miescher (eds), *Africa After Gender?*, Indiana University Press, Bloomington, IN.

Collins, H. P. (2004) *Black Sexual Politics, African Americans, Gender, and the New Racism*, Routledge, New York, NY.

Collins, J. (1994) *The Ghanaian Concert Party: African Popular Entertainment at the Cross Roads*, University of Michigan Press, Ann Arbor, MI.

—— (2000) 'The Generational Factor in Ghanaian Music: Past, Present and Future', plenary paper at conference on 'Playing with Identities in African Music', Nordic African Institute, Turku/Abo.

Dogbe, E. (2002) 'Visibility, Eloquence and Silence: Women and Theatre for Development in Ghana', in J. Plastow (ed.) *African Theatre: Women*, James Currey, Oxford.

Ezumah, N. N. (2009) 'Doing Women's Studies: Problems and Prospects for Researchers and Activists in Nigeria', in A. Adomako Ampofo and S. Arnfred (eds), *African Feminist Research and Activism: Tensions, Challenges and Possibilities*, Nordic Africa Institute, Uppsala.

Hobson, J. and R. D. Bartlow (2008) 'Introduction: Representing Women, Hip-hop, and Popular Music', *Meridians: Feminism, Race, Transnationalism*, Vol. 8, No. 1, pp. 1–14.

Kieya (2007) 'Rewriting Rap to Empower Teens', www.wakeupnowblog. blogspot.com/2007/11/hiphop-empowerment.html (accessed 25 July 2008).

Kong, L. (1995) 'Music and Cultural Politics: Ideology and Resistance in Singapore', *Transactions of the Institute of British Geographers*, Vol. 20, No. 4, pp. 447–59.

Mama, A. (1996) 'Women's Studies and Studies of Women in Africa during the 1990s', Working Paper No. 5 (96), CODESRIA, Dakar.

McFadden, P. (2003) 'Sexual Pleasure as Feminist Choice', *Feminist Africa*, No. 2, pp. 50–60.

Newell, S. (2000) *Ghanaian Popular Fiction*, James Currey, Oxford.

Pereira, C. (2003) '"Where Angels Fear to Tread"? Some Thoughts on Patricia McFadden's "Sexual Pleasure as Feminist Choice"', *Feminist Africa*, No. 2, pp. 61–5.

Simone, A. (2008) 'Some Reflections on Making Popular Culture in Urban Africa', *African Studies Review*, Vol. 51, No. 3, pp. 75–90.

Singhal, A. and E. Rogers (1999) *Entertainment-Education: A Communication Strategy for Social Change*, Routledge, London.

Vambe, M. T. (2000) 'Popular Songs and Social Realities in Post-Independence Zimbabwe', *African Studies Review*, Vol. 43, No. 2, pp. 73–86.

8
Subversively Accommodating
Feminist Bureaucrats and Gender Mainstreaming
••
Rosalind Eyben

> It's not that gender mainstreaming has failed but that we have failed
> to mainstream gender. (Comment made at a meeting of the DAC
> GenderNet, July 2006)

Gender mainstreaming was championed in the 1990s as a strategy
for infusing mainstream policy agendas with a gender perspective
and transforming the institutions associated with them. Its radical
promise came to be dimmed over the course of a decade in which
it became increasingly evident that the desired results were simply
not being achieved. The run-up to Beijing Plus Ten, in 2005,
provoked a moment of significant reflection among international
development researchers and practitioners. The overall conclusion
was that the transformational promise of Beijing had failed to
bring about a policy shift in favour of women's empowerment.
By 2006, a spate of evaluations had depressed feminists working
inside large development bureaucracies. Findings confirmed a
failure to sustain the interest and commitment of governments and
international development agencies in women's empowerment.
Had they been too ambitious when seeking to transform their
bureaucracies? Would more modest objectives achieve more
in the long run? Some feminists inside development agencies
argued that buying into the prevailing discourse of efficiency
and effectiveness might be the quicker route to persuading their
organizations to take 'women's empowerment' seriously.

The mood has shifted. 'Gender equality and women's

empowerment' have re-established themselves in international development agencies as important goals to which senior management appears to be paying serious attention. The establishment of UN Women was an impressive result. Many would not have predicted that so many governments, including the UK, would have lobbied so hard in the UN corridors to secure such an attitudinal change in international development policy. Today, feminist bureaucrats can argue that opting for an instrumentalist strategy is proving a success – at least within its own terms. It has influenced policy thinking. As one put it to me, 'Success is getting people to say things that you didn't think they were going to say.'

Much of the debate concerning the effectiveness of mainstreaming is about whether it is understood as working within existing paradigms or changing them. Is it possible to secure the desired policy action by 'infusing' gender into existing ways of doing and organizing things – and by so doing to incrementally secure real gains for women? Or will transformative policies for women's empowerment only be achieved through discursive and organizational transformation? Rather than reaching a firm view on this question, this chapter reflects on the limits and possibilities of the way in which 'policy' is understood in debates about gender mainstreaming. It draws on the author's engagement in policy processes and interviews with people in a range of aid organizations to examine the understandings that those involved in making, advocating and implementing policies for gender equality and women's empowerment bring to bear on their efforts. It examines assumptions about policy change as a pathway of women's empowerment and goes on to explore a shift from a focus on institutions to a focus on actors and agency, and on strategies, tactics and manoeuvres.

The debate

Most work on conceptualizing policy in relation to women's empowerment has been undertaken in relation to the nation state. In that context Goetz and Hassim (2003) critique the liberal emphasis on the power of voice that does not consider the broader societal and institutional arrangements that shape the possibility of voice – an emphasis that also privileges bureaucratic arrangements for installing gender equality policies over the role of organized politics. Thus, she argues, successful policy change for women's empowerment depends upon three interrelated factors: the nature of civil society and the status and capacity of gender equality advocacy within it; the nature of the political system and political parties; and the nature and power of the state, including the bureaucratic machinery.

There has been a strong feminist tradition of questioning whether the bureaucratic form of organization is by its very nature oppressive to women as the 'institutional arm of male dominance' (Calas and Smircich 1999; Ashcraft 2006). We might see bureaucracies as instruments of discipline that work to maintain the status quo, sometimes despite the best intentions of those working for change from within. Thus feminists face the dilemma of engaging with the state machinery so as to change it, while devoting most of their time to performing the tasks that the bureaucracy requires of them, after which the machinery fails to deliver the hoped-for transformations.

Standing (2004) argues that donors' conventional approach to policy leads to their failing to think through how bureaucracies actually work in many aid-recipient countries, with gender 'focal points', tools and checklists becoming part of a self-perpetuating industry that depoliticizes and makes technical what had begun as a political agenda. Gender mainstreaming objectives 'which place the onus on the bureaucracy to drive social transformation, especially where the political legitimacy of the institutions of government is already fragile, will therefore continue to run into the hot sands of evaporation' (2004: 84). She further argues that donors are naïve about the causal links between policy intention and policy outcome, and unrealistically confident that gender and development planning can identify women's interests and devise pathways to advance them.

One reason why the idea of gender mainstreaming has not delivered on its expectations may be that feminist activists were over-influenced by the notion of policy as a package that can be transferred to another context without turning into something different. Where only token compliance is required, the transfer of policy may appear to have taken place, but if we understand policy as a site for resistance and contestation we might find the effects to be quite different. A concept of top-down linear policy implementation can seriously constrain an imaginative search for more appropriate understandings of the context and possible responses to that context. In a gender audit of the work of the UK Department for International Development (DfID) in Malawi, Moser and her co-authors (2005) refer to 'evaporation and invisibilization' of DfID's policy intentions as they were carried through in the programmes it partners with the Malawi government. The authors consider the lack of internal capacity in DfID as a factor that shapes this outcome, and note the need for staff training as well as additional tools and methods. This technical response to the problem is likely to be the one most acceptable to senior management – even if they do not implement the recommendations – particularly in the absence of any political commitment from the Minister and any strong external constituency for change. Without that political commitment and strong civil society mobilization, it is very easy for gender equality work to slide down the slippery slope from an incremental approach to changing the paradigm, to becoming entirely instrumentalist. However, some would argue that even this is better than nothing; and in the longer term it may even produce the transformative effects unwanted by senior management, but secretly desired by the closet feminist.

In recent years, these arguments have gained ground. There has been a marked shift towards an instrumentalist perspective on gender equality and women's empowerment in the international development policy arena. The language of rights has disappeared from many official aid agencies' gender equality strategies. Those with gender briefs inside international agencies conclude that the only pragmatic way to work in this increasingly constrained environment is to fall back on the old efficiency arguments. As one participant in the DAC GenderNet meeting in June 2006 put it, 'The Paris Agenda is about increased aid, donors want countries to have economic growth as a result of that aid, and therefore if we want gender on the agenda we have to show how gender equality is important for growth.' Gender mainstreaming is becoming instrumental, based on the assumption that organizations will fail to deliver their other policy objectives, such as economic growth or girls' education, unless gender issues are addressed. The mainstreaming strategy being adopted *de facto* is to change procedures and introduce incentives rather than to change discourse, values and power relations. But can the two be separated so neatly? Are there possibly unpredictable effects when feminist policy actors are on the one hand committed to changing discourse and power relations, while on the other hand acting pragmatically to secure small instrumental changes?

Insider activism

Gender mainstreaming can be understood as a concept, a policy and a practical way of working. Much of the debate about gender mainstreaming has focused on the last of these and concluded that it has failed as an instrument of transformation, because it has had to work within existing paradigms and organizational forms. As such, it appears to have made only modest changes to the status quo. On the other hand, according to Porter and Sweetman (2005) there has been little evidence to date that a more radical approach, with an explicit transformative agenda, has been successful either. For some feminists 'the failure' of mainstreaming in global development institutions has led to the conclusion that it is a waste of time and energy to engage directly any further with them. True (2003: 368), among others, disagrees:

The question is… not *how* feminist scholars and activists can avoid cooption by powerful institutions, but whether we can afford *not to* engage with such institutions, when the application of gender analysis in their policymaking is clearly having political effects beyond academic and feminist communities.

Rejecting gender mainstreaming as it is currently represented need not imply ignoring the potential of development organizations as a pathway of empowerment. Can we make that potential more visible by replacing our concern with gender mainstreaming, with addressing how power works in policy processes, and by focusing less on organizations and more on the agents that inhabit them, and on what *they* can do to realize some of the more radical potential of gender mainstreaming?

In a discussion of the quest for gender equality, Gita Sen (2006) asks whether social activism is the key to effective translation of research-based knowledge into policy and if so, what combinations of research and activism are required in different circumstances. For Sen, research relates to struggles over discourse, whereas activism is about struggles for institutional change. She notes that attempts to combine research with activism tend to be regarded askance, possibly because the disappearance of a neat division of labour places the actors in a position of competing for resources and recognition. She concludes that where social transformation is sought, both researchers and activists are essential but that the relationship between them can be complex.

In international feminist circles, Sen's understanding of 'activist' is common. Self-labelling as 'activist' by those working for policy change within large bureaucracies – international NGOs, governments and multilateral organizations – can be contentious for those whose activism is from within academia or the grassroots. Certainly, when I was in such a position, I saw myself as an activist, part of the women's movement, forming and working through transnational networks and employing very similar tactics. This controversy may concern a distinction between those who understand the political strength of activist networks to be their openness and potential to cut across formal state–society boundaries, and those who recognize bureaucrats as possible allies and donors but see them as on the other side of an unbridgeable divide.

The politics of making networks for radical shifts in policy for women's empowerment requires not only reflexivity, patience and stamina, but also 'consideration of the role and identity any one of us can most usefully assume in a particular context. This calls for thinking about the scope of possible action and about questions of power, vision and agency…. Everything in strategy has to be guessed at and presumed' (Sen 2006: 134).

In what follows I identify, in no particular order, a range of strategies and tactics that are being used by bureaucratic actors to negotiate change. I suggest that precisely because everything in strategy is largely unpredictable, we may not be able to determine in advance, for example, whether or not getting a senior manager to say something different will be a pathway of change.

Negotiating change

Discursive ambiguity has long been deliberately practised as a means to create and sustain a broad-based policy constituency and to manage conflicts within that constituency (Rydin 2005). Someone in a position of authority in a complex and dynamic environment might consciously choose discursive ambiguity to strengthen support for a vaguely defined common goal such as gender justice or women's empowerment. In such circumstances, the strategic actor facilitates space for others to make their own assessment of their situation and to choose and act upon the meanings *they* associate with this discursive goal, each from their own location and vantage point. Such a strategy can generate creative responses of the kind the strategic actor is seeking, although she would not have been able in advance to say what she would have liked these to be.

Strategic ambiguity presents a rather different face and runs other risks in conditions of recognizable discursive differences. Here it 'provides a mode of exerting influence over stakeholders to stimulate desired behaviours necessary for the implementation of strategy' (Davenport and Leitch 2005: 1619). Some feminist bureaucrats in international development agencies have deliberately remained vague on what gender equality is and how to do it, in the hope that other actors such as economists in the World Bank may find themselves making choices concerning investment in 'women's economic empowerment' – in accordance with the Bank's Gender Action Plan – that eventually might lead to rights-based outcomes. For such a strategy to work it is essential to avoid clarity, including, for example, new guidance or principles that are too specific as to why gender equality is important. The risks of this approach arise from the capacity of another set of actors to impose *their* meaning in the absence of a countervailing narrative. Thus, the policy activist must feel reasonably confident in her institutional power analysis that ambiguity is the optimal means to safeguard room for manoeuvre, in circumstances where there is little chance of securing collective agreement to her desired meanings.

Social movement theory tells us of the importance of *deconstructing terms and ideas that have become taken for granted* so as to reveal that what was understood as 'natural' is no more than a social construct and thus amenable to change. In this way, an issue can be reframed so as to expand the imaginative horizon of what it is possible to change. Issues that may not previously have been visible can then be put on the policy agenda.

Opportunities to achieve this kind of outcome are enhanced if the wider discursive environment has become unstable, for example in times of religious or political upheaval when many ways of doing and believing are put into question. A number of contradictory trends in the global policy environment indicate that some policy actors are *seizing the moment of discursive instability*, as manifested by the recent resurgence of concern and interest in gender equality strategies in the context of the global economic crisis.

One such trend, arising from the invasion of Iraq and other incidents, is the growing scepticism regarding 'evidence-based policy', providing an opportunity to introduce other ways of knowing and acting for transformative change. Another trend that appears to contradict the first is the current emphasis – as manifested in the 'Paris Declaration on Aid Effectiveness' – on technical managing for results that ignores political contexts and in which outcomes must be predetermined, 'concrete and measurable' (World Bank 2006). Another opposing trend is the increasing global policy interest in citizens' voice and participation – an interest that appears to provide an environment for a diversity of ways of knowing, in which inclusive and deliberative dialogues are the basis for responsive and appropriate policies in a dynamic and often unpredictable political world.

These contradictions are signs of an unstable discursive environment that reduces the potential for policy to sustain the status quo and opens up possibilities for reinforcing efforts to change the discourse. The implications for practice are that each episodic moment must be handled with full consciousness of the risk of reinforcing the status quo by offering no resistance to the dominant discourse, while being aware of the risk to credibility, job or research grant of manifesting open resistance. The strategic solution is to use what Clegg (1989) describes as '*outflanking manoeuvres*' to reinforce discursive change and to further unsettle the status quo. The strength of this concept is its focus on political activity rather than, as in 'gender mainstreaming', on organizational change. It sees networks and alliances across and between organizations as the instruments for changing power, while formal organizations (perhaps with their own conservative networks) tend to be preservers of the status quo.

Feminists working inside international organizations can *mobilize human and financial resources through alliance building,* being aware of and making use of networks within and beyond their own organization to support their agenda. Alliances with civil society networks help the latter gain access to financial resources. Facilitating an alliance of lobbyists' access to policy spaces is strategic, provided the transformative agenda is a clear shared goal and that both the insider activist and the alliance leaders do not let the logic of the bureaucracy co-opt the alliance to its own agenda of conserving the status quo.

For example, in 1985 an informal network of feminists lobbying the UK government on women in development matters formalized itself into a development section within the Women's Organizations Interest Group (WOIG) of the National Council for Voluntary Organizations. In a path-breaking decision in 1986, the newly appointed Minister for Overseas Development, Chris Patten, instructed his officials to hold regular meetings with the WOIG; these meetings with the gender lobby continued up to the 1995 Beijing Conference. During that time the WOIG transformed itself into the National Association of Women's Organizations (NAWO).[1] Many of the civil servants who were persuaded to meet the lobby at our regular meetings saw it as adversarial, as indeed did some of the members of the lobby. Nevertheless, when working for DfID, I came to trust some of the leaders of the lobby, in whom I could confide and to whom I could provide advice about how to handle the meetings for securing maximum policy advantages. Eventually, when I had the budget to do so, I arranged for the lobby to receive a government grant – 'to help with the preparations for Beijing' – which they and I interpreted as resources for more effectively lobbying DfID.

Networking has of course long been a staple of feminist global action (Tickner 2001; Moghadam 2005). It reflects a tradition of working through trust-based alliances in opposition to the dominant discourses and formal structures that the networks are resisting and seeking to change. Successful networking requires an intensive investment in relationships, which must be balanced with the time required by practitioners and researchers for their organizational and professional obligations.

The effective policy activist *identifies the opportunities for introducing discursive shifts within the dominant rules of the game.* The selective use of instrumentalist arguments can be part of a game plan for changing these rules. An example is the global campaign against violence to women. As part of that campaign, the World Bank's

1993 *World Development Report* was used to demonstrate that such violence brought health and economic costs. Instrumentalist as this approach seemed to some, within mainstream organizations such as DfID, it made violence against women at last a permissible subject of discussion, providing an entry point for subsequent recognition that this was a human rights issue. Equally, policy activists working inside mainstream organizations may keep an apparent distance from activists outside, while using the 'threat' of radical movements as an incentive for organizational change and new policy responses. When working in DfID, I frequently made the radical women's lobby out to be more of a menace to the status quo than it really was – 'we risk getting some really difficult parliamentary questions unless we change our position on this'.

Those who hope that international aid can be an instrument of social transformation see the emphasis on bureaucratic efficiency in the current aid architecture, embodied in the Paris Declaration, as a setback. Yet the discourse associated with the Declaration provides opportunities for creating discursive shifts in the rules of the game while appearing to demonstrate full commitment to the Paris agenda. The discourse is sufficiently ambiguous to provide the opportunity for imaginative engagement to turn Paris on its head. For example, the emphasis on results, broad-based ownership and accountability has been seen by some feminist bureaucrats as a chance to ask 'Results for whom?' and 'Accountability to whom?'

The safest spaces for learning, sharing and plotting are those established for another more conservative purpose, which the feminist policy actor is then able to *subvert*. In addition to the conspiracy being less obvious because it is taking place within the existing organizational arrangements, it is likely that such spaces can be financed from existing budgets. As in judo, the conspirators are making use of their opponents' resources. The activist's time is covered as part of her routine duties and she will write a conventional back-to-office report that omits the subversive component of the meeting. Nevertheless, constant attention is required to avoid the space being captured to perform its ostensible purpose. This may happen if gender specialists who are conservative instrumentalists rather than feminists seek to use the space for their own ends. A case in point is the conservative women's networks engaging in UN institutional spaces who seek to roll back global policy norms on reproductive rights (Mullings 2006).

In a situation of discursive instability, those working to sustain the status quo need to be as imaginatively active as those working for change. They are also likely to use many of these same tactics of outflanking through networks, exploiting contradictions and creating safe spaces for conspiracy. They may co-opt transformative discourse, using terms such as 'empowerment' to reinforce a conservative position (Cornwall and Brock 2005). They may even persuade feminists that they share the same goals and extract from them scarce financial and human resources for research and to get access to other policy spaces which they can then subvert – all in the guise of representing organizations or networks that share a transformative agenda and are just having to use instrumentalist language as a cover. Indeed, in some cases, policy activists may find themselves supporting the status quo while still believing they are changing things. Many would argue that feminist engagement with the World Bank is such a case (True 2003).

Of course, it is rarely so black and white. Actors' ideas change over time and they may become more or less radical depending on whom they associate with, and the effectiveness of communication efforts by the networks mobilizing for change. Nevertheless, subversive steps may need to be taken to keep open spaces for such developments to take place. A well-positioned policy activist responsible for developing the agenda and inviting the participants to an international meeting may feel institutionally compelled to invite the opposition – but can then suggest that the meeting could benefit from the presence of a 'critical friend' to reflect at an appropriate time on the key emerging issues. Another tactic is to draft the speech of the important personality invited to open the meeting and who, unaware of the issues being debated at the meeting, unknowingly provides discursive ammunition to neutralize the presentations of the opposition.

The opposition, of course, will use its own tactics, discursive or otherwise. The policy activist needs to be alert to the possibility of dirty tricks. Once, when I was leading a group of policy activists on a visit to lobby for change in a certain global organization, I was told by someone from that organization, hostile to the purpose of our visit, that he had just received a call from the director-general's office that our scheduled meeting with the director-general – the highlight of our visit – had been postponed for half an hour. When we therefore duly arrived 30 minutes later than originally foreseen, we discovered that no such message had ever been sent and that we had lost the chance of meeting the director-general.

Conclusion

In her comprehensive review of gender mainstreaming, Walby (2005) argues that unless organizations work through the contradictions between a desire to use gender for instrumental reasons and their desire to promote gender equality in its own right, gender mainstreaming will tend to support the status quo. However, I believe the issue to be more complex. These very contradictions can provide opportunities for policy change. Large organizations are heterogeneous 'battlefields of knowledge', full of contradictions and struggles; a policy activist would seek to manage and exploit these contradictions rather than resolve them. These contradictions between the instrumentalist and transformative agendas can be managed by using the instrumentalist agenda to make the status quo case for mainstreaming, while hoping and working towards more transformational goals, concerning which the activist stays silent except with co-conspirators.

Thinking about policy and social change in a manner that embraces rather than ignores contradictions calls for staying 'open to paradox'. This suggests that outflanking manoeuvres must be guided by improvisation. As in jazz, the players have a shared idea of what they might play, but the interaction of the instruments as they perform is different each time, so the score becomes a living reality rather than something determined in advance (Clegg *et al.* 2002). We might call this 'planned improvisation' that responds to the dynamics of the political environment. Because there is a shared vision but plans must constantly change, trust is a fundamental ingredient; who you choose to play with shapes the outcome. For feminist policy actors this requires an intensive investment in long-term relationships that often become supportive friendships.

Women's empowerment is often treated by international agencies as something that can be designed as a policy blueprint, rolled out and scaled up. This chapter suggests that what actually happens where policy is conceived, negotiated and shaped may be altogether different. This chapter seeks to show that individual agency matters. This is rarely recorded in the world of development policy, where change is attributed to the system, not to individuals. Paying closer attention to agency brings into focus the changes that can occur through bureaucratic activism. While feminists working for global social change need not support the discourse and practices of international development organizations, they should definitely watch for opportunities for these organizations to be pathways of empowerment.

Despite strong misgivings concerning the depoliticization of gender mainstreaming and the return of instrumentalist policies for women's empowerment, feminist researchers and civil society activists should not dismiss the efforts of feminists employed within development bureaucracies who struggle to keep women's rights on the international development agenda.

Acknowledgements

I am most grateful to Andrea Cornwall for her support and editorial advice in drafting this chapter. This chapter was previously published as an article in the *IDS Bulletin*, and we are grateful to Wiley-Blackwell for their kind permission to republish it here.

Note

1 The present Gender and Development Network was subsequently established, in which gender specialists from the major British development NGOs participate.

References

Ashcraft, K. (2006) 'Feminist-Bureaucratic Control and Other Adversarial Allies: Extending Organized Dissonance to the Practice of "New" Forms', *Communication Monographs*, Vol. 73, No. 1, pp. 55–86.

Calas, M. and L. Smircich (1999) 'From the Woman's Point of View: Feminist Approaches to Organization Studies', in S. Clegg and C. Hardy (eds), *Studying Organization, Theory and Method*, Sage, London.

Clegg, S. (1989) *Frameworks of Power*, Sage, London.

Clegg, S., J. Vierra da Cunha and M. Pinha Cunha (2002) 'Management Paradoxes: A Relational View', *Human Relations*, Vol. 55, No. 5, pp. 483–503.

Cornwall, A. and K. Brock (2005) 'What Do Buzzwords Do for Development Policy? A Critical Look at "Participation", "Empowerment" and "Poverty Reduction"', *Third World Quarterly*, Vol. 26, No. 7, pp. 1043–60.

Davenport, S. and S. Leitch (2005) 'Circuits of Power in Practice: Strategic Ambiguity as Delegation of Authority', *Organization Studies*, No. 25, pp. 1603–23.

Goetz, A. M. and S. Hassim (2003) 'Introduction: Women in Power in Uganda and South Africa', in A. M. Goetz and S. Hassim (eds), *No Shortcuts to Power: African Women in Politics and Policy Making*, Zed Books, London.

Moghadam, V. (2005) *Globalizing Women: Transnational Feminist Network*, Johns Hopkins University Press, Baltimore, MD.

Moser, C., O. M'Chaju-Liwewe, A. Moser and N. Ngwira (2005) 'DfID Malawi Gender Audit: Evaporated, Invisibilised or Resisted?', report submitted to the Department for International Development, London.

Mullings, B. (2006) 'Difference and Transnational Feminist Networks', *International Studies Review*, No. 8, pp. 112–15.

Porter, F. and C. Sweetman (2005) 'Editorial', *Gender and Development*, Vol. 13, No. 2, pp. 2–10.

Rydin, Y. (2005) 'Geographical Knowledge and Policy: The Positive Contribution of Discourse Studies', *Area*, Vol. 37, No. 1, pp. 73–8.

Sen, G. (2006) 'The Quest for Gender Equality', in P. Utting (ed.),

Reclaiming Development Agendas: Knowledge, Power and International Policy Making, UNRISD/Palgrave, Basingstoke.

Standing, H. (2004) 'Gender, Myth and Fable: The Perils of Mainstreaming in Sector Bureaucracies', *IDS Bulletin*, Vol. 35, No. 4, pp. 82–8.

Tickner, J. A. (2001) *Gendering World Politics*, Columbia University Press, New York, NY.

True, J. (2003) 'Mainstreaming Gender in Global Public Policy', *International Feminist Journal of Politics*, Vol. 5, No. 3, pp. 368–96.

Walby, S. (2005) 'Gender Mainstreaming: Productive Tensions in Theory and Practice', *Social Politics*, Vol. 12, No. 3, pp. 321–43.

World Bank (1993) *World Development Report*, World Bank, Washington DC.

—— (2006) *Gender Equality as Smart Economics: A World Bank Group Gender Action Plan*, World Bank, Washington DC.

9

Reciprocity, Distancing and Opportunistic Overtures

Women's Organizations Negotiating Legitimacy and Space in Bangladesh

Sohela Nazneen and Maheen Sultan

Women's organizations are vehicles for women collectively to formulate and voice their demands for rights and empowerment to their community, society and the state. This chapter shows how in the last decade women's organizations in Bangladesh became effective advocates of women's interests and empowerment by negotiating their position and establishing their strength and legitimacy. They were able to further the gender justice agenda at various levels and achieve increased recognition for these demands, and policy changes to ensure women's rights.

The 1990s were perceived by various women's movements in Bangladesh as a 'golden age': a time when there was scope for raising feminist issues with the state. The discourse around the Fourth World Conference on Women in Beijing in 1995 and the resulting Platform for Action encouraged the state to enter into engagement with these actors. There was increasing recognition of such organizations as legitimate interlocutors. In addition, the period of democratic transition beginning in 1990 meant that relations with the state were perhaps less confrontational. However, the state's attitude to gender equity has been contradictory: at times it has enacted progressive laws, yet at others it has been distinctly patriarchal, acting to sustain male advantage (Jahan 1995). The state is built on a hierarchical structure featuring gender and class, and patron–client relationships are still the dominant form of social organization (Goetz 2001;

Nazneen 2008a). Further, aid dependence and the politicization of the civil bureaucracy have severely undermined the capacity of the state. Almost all civil society organizations are polarized along party lines, which undermines the capacity of the actors to articulate collective interests (Hassan 2002; Nazneen 2008b).

It is within this context that we explore how three national-level women's organizations mobilize various constituencies, including their own members, and negotiate with political parties, state bureaucracy and allies in civil society to achieve gender justice goals. In examining how Bangladesh Mahila Parishad, Naripokkho, and Women for Women mobilize various constituencies, our research focused on two processes: how they create support for their cause ('activation of commitment', Ryan 1992) and how they create meaning around an issue.

We argue that the manner in which the organizations package the issues selected by them, and the strategies they use to engage with the state, political parties and civil society, are influenced by a number of factors: the nature of state and civil society relations; the incentives and costs incurred in promoting issues related to gender justice; the strength of personal connections the organizations have with these actors; and the opportunities provided by various developments in the international human and women's rights arena. The contradictory positions of the Bangladeshi state on gender equity issues, aid dependence and politicization of the civil bureaucracy have led the feminist organizations to engage with them in an opportunistic manner, seizing chances as they arise to further their cause. This behaviour is motivated by the need to maintain autonomy, legitimacy and dependence on personal connections to access state machinery.

Generally, the organizations have tried to distance themselves from the political parties and have not directly lobbied for their issues to be incorporated within party agendas. This is due to the fear of losing autonomy and also legitimacy as non-partisan actors, and to the failure of the organizations to establish themselves as major players within the political system. Relations with civil society are based on mutual reciprocity, personal obligation, legitimacy concerns and asymmetrical power relations. In conclusion, we reflect on the extent to which the strategies used defined and broadened constituencies, and were useful in ensuring the legitimacy of the cause and the sustainability of the different movements.

Case study organizations

The three organizations chosen for the study – Women for Women (WFW), Naripokkho (NP) and Bangladesh Mahila Parishad (BMP) – are influential role models for other organizations, and the diversity of strategies they use for constituency building and mobilizing provide interesting insights. For our research focus we asked the organizations to select one issue on which they were mobilizing successfully.

BMP was established in 1970 and is the largest women's organization in Bangladesh. It has a clear command structure with a hierarchical decision-making and implementation process. It has strong links with leftist political parties. We analysed their work on the political empowerment of women. Demands have evolved over time but now include the reservation of 100 parliamentary seats for women; increasing the numbers of women in decision-making bodies; an obligation on political parties to ensure that 33 per cent of nominations for parliamentary elections are women; and the facilitation of women's involvement in local government.

NP is a small organization, formed in 1983, and committed to promoting women's equality to transform existing unequal power relations. It has a participatory style of decision making. We analysed their campaign against acid violence. Key aims for them include changing social attitudes, with special attention to the cultural representation of women. They sought adequate treatment of women and to transform their status in public perception from victims to survivors.

WFW is the smallest of the organizations studied. It was established in 1983 and mainly focuses on policy advocacy. In the light of its long record of work on mainstreaming gender, it decided to mobilize around the implementation of the Convention on the Elimination of Discrimination Against Women (CEDAW). As part of the Beijing conference follow-up, CEDAW was seen as an instrument that would help the women's movement in its attempt to make the state understand discrimination and its impacts, and to reform its laws in that light.

Methods

Our objective was to capture the diversity of strategies used by the selected women's organizations for creating and mobilizing support around particular issues. Our starting point was to explore the movement-building process through the eyes of activists. This is why a single issue was chosen for each organization. As our work progressed, we realized that, though these organizations were diverse, commonalities in the strategies they used could show how structural factors influence organizational behaviour, which became a key focus in our research.

The research process was reflexive, reiterative and action-oriented. One objective of the research was to understand how organizations build support, and to help them develop a more sophisticated analysis of the process – and this explains our emphasis on action orientation (Cook and Fonow 1991). Each organization selected issues on which they felt they were successful in mobilizing support. Since answers to the research questions required insider knowledge, open-ended interviews with key people were a major source of data collection. These were followed by further interviews and documentary analysis. Previous research on organizational history and construction of organizational timelines helped to contextualize these issues within the broader societal context.

Our own insider status (one of us is a member of NP and the other has connections with both BMP and WFW) helped us to gain access, create space for the interviewees to reflect freely, and build an easier rapport, since we were seen as people with knowledge of the organizations and the feminist movement. On the other hand, our outsider perspective as researchers and the theoretical grounding of our work gave us another lens through which to evaluate the organizations' actions and be aware of our own subjectivities.

Packaging: 'naming and framing' the issues for mobilization

How an organization packages or 'names and frames' an issue (Gamson 1975) plays a key role in building consensus among its members and allies. Naming and framing is influenced by the ideology of the organization, the nature of its allies and supporters, and the type of emotion the organization wants to evoke from its constituents (Taylor and Rupp 1991). Packaging plays a part in building trust and solidarity amongst its members (Tarrow 1998).

The organizations used different tactics in packaging their issues. The BMP framed the debate around women's political participation in terms of 'entitlement'. The emphasis for BMP's core constituents of members and locally elected female representatives was that in order for women to enjoy equal economic and social rights they needed to participate equally in decision making. Barriers to women's political empowerment were presented as an injustice. The emphasis on these aspects aimed to do the following:

> [M]ake our members and women realize that unless women have the decision-making power they will not be able to change their position in other areas such as economic and social.... The women representatives are aware about their rights being denied. They cannot carry out their duties because of the discrimination they experience at the hand of their male colleagues and at the institutional level. It creates anger and frustration among them about the injustice. We are there to provide support and to create a general awareness among women about this injustice. (Interview, BMP 1, 14 July 2008)

This injustice framing was crucial in building solidarity among members, representatives and women in general. These particular framing strategies were also used in other women's organizations and civil society, as there is very little disagreement amongst them on demands regarding this issue.

However, for political parties and the state, BMP used more strategic methods – by reminding them of their manifesto promises and highlighting gender biases within the political system. The BMP acts as a lobbying organization on this issue because the major political parties do not share the same commitment to women's political empowerment. However, they may respond if BMP can show the benefits of supporting this agenda. The reform of state agencies opened up a space for lobbying and the state executive branch is a key instrument for change.

The results of this packaging have been mixed. BMP have been successful in consolidating support amongst members and, to some extent, civil society. The campaign has evolved and spread: the issue is now widely recognized. However, they have had less success with the state and political parties. Holding the parties to account for promises made has been difficult. The parties do not see any significant risk in terms of votes from reneging on these points. In addition, BMP have been unable to address the perceived political cost of opposition from within parties, and the potential loss of seats to other parties due to increasing reserved seats for women.

NP wanted to frame issues around the acid survivors' movement by campaigning for survivors' medical treatment, rehabilitation and justice needs to be met by the state. But gender-sensitive service delivery and justice are not their only goals: they also want to create social awareness of the crime itself, and to evoke empathy with the survivors as people. Thus, NP framed the issue as a matter of social justice, stressing the suffering experienced by both survivors and their family members, and thereby creating space for and legitimating demands on health care and legal needs, but also on crime prevention. This framing emphasized the need to reflect on a society which gave rise to, enabled and tolerated such a heinous crime.

NP deliberately tried to evoke empathy for and protectiveness towards the survivors among service providers in order to motivate them into creating an enabling environment. One NP activist explained:

> [O]ur target was to use emotions, and we used it to our advantage [advantage of the survivors]. We encouraged the girls to speak out, to describe their traumas, pains, their family. It is difficult to ignore if you see it, if you hear it, if they are a person to you. (Interview, NP 2, 10 September 2008)

Another reason for using this strategy was to circumvent the judgements made by service providers about the moral character of survivors (usually young women). This was particularly useful in court, where these issues were raised by the defence. One NP member detailed her strategy:

> If I had tried to challenge society's views about who a good girl is I would have hit a wall! Instead I tried to use emotions. I argued that whether one was involved did not mean that she deserved to have acid thrown at her. Her misdemeanour does not match the treatment she received. That the defendant's lawyer who is like her father/brother ... should not be making such dirty insinuations. (Interview, NP 3, 14 September 2008)

Since the stress was on evoking empathy for the survivors, NP did not confront the social definition of the acceptable behaviour of a 'good girl'. Issues around adolescent romance and sexuality were explored with the survivors in 'safe' environments, not necessarily in the public domain (Interview, NP 4, 2 December 2008). However, NP did try to link the decision of a young woman to say no to a romantic proposal or the right to end a relationship to issues around bodily integrity and reproductive rights. This was raised during rallies and meetings held on International Women's Day and at other forums. The slogan used was 'Shorir amar, shidhanto amar' (My body, my choice).

Women for Women (WFW) chose to frame the full ratification and implementation of CEDAW as a 'bill of rights for women' for its key civil society constituents (Interview, WFW 1, 30 July 2008). The various CEDAW articles were linked to the articles of the Beijing Platform for Action (PFA), in order to contextualize and illustrate the nature of discrimination faced by women. This helped to concretize the issue at the grassroots level. A WFW member explained the process:

> [W]e worked on CEDAW, where it came from, what does it say, how would women benefit. We went to the field. The first question we got was 'What is CEDAW?' We started by saying it was a dalil (legal document), and they thought it was a deed for land! So we decided to link it to women's rights issues, to the PFA. (Interview, WFW 3, 30 July 2008)

When presenting to the state, WFW deliberately chose to take a 'legalistic' approach in framing the issue. This was to avoid any accusations of being anti-Islamic and to create space for negotiation. The full ratification of CEDAW and the obligation to ensure gender equality were presented as mandatory, since the state is a signatory to the Convention. A WFW member observed:

> Our arguments are not based on emotions and nor are they targeted to evoke any emotional response, but to convince a person through logical argument.... Our examples show how the religious personal laws can be discriminatory; why the government is accountable under CEDAW to address gender inequality.... We used the constitution to argue our case ... we approached the government and the state diplomatically, keeping the pressure on, because of the conservative elements. (Interview, WFW 1, 30 July 2008)

WFW was able to keep pressure on the bureaucrats until the early 2000s, although it is now decreasing, without incurring any backlash from fundamentalist quarters. Personal connections may have influenced this. However, the stress on the state being under international legal obligation, and on secularism, have limited this issue to concerned women's groups, particular state officials, and certain sections of civil society. It has not been accepted by any of the political parties as a mainstream issue, neither has it been included in the wider civil society arena.

The organizations were successful in creating solidarity and support amongst their allies and other civil society groups by approaching only 'like-minded' groups and packaging the issues in an uncontroversial manner. In negotiating with the state, the strategies helped the organizations avoid controversy and afforded them access, particularly as officials saw the issues as worthwhile and unthreatening. This indicates that the organizations correctly assessed how to appeal to the state, and had a clear grasp of the national and international context.

However, the 'packaging' strategies have had limited success in creating space for a 'women's agenda' within the political parties – largely because these issues remain costly to address politically, and because the organizations fear the implications that political associations may have for their standing.

Alliance building with civil society: reciprocity, legitimacy and hierarchy

The three organizations created alliances with civil society organizations, particularly women's organizations, as a means of building support for their issue, and strengthening the case that they were advocating, thus increasing pressure on the state. In the context of a polarized civil society, alliance building is risky since the legitimacy of an organization is affected by whom it includes and trusts as an ally. An unspoken but implicit principle for entering into and forming alliances is that of reciprocity. These factors fuel the need to control and set the agenda, and create tensions within the alliances. The legitimacy of an organization to form an alliance and bring together a group of organizations around a specific issue has to be established. This also brings in the question of hierarchy, with certain organizations having more weight through greater resources in terms of information, connections, mobilization potential and visibility than others.

In the case of Naripokkho's movement against acid violence, several types of alliances were formed, although these were not consciously created by NP. The most formal alliance has been the Acid Survivors Foundation (ASF). The main objective was to bring together the organizations working to combat acid violence while coordinating and bringing together the services and advocacy that were needed by the acid survivors. NP decided that the role of service provision was not part of its mandate, but wished to ensure that an advocacy platform be built around this. There were mixed views around the role the ASF would play, and NP was left feeling sidelined in the design and running of the Foundation, despite being one of its initiators.

NP members and volunteers also promoted the building of networks among survivors, the main objective being to contribute to their sense of empowerment and facilitate the transition from being victims to being survivors. This networking is continuing among the survivors.

Strategic alliances were created with the media to ensure more positive coverage. Although first attracted by the news value and sensationalism of the issue, some media institutions became genuinely committed to combating acid violence. *Prothom Alo*, a national daily, has since created a fund from which they make regular grants to acid survivors. Internally NP had to struggle with issues of how the women would be represented and whether the sensationalization would objectify them, but the survivors themselves wanted the media attention and felt in control of the interactions. The protection NP had wanted to give was neither needed nor wanted (Interview, NP 4, 2 December 2008)!

Other alliances formed included those with doctors and international organizations that mobilized resources for the acid survivors. A number of doctors, both in Bangladesh and overseas, as well as institutions such as the Dhaka Medical College Hospital and Gonoshasthya Kendro Hospital, became committed to providing care for the victims on a voluntary basis, and this even led to the creation of a specialized burn unit at Dhaka Medical College Hospital.

For BMP, the Shamajik Protirodh Committee (SPC or Social Resistance Committee) was set up in 2001 in response to the electoral violence against minorities occurring at that time. The SPC then took on the issue of women's political empowerment. BMP felt that they would be stronger and less exposed to backlash if they were joined by other organizations. These alliances were seen as instrumental and context-specific. A BMP member said, 'If a strong democratic government were to come along then slowly this platform will dissolve ... it won't be as essential' (Interview, BMP 3, 29 July 2008).

BMP recognizes that there are issues on which the SPC members respond more easily and on which they can have joint positions. There would seem to be an increasing acceptance of differences of approach. There are attempts to negotiate, discuss and come to common understandings. When BMP spokespersons were asked if there were conflicts between different organizations, the response was 'Each organization deals with various issues in their own way. There are differences' (Interview, BMP 3, 29 July 2008). However it was perceived that now the organizations were more willing to work with each other:

> Organizations have a more similar understanding of issues than before and perhaps the context has brought together organizations and helped them to work together. There is a greater unity among the organizations now.... There is greater maturity now and demands are stronger.... The blockages from government – not keeping their promises – has raised people's awareness ... the alliance between organizations, the coalition has become much stronger. (Interview, BMP 1, 14 July 2008)

BMP has been successful in garnering media interest in women's political participation. The media follow developments around the issue and can amplify the efforts of the women's organizations and hold up to public scrutiny the roles the parties or the government play or do not play in furthering women's interests.

WFW has formed and participated in fewer alliances than the other two organizations. One major exception was the work they did to reach out to women's organizations during the pre- and post-Beijing process, including grassroots organizations. The results of a needs assessment process showed that there was a lack of information on the Beijing process and CEDAW. In response the National Committee for Beijing Preparations (NCBP) was created, which later became the National Committee for Beijing Plus.

The NCBP network created an outreach for WFW. They saw the NCBP members as allies who believed in the same issues. At national level, WFW has to struggle (as do other national-level women's organizations) to establish its identity and legitimacy to lead on a particular issue, but little contestation comes from the organizations outside Dhaka, who are happy to be included in as many alliances as possible.

> Problems related to smooth functioning do not take place with organizations based outside of Dhaka. However, the problems rise with Dhaka-based organizations. These organizations at times do not focus on the larger picture but want to highlight their own achievements. There is conflict over 'who owns' the issue. So the network is not as supportive as it could have been. (Interview, WFW 1, 30 July 2008)

WFW belongs to another alliance related to CEDAW – the Citizen's Initiative for CEDAW, which drafted the Alternative Report for the CEDAW Committee in 2009. This allows WFW to be part of a larger group, enabling it to influence the analysis of the country context and progress using the CEDAW conceptual framework, and also to use the platform to lobby for the removal of remaining reservations to CEDAW.

While WFW has contacts in the media and working relations with the Nari Sangabik Kendra (Women Journalists Centre), for which WFW has provided training, there is disappointment that their alliance with the media is not stronger, and that the media have not taken on a more proactive and progressive role (Interview, WFW 2, 16 August 2008).

We can see that the strategy of forming alliances is a common one, with varied degrees of specialization, sustainability, institutionalization and effectiveness. These alliances have given the organizations additional visibility and credibility, and increased outreach beyond their organizational membership to smaller and often local-level organizations with mutual benefits to each (Goetz and Hassim 2003). Expectations of mutual benefit and an unspoken principle of reciprocity have motivated members. Both NP and BMP were conscious of differences of opinion within the alliances and made conscious efforts to manage and address these differences.

Relations with political parties: costs of engagement versus non-engagement

There are divergent views in the women's movement about engagement with political parties and how far they can protect their autonomous voice. WFW and NP were similarly dismissive of the parties and felt they had very little to gain but everything to lose from engagement. BMP took the opposite view, seeing the parties as allies who would espouse their cause. Consequently, they adopted two very different strategies to begin with, but the BMP's disillusioning experience has led to convergence.

In spite of BMP's success before the 2001 elections in getting both major parties to agree to reserved seats for women, neither party implemented this. The parties perceived the costs in terms of erosion of their male power base to be higher than any potential benefits of ensuring women's effective representation. There has since been a gradual disillusionment and a feeling of betrayal as the various political parties have failed to deliver. 'Now we do not attend the meetings of the two big political parties. The nature of politics has changed. But we now have our own politics … the women's movement has its own politics' (Interview, BMP 3, 29 July 2008).

Strategically, BMP continues to work with the centrist and leftist parties, and is willing to work with the party in power, trying to identify the right contacts. However, there is regret that none of the parties lives up to their expectations. The parties that BMP members feel reflect their own political positions are thought to be very weak or even insignificant.

Both NP and WFW were concerned about losing credibility if they engaged with the parties. In the polarized national context mentioned previously, the organizations have had to 'jealously guard their non-partisan position' (Interview, NP 4, 2 December 2008) and fight off party labels that have been applied to them from time to time.

NP consciously avoided engaging with political parties. An interviewee pointed out that the organization 'did not know how to speak the language the politicians would understand' (Interview, NP 4, 2 December 2008). They did, however, interact with local politicians and found it easier to engage on concrete issues rather than with the national-level party and its politics. NP sees this avoidance as a common failing of feminist organizations. WFW also acknowledged that their relationship with political parties was weak. 'We were unable to use political contacts. We tried many ways through NCBP, we arranged seminars, but never got their support' (Interview, WFW 2, 16 August 2008). There was no follow-up.

Thus the organizations were all negative about the political parties and their lack of responsiveness and commitment to gender equality in general, and to the issues they were pursuing. The political parties do not seem to consider the women's organizations as part of their constituency, and do not feel the need to justify their actions or indifference. BMP's agenda on political participation has become part of party rhetoric, but there does not seem to be any real commitment towards it. CEDAW has not entered the political vocabulary. However, issues of violence against women are increasingly addressed in the documents of the parties – but whether this is in response to the women's organizations' demands or to the wider social mobilization is not clear.

While there may have been costs in engaging with political parties, there are also costs in failing to do so. The potential influence of the women's organizations is limited, and they do not have access to the mainstream political party agenda. In the face of the current stalemate in relations with the parties, none of the three organizations seems to have come up with any new forms of engagement.

Engagement with the state: opportunism or pragmatism?

The women's movement in Bangladesh has strong views about engagement with the state. On what terms? For what purposes? And also: which state? Before 1990, the debate focused on whether engagement with an autocratic state meant legitimizing it. Now, it has shifted to how and what types of engagement with the state can bring about greater accountability, responsiveness and change. This shift is in the context of a 'Third World state' that is the main development actor and responsible for the fulfilment of various responsibilities.

For WFW, especially on an issue such as CEDAW, the state had the primary role to play. WFW was able to benefit from close relations with the bureaucracy and from the presence of their own members in positions of influence at crucial points in time. The argument for the full implementation of CEDAW was based on a reference to the national constitution. WFW showed that it was in the government's interest first to ratify CEDAW, then to report on it regularly, and to move towards removing the remaining reservations. International reputation has always been important to the government, whichever party is in power, and the costs were perceived to be limited since it has been able to sign such conventions without needing to implement them in national laws or policies. The women's organizations have tried to increase the costs by using the CEDAW Committee platform to shame the government publicly for not living up to its promises to remove the reservations and undertake modification of national laws to be in conformity with CEDAW.

The rationale behind NP's strategy to make the state responsible for ensuring women's rights is sustainability – 'because we might be here today as an organization (and gone tomorrow), but the government machineries will stay' (Interview, NP 3, 14

September 2008). One of the interviewees explained: 'We were not against the state. Our role was to enable the state. So the issue was developing capacity' (Interview, NP 3, 14 September 2008). They felt that public offices needed to be strengthened and encouraged to deal with cases of acid violence. An interviewee explained: 'We cannot create an alternative system. We need to fix the (existing) system' (Interview, NP 3, 14 September 2008).

Invariably, influencing the government is difficult, time-consuming and laborious. Experience has shown that there is a wide gap between policy and implementation and that, unless there is constant pressure, many of the legal or policy level gains remain paper victories. NP's strategy emphasized the creation of working relations with various levels of the state – for example, the police and the hospitals. One member, commenting on the responsiveness of government officials at these levels to the issue of acid violence, said that it was much warmer than the organization had experienced before (which can be explained by the framing of the issue), and that 'active citizenship' could lead to a qualitative improvement in services (Interview, NP 4, 2 December 2008).

Coming from a political background, BMP found it harder to engage with the state, especially during periods when they did not approve of the political ideology of the regime. After initial reluctance, BMP decided to work strategically with the state apparatus and continued to take up opportunities to petition and lobby the state. An interviewee explained:

> If we want to change laws then we have to go to the 'state apparatus'. We will have to approach the PM and ministers. We cannot avoid the state structure to bring about such changes. (Interview, BMP 2, 18 July 2008)

The pressure was kept up despite their reluctance to engage and fears of being negatively received: 'kanai diaichi tula, pithai bendhaichi kula' ('we shut our ears with cotton and padded our back against blows' (Interview, BMP 2, 18 July 2008).

BMP interviewees pointed out that the state acknowledges them as legitimate spokespeople for the women's movement:

'We are sometimes called by the state to give our opinions on various subjects – for example, the Women's Development Policy' (Interview, BMP 1, 14 July 2008). However, on the issue of political empowerment the state never called BMP; instead, they have approached the state:

> We have worked with all the political governments. In the last government, we were never able to meet the Prime Minister but her Law Minister. In the AL government, we were able to meet the Prime Minister. The impact in both cases was nil. But for a demand such as ours we had to approach the government. (Interview, BMP 2, 18 July 2008)

All three organizations have been able to engage strategically and substantively with the state and bring about various changes. They have tried to establish state responsibilities in a number of areas, recognizing that some issues can only be addressed by the state. For WFW it has meant using the opportunities afforded by the CEDAW reporting procedures to follow up on full ratification and implementation. For NP, engagement was at various levels and in various forms: from service monitoring to policy advocacy. For BMP, it meant sustaining the momentum through contact with whatever party came into power. The organizations have been both pragmatic and opportunistic in their engagement, and the state would seem to be dealing with them in the same manner – calling on them as and when needed, and choosing to ignore them when it suited it to do so.

Personal networks: access and sustainability issues

Given the social and political context of Bangladeshi society, personal networks emerged as a key tool that all three organizations used for access. In movement building, personal networks play an important role in determining who decides to join (Tarrow 1998). Personal connections, either familial or of other types, create a sense of obligation to reciprocate and evoke trust, which are key factors in influencing people to act. In the case of the three organizations, the networks helped to open up policy and organizational spaces to present their case.

NP used personal networks in approaching the state to overcome initial resistance in accessing state service provision; to manage disagreements among the service providers about NP's role; and to create an immediate impact on the issue. Initially, NP's proposal to monitor health-care service providers and police stations was resisted by government employees. They feared that monitoring could reveal failings. However, the members' personal relations with hospital and police heads ensured the required permission:

> We had gained access because X or Y knew someone – either the Law Minister or the health secretary or the senior physician…. [W]e knew we had to get the big heads first to agree with what we were doing. The initial meetings were difficult and chaotic as each group – doctors, lawyers, police – blamed the other. (Interview, NP 2, 10 September 2008)

Many of the WFW members are academics and have family or former students working within the state bureaucracy, and this created an opportunity for them to lobby key people. A WFW member explained:

> All of us have links with the bureaucracy…. [A] lot of the government secretaries are our students. Some of them were our juniors [when studying at the same university]. Our family members work as state officials. We used that network…. If we asked for a meeting, if we made a request … they could not just overlook it. (Interview, WFW 1, 30 July 2008)

Moreover, in the 1990s when WFW started working on CEDAW, many of the WFW members were in key positions. This allowed them to bring up gender equity issues in various state forums, build rapport with key officials, and identify obstacles. One WFW member observed:

> We had the right people in the right places. They were in strategic positions… We were in the Planning Commission, also working in donor agencies. We were able to bring in gender issues at different levels of policymaking process. Since we were in key positions, we

did not face bureaucratic resistance. We could negotiate. (Interview, WFW 2, 16 August 2008)

Interviewees from BMP pointed out that, in dealings with the state, personal networks are the primary strategy that produces results. Garnering support among the political parties was also done on the basis of personal networks. One interviewee explained that personal connections with party leadership were used on a strategic basis:

> We try and work with people who are progressive within the party, whom we may have known. (Interview, BMP 2, 18 July 2008)

The presence of particular individuals within a group determined whether BMP would ask them for cooperation. The interviewees explained that this selection approach was due to the partisan nature of Bangladeshi civil society and the cost it implies. One BMP member commented:

> We do not approach groups, we approach individuals who are progressive, who believe in women's empowerment.... Given that a lot of the groups can be partisan, our allies are not groups but specific persons who we can trust. (Interview, BMP 2, 18 July 2008)

Interestingly, NP and WFW interviewees did not state categorically that they approached allied organizations on the basis of whether they had personal contacts in these organizations, but based their selection instead on what types of services these organizations could provide to the core constituents. However, the effectiveness of NP or WFW within these alliances, and the nature of their relationships with allies, are influenced by personal connections that induced trust and a sense of obligation. Personal networks have expedited the process of accessing the state, and in certain cases ensured collaborative relations. However, they have not been effective in dealing with political party leadership. This is partly because for some organizations, such as WFW, the party leaders were not from the same social background. Despite their use of personal networks, BMP's experience shows that they were marginalized in mainstream politics.

The above discussion raises questions about the impact personal networks have on issues such as sustainability and the success of a movement. Undeniably, the strength of personal networks facilitated advocacy and aided mutual reciprocity in building alliances. It was also effective in mobilizing insiders within the state structure and overcoming resistance within state bureaucracy. However, it may also adversely influence sustainability and effectiveness, if gains made in negotiating with the state or political parties rely on personal links with individuals; if the individuals leave, then the organizations' effectiveness may diminish. All interviewees recounted instances where this has been the case. In spite of these risks, in the context of Bangladesh networking remains an effective strategy.

Conclusions

We sought to gain insights about constituency-building strategies and their outcomes through in-depth analysis of three women's organizations. Our analysis shows that strategic packaging and engagement with supporters and allies have allowed these organizations to establish legitimacy of voice and space for a particular issue. Their strategic engagement allowed them to promote demands for gender justice and mobilize a wider audience than their own membership and like-minded groups. The fact that they were able to make opposing these agendas difficult for other organizations shows the strength of the constituency-building process.

Though these organizations mobilized supporters for different causes, their strategies in dealing with the state, political parties and other civil society groups were similar. It is this similarity that draws attention to the importance of wider contextual factors – a polarized civil society, the nature of the state, and so on – that influence the decisions of organizations in movement building. Alliance building is not without issues. Power asymmetries and how struggles for legitimacy fuel the need of the larger organizations to control the agenda-setting process are an obvious example. Equally, personal networks – although playing a key role in mobilizing – raise questions about sustainability. Moreover, non- or ineffective engagement with political parties has had certain costs in terms of reducing influence.

All the organizations studied had a broad understanding of their constituencies. This included membership, NGOs, civil society, state officials, political party leaders and the media. This particular way of understanding is a departure from how traditional membership-based organizations identify their constituencies. The strategies of packaging and alliance building were influenced by this understanding. The organizations sought to reach out to these diverse groups and align them on their side. This entailed making certain compromises, such as how issues were 'named and framed' and how meanings were negotiated with allies. This left certain issues out of the public debate that perhaps needed to be raised. However, these well-chosen compromises help the organizations to create space and legitimacy to put forward issues and agendas further down the line.

The strategies used to mobilize support and build constituencies in favour of the specific demands contributed towards advancing the agenda for women's empowerment in Bangladesh. The analysis has shown that while doing so the organizations studied also gained greater legitimacy and strength for themselves as advocates of women's interests. Strategies for empowering women need to take into account the role played by such organizations as mediators and channels of women's voice and demands, and therefore appropriately acknowledge and support them.

Acknowledgement

This chapter was previously published as an article in the *IDS Bulletin*, and we are grateful to Wiley-Blackwell for their kind permission to republish it here.

References

Cook, J. A. and M. M. Fonow (1991) *Beyond Methodology: Feminist Scholarship as Lived Research*, Indiana University Press, Bloomington, IN.

Gamson, W. (1975) *The Strategy of Social Protest*, Dorsey Press, Homewood, IL.

Goetz, A. M. (2001) *Women Development Workers*, University Press, Dhaka.

Goetz, A. M. and S. Hassim (2003) *No Short Cuts to Power: African Women in Politics and Policy Making*, Zed Books, London.

Hassan, M. (2002) 'The Demand for Second Generation Reform: The Case of Bangladesh', PhD thesis, University of London.

Jahan, R. (1995) 'Men in Seclusion and Women in Public: Rokeya's Dreams and Women's Struggles in Bangladesh', in A. Basu (ed.), *The Challenges of Local Feminism*, Westview Press, Boulder, CO.

Nazneen, S. (2008a) 'Gender Sensitive Accountability of Service Delivery NGOs: BRAC and Proshika in Bangladesh', PhD thesis, University of Sussex, Brighton.

—— (2008b) 'Group Discrimination at Elections: Bangladesh', in D. Mendis (ed.), *Electoral Process and Governance in South Asia*, Sage, London.

Ryan, B. (1992) *Feminism and the Women's Movement*, Routledge, London.

Tarrow, S. (1998) *The Power in Movement*, Cambridge University Press, Cambridge.

Taylor, V. and L. J. Rupp (1991) 'Researching Women's Movements', in M. M. Cook and J. A. Fonow (eds), *Beyond Methodology*, Indiana University Press, Bloomington, IN.

10
Empowerment as Resistance
Conceptualizing Palestinian Women's Empowerment
●●

Eileen Kuttab

Interpreting the concept of women's empowerment in the context of the Occupied Palestinian Territories (OPT) calls for an unconventional and critical approach. The drastic changes over the last two decades in the global economy, and the resulting impact on social and economic structures, have reproduced the concept of empowerment within a neo-liberal paradigm that emphasizes the Women in Development (WID) approach (Young 1993). Hijacking its original emancipatory meaning and intent, international institutions such as the World Bank, UN organizations and the donor community have taken up the term and used it to unify and mainstream, along with their own financial philosophy and conditions (Kuttab 2008). Although in the 1970s the concept was explicitly used to frame and facilitate the struggle for social justice and women's equality through transformation of economic, social and political *structures*, today it is often narrowly interpreted as 'participation in decision making', increased access to productive resources, and 'expanded choices' of *individual* women (Bisnath and Elson 1999; Nussbaum 2000; Abu Nahleh *et al.* 2003).

This definition of empowerment has been adopted mechanically by local women's organizations in the OPT, as in other developing countries. In this context, a process of adopting global definitions, interpretations and practice has resulted in an unconscious compliance with the global agendas. It has led to the accommodation and substitution of local priority issues, and to the employment of the traditional WID approach in ways that conform to reformative and instrumentalist rather than transformative and radical understandings of the term, and to individual instead of collective empowerment (Sen 1993; Oxaal and Baden 1997). The practice of this version of empowerment has resulted in limited changes in gender relations and gender roles, and produced women overburdened with yet more work; it has connected their productive and reproductive roles within the household economy, and at the same time isolated them socially from playing a role in public life. In addition, the adoption of this concept has affected local agendas in a way that has alienated them and made them irrelevant to their constituency.

From instrumentalism to resistance: defining empowerment in Palestine

The adoption of an instrumentalist definition of empowerment in this context is especially unfortunate in view of the OPT's unique situation of 'de-development' (Roy 1987). De-development is the consequence of being subjugated to Israeli colonial occupation for the past sixty years and the absence of an independent state and national sovereignty. This situation has resulted in structural deformities and limitations, patriarchal domination and the wide gender gap, and spatial segregation and social fragmentation within the Bantustan political geography. These conditions have worsened in the period after the 1993 Oslo peace agreement, with the construction of the separation wall, segregation of the different areas of the West Bank and Gaza, and restrictions on mobility through siege policy and checkpoints.

All these factors have been either ignored or marginalized in development analysis. The OPT has come to be imagined as a post-conflict situation, which represented a golden opportunity for structural adjustment and an open door for international organizations and the donor community. Although the flow of funding was mainly political, aiming to stabilize the peace process, the kind of funding, and the discourse that came with it, have affected and alienated many civil society organizations, including women's organizations.

These conditions have meant that any kind of real empowerment has been impossible to attain in a colonized society with continuous crisis. Nor can conventional paradigms of empowerment help us understand how women themselves express empowerment within conditions of oppression without taking a position that there is no empowerment under occupation. Yet Judith Butler's words, published in an interview in an Israeli newspaper during her visit to the Palestinian Territories in February 2010, can help in understanding how, when and why women can be empowered through resistance and in conditions of subjugation. She says:

> It seemed that if you were subjugated, there were also forms of agency that were available to you, and you were not just a victim, or you were not only oppressed, but oppression could become the condition of your agency. Certain kinds of unexpected results can emerge from the situation of oppression if you have the resources and if you have the collective support. (*Haaretz*, 24 February 2010)

These words can help us to understand the situation of Palestinian women and the conditions under which they can be empowered through redefining empowerment to suit the context, and not through adapting alienating concepts to distort reality.

In this context, it is therefore possible to adopt a definition of empowerment that retraces historical roots in definitions emphasizing agency and radical change. Implicit in the concept of women's empowerment is also the notion of power – one that is as connected to authority, domination and/or exploitation as it is to the exercise of power in collective action or for liberation (Kabeer 1999, 2001). Such a concept does not adopt global definitions mechanically, but is linked to everyday resistance to occupation. It is framed within coping strategies and steadfastness. Such a definition would be more authentic and relevant in the Palestinian situation, and would speak to the everyday struggle for survival in Palestine, to assert national and gender identity, and to claim women's rights as an integral component of the national struggle.

Meanings of women's empowerment in the Palestinian context

Based on the findings of a previous work produced in 2003 investigating the use of the concept of empowerment in different women's organizations (Abu Nahleh *et al.* 2003) – and on a recent study within the Pathways of Empowerment Research Programme project aimed at understanding women's empowerment as understood and expressed by women's organizations in different contexts – a series of focus group discussions and interviews were conducted in order to understand the origin, meaning and use of the concept in the Palestinian context. A series of indicative quotations from these interviews reveals some of the differences of perspective that emerge in this context.

The first perspective is offered by an executive member of the Union of Women's Committees – a leftist organization that is considered radical and has maintained its grassroots structure and original discourse:

> The concept of empowerment is a new concept that has been suddenly imposed on us after Oslo and channelled through the aggressive wave of funding of projects to women's organizations. Historically we have worked towards empowering women (before the use of the concept) through a point of view that says that women are equal partners with men, they have the same rights and duties, and should engage in all different roles that are required of them to sustain the resistance and claim their gender identity. This was the situation of women in the first Intifada when all women young and old engaged in the struggle according to their capacity and view of their role in the resistance. So our conceptual reference was comprehensive and radical, working through decentralized democratic structures that give opportunities for women to become activists politically and socially, and challenge the male and patriarchal structures of the society. We have prepared and promoted candidates

for elections for public office, and activated women economically through cooperatives as units of production.

We also see women's empowerment through their work in affecting other women and raising their awareness of their rights, in a gender perspective to impact gender roles and gender relations within the household as an entry point to women's liberation. This is the kind of empowerment that we enhanced without using the label or the concept. At the same time it was a process that was not timed within a project that can end at a certain point when women are not yet ready to claim their full rights or continue to build their case. To us, this process is a process of radical citizenship (without a state under occupation) and a national and political responsibility of all citizens to resist the occupation and attain their rights through building a democratic community. This process by itself is a challenge to the way empowerment is being used and practised nowadays, that focuses on individuals and not the collective and hence cannot have a transformative nature, and at the same time maintain the institutional borders closed to any radical change to be able to receive foreign funding.

To us in the union, empowerment is a tool and an objective at the same time. The empowered woman can defend her rights and at the same time engage in the struggle for attaining the rights of other women. We define empowerment as a revolutionary process and as part of social struggle against occupation, and patriarchy. It is the collective empowerment that can mobilize and organize women to reach their goals. We don't design projects or programmes according to international organizations, but according to the needs and interests of women and try to find alternative resources to international funding. This as a whole is a comprehensive process of empowerment.

These words exemplify the historical use of the concept of empowerment in this context, one that focuses on the process and agency and on engagement in national resistance for social liberation. This kind of empowering process is gradual but radical, and comprehensive, does not compartmentalize issues but sees their interrelatedness, and situates the process within its real context, considering the colonial status of the OPT as one of the structural and national obstacles.

A member of the Union of Women Committees for Social Work, who is considered to be mainstream and secular, defined empowerment as follows:

> Empowerment is the capacity to take decisions and execute them freely and in order to do this the women should be economically, socially and politically empowered. Empowerment is the capacity to have a comprehensive knowledge on all issues and all levels. When a woman can perform excellence in the work she does, then she can impose her personality and respect and this can solve the problems and give her the power to challenge. An empowered woman is the one who has the capacity to perform well, and who can manage a meeting, and can conduct training and so on. Most women are empowered through their individual effort but the institution can be supportive. Empowerment is dependent on funding: if the committee is able to get funds, they can be more successful and empowered. As the concept is reflected through the donor community, we adopted their definition to be able to fund our projects.

Although she has integrated the social, political and economic levels in a comprehensive empowerment process, she has emphasized individual and personal traits, which are thought to be important for women's empowerment, and which can also enhance collective empowerment. Yet the concept is not clear to her, and she considers foreign funding as a powerful tool for empowerment.

A member of the Palestinian Women's Working Committee – a leftist organization that was among the first to institutionalize and professionalize women's activism – who is also a member of Women against Violence forum, defined empowerment in these words:

> Empowerment is based on power, which can be realized through three factors: knowledge of oneself, has the necessary confidence in achievement and work, and be a member of a collective to realize citizenship, this is how you can be empowered.

Although she is on the left and appreciates the transformative power of empowerment, she stressed the personal traits, but saw the linkage between individual and collective as important to empowerment.

Finally, an employee of the Ministry of Women's Affairs, who had been a member of a left political party, was asked about the concept of empowerment. She said:

> Empowerment is a continuous process that aims to enhance women's capacity for decision making. Empowerment begins with individual empowerment through capacity building and then it should be integrated with collective empowerment in order for change to happen. If the status of women does not change, then empowerment is not real.

These are different interpretations of empowerment that combine individual with collective empowerment as interrelated processes. While some put more emphasis on the collective, others feel that the individual charisma is also important. It is worth noting that foreign funding, emphasized by some as an obstacle to enhancing transformative empowerment, is believed by others to be a powerful tool for empowerment. These are simple examples of how different women's organizations perceive the process of empowerment through the lens of their political affiliation and ideological framework.

Empowerment on three levels

Three kinds of empowerment are addressed in the programmes of Palestinian women's organizations: political, economic, and legal empowerment. Many organizations target individual and collective empowerment as parallel strategies (Abu Nahleh *et al.* 2003). Variations in the ways different development actors conceptualized empowerment reflect the relation between political and ideological frameworks and readiness to adapt to global agendas. For instance, the definition of political empowerment was broad enough to include the term 'political' in its classical context linked to politics, or to any activity related to the national struggle and defined as political, or to participation in a decision-making process. Issues of gender, human rights, and women's rights, including women's agency and leadership, have also been defined as part of political empowerment. Definitions of legal empowerment reflected a wide range of issues, including the provision of social, psychological and legal services for women, legal literacy and education on legal rights, strengthening of women's identity, protection from abuse and violation of rights, and advocacy through campaigning and influencing legislators and decision makers for protection of rights (*ibid.*).

In contrast, definitions of economic empowerment focused mainly on economic independence as an important prerequisite to women's empowerment, although it was the least integrated in programmes of women's organizations. Some took the rights perspective as a basis for economic empowerment, considering women's participation in the labour market or decent work as a right that should be granted and protected. Women's micro-credit institutions have mushroomed in Palestine, to grant credit for women entrepreneurs in order to empower them economically. But studies conducted by the Institute of Women Studies at Birzeit University (World Bank 2010) showed these schemes to be no more than poverty alleviation schemes that did not result in empowerment, but added burdens on women with limited outcome. By focusing on individual empowerment as a separate activity not connected to collective empowerment, they emphasize the instrumentalist rather than the transformative approach of empowerment.

Alternative perspectives on empowerment

In 1987 when the first Intifada (uprising) erupted, the women's movement, like other mass-based organizations, was able to respond to people's aspirations towards independence through integrating national and social liberation struggles, and with decentralized structures and outreach. Neighbourhood and popular committees successfully mobilized different sectors of the society, using their experience and commitment to respond on the one hand to the urgent needs of the struggle and, on the other, to promote social and political consciousness. Mobilization of women occurred on two levels, raising national and political consciousness through organization and participation in the struggle, and building and expanding women's own spaces by raising gender consciousness and claiming women's rights. Some radical women's committees put the two levels into one strategy, addressing women's economic needs and desires through building women's cooperatives, and at the same time fulfilling national slogans like self-reliance and a boycott of Israeli goods.

Women in these organizations asserted their social and economic rights as women, making economic empowerment an integral part of political and social empowerment. Working in cooperatives exposed women to public life in terms of the market. They were able to build solidarity and cooperative relations among themselves, understood and acted towards changing gender dynamics within the household, and became involved politically in community issues and concerns (Kuttab 2006). This comprehensive process of empowerment is part of their resistance and coping strategy under occupation, on one hand, and their development of political, economic and social spaces on the other. Mobilizing and organizing women in a movement that understands the dialectical relation of the three levels of women's oppression – the national, social and class levels, representing the triangle of oppression of Palestinian women – becomes necessary as a condition of resistance and transformation.

Competition over funding and fears for the continuity of their work imprison today's Palestinian women's organizations within the global boundaries of the concept and its practice. However, there are new, more creative, kinds of activism that have been strengthened after the Al-Aqsa Intifada of 2000, which recall the forms of mobilization and organizing that were so much part of earlier women's movement activism in Palestine. Mixed-sex Community Based Organizations (CBOs) are being formed, and are seeking to introduce new dynamics to challenge traditional patriarchal community institutions. These CBOs are a culmination of 'Neighbourhood Corners', which grew out of a very simple idea, launched by Bisan Center for Research and Development in Ramallah, that 'if you give people physical space or place to gather, they will begin to exchange ideas and plan activities that meet their needs'.

These organizations have built the concept of alternative development through a strategic process of helping communities articulate their own needs, strategize solutions, and implement these while building leadership and organizational capacity. This in itself is the process of empowerment, as it depends solely on young people who are community members, authentic enough to find empowerment in a collective effort depending on the internal resources available in the local community. Through brainstorming sessions using popular education, and action research that can facilitate understanding their environments, they are able to discuss and carry out alternative development practices. Solidarity, complementarity and partnership become the equation for collective empowerment that can be transformative and bring the desired outcomes. Although they are new and it is difficult to evaluate their performance, CBOs hold hope for the future.

Conclusion

There is a clear understanding amongst Palestinian women's organizations of the concept of empowerment, irrespective of whether it is stated or defined, implicitly addressed in their work or explicitly mentioned in their brochures and programmes. This familiarity with the concept is due to their exposure to the international discourse that comes not only with grants, but also with projects for implementation. They use the concept in a flexible manner, reflecting a broad range of meanings. The three main kinds of empowerment that were mentioned − political, economic and legal empowerment − address a wide range of issues and facilitate working on a wide range of programmes, often with a focus on individual women rather than women as a collective.

Some organizations see individual empowerment as a prerequisite for collective empowerment. Others feel that collective empowerment is more important to focus on, as it results in the transformation of the structures that subjugate women. However, what becomes evident from the Palestinian context is the need to tie empowerment to the everyday resistance to the colonial occupation, and see it as part of a comprehensive process that relates national resistance to social and economic independence.

'Participation in decision making', increased access to productive resources and 'expanded choices' of *individual* women – the components of neo-liberal empowerment – will not be sufficient for the empowerment required to transform the economic and political structure and affirm women as equal partners and citizens (Bisnath and Elson 1999: 2). Women want not only access to resources, but also control over them. They want not only to participate in decision making through quotas for women, but to do so with full rights as equal citizens. Women don't want to work in any employment opportunity, but to be employed in protected and decent work. In such a situation women become empowered, and this is why this kind of empowerment cannot happen under colonial occupation and patriarchal domination. It is difficult to attain a degree of empowerment if the occupation does not end, and if stability and security do not prevail. There can be no empowerment in a situation where access of women to economic opportunities is not linked to change in gender roles and gender relations. As Palestinians have no independent state, it becomes even more problematic for women to attain independence, equality and social justice without the intervention of the state and the protection of the law.

The institutionalization and professionalization of women's issues through adopting global agendas presents a difficult dilemma for the women's movement. Particular issues arise in developing a strategy that can address both gender issues within the emerging patriarchal political system and the very real conditions of occupation and colonialism that men and women face on a daily basis (Kuttab 2008). The main obstacle to achieving liberation and democratic transformation is the condition of alienation that renders people as powerless and marginalized, excluded from the political process.

Ultimately, liberation from the occupiers and emancipation from structures of domination from within can only be achieved through the wide participation of people in the political process through overcoming political alienation and freeing the civil society from the grip of the donor community and the state (Kuttab 2006). If women's organizations continue to speak of equality and empowerment in the abstract and in isolation from national liberation issues, and accommodate the global agenda as the only agenda, it will continue to be distant from the masses and the needs of the masses. To make women's issues legitimate societal issues, the women's movement and women's organizations should go back to their original agenda of balancing the national and the social in a workable formula that can empower women in everyday resistance against colonial occupation, and at the same time address patriarchy and class exploitation as an integral part of the struggle.

Acknowledgement

This chapter was previously published as an article in the special issue of *Development* on Gender and Empowerment. We are grateful to Palgrave Macmillan for their kind permission to republish it here.

References

Abu Nahleh, L., E. Kuttab and L. Taraki (2003) 'Women's Empowerment: Between Theory and Practice at the International and Local Levels', discussion paper (unpublished).

Bisnath, S. and D. Elson (1999) 'Women's Empowerment Revisited', background paper for *Progress of the World's Women: A New Biennial Report*, http://www.undp.org/unifem/progressww/empower.html.

Kabeer, N. (1999) 'Resources, Agency, Achievements: Reflections on the Measurement of Women's Empowerment', *Development and Change*,

Vol. 30, No. 3, pp. 435–64.

—— (2001) 'Reflections on the Measurement of Women's Empowerment', in *Discussing Women's Empowerment – Theory and Practice*, Sida Studies No. 3, Novum Grafiska AB, Stockholm.

Kuttab, E. (2006) 'The Paradox of Women's Work: Coping, Crisis, and Family Survival', in L. Taraki (ed.), *Living Palestine, Family Survival, Resistance, and Mobility under Occupation*, Syracuse University Press, New York, NY.

—— (2008) 'Palestinian Women's Organizations: Global Cooption and Local Contradiction', *Cultural Dynamics*, Vol. 20, No. 2, pp. 99.

Nussbaum, M. (2000) *Women and Human Development: The Capabilities Approach*, Cambridge University Press, Cambridge and New York, NY.

Oxaal, Z. and S. Baden (1997) 'Gender and Empowerment: Definitions, Approaches and Implications for Policy', Bridge Report No. 40, Institute of Development Studies, Brighton.

Roy, S. (1987) 'The Gaza Strip: A Case of Economic De-development', *Journal of Palestine Studies*, No. 17, pp. 56–88.

Sen, G. (1993) 'Women's Empowerment and Human Rights: The Challenge to Policy', paper presented at the Population Summit of the World's Scientific Academies.

World Bank (2010) 'Checkpoints and Barriers: Searching for Livelihoods in the West Bank and Gaza. Gender Dimensions of Economic Collapse', report, Sustainable Development Department, Middle East and North Africa Region.

Young, K. (1993) *Planning Development with Women*, Macmillan, Basingstoke.

11

Crossroads of Empowerment

The Organization of Women Domestic Workers in Brazil

Terezinha Gonçalves

As I thought about this chapter and talked with Creuza Oliveira, the ex-president of the National Federation of Domestic Workers (FENATRAD) about the trajectory of domestic workers organizing in Brazil, we both came to realize that there are many crossroads in a woman's life. These crossroads are places and moments where privilege and inequality are highlighted. The Brazilian city of Salvador, where we both live, is a place where Afro-Brazilian culture holds great influence and crossroads have a particular cultural significance – imaging places or moments where (or when) you are presented with a choice, or the power to make a choice. In women's lives there are other crossroads, those that often do not offer an opportunity to choose or change something in their lives, and in which their own power may be absent. At these crossroads, intersections of gender, race and social class provoke an accumulation of inequalities that may make it hard to surpass the obstacles women face in their pursuit of pathways of empowerment.

The experience of being a woman is socially and historically constituted. There are girls who start their lives working very hard, without any chance to grow up, get a good education, and choose a profession. In Brazil it is very difficult for non-white women to complete their education and get a real chance to choose their destiny. Becoming a domestic worker is rarely a choice. This choice or lack of choice is the first crossroads that domestic workers face. For myself, a white middle-class woman, there were many choices when I reached that early crossroads. When I was born my family made many plans for my future: to go to a private school and become a prominent professional. My grandma always told me, I'll never forget: 'Never get married! Marriage is not a good business for any woman; get a good profession, be a doctor, be a lawyer, be a journalist.' In my home there were five domestic workers taking care of everything and there was one domestic worker whose only job was to take care of me. She was called 'Maria Pequena' (Little Maria), because she was only 12 years old at that time. She carried me everywhere: to play, to kindergarten, to bed, to be fed. She was a child taking care of another child. She did not know how to read or write. After some years she married and went back to her mother's house, back to the same poverty that had first brought her to my house.

Creuza Oliveira, like Maria Pequena, started work when she was still a child. At the age of ten, she began looking after other children. She remembers the loneliness of being the only child in the house who received no affection, of the birthdays forgotten, of the daily humiliation of having her own separate plate and cup that were kept under the kitchen sink, of never being able to play, or to study. She remembers those days: 'They called me a stinking girl, black girl with "bad hair".... Any child who grows up hearing this believes that it is the truth.' She was the same age as the family's children; she represented centuries of social inequality separating the two realities. Until the age of 15, she never received any money for her work, only food and old clothes. It was not until she was 21 that her documentation as a worker was signed for the first time. She suffered violence, from psychological violence to deferred payment and even sexual abuse. In her activism, Creuza has sought ways to put an end to successive generations of young black girls becoming domestic workers. But, she reflects: 'Exploitation is a difficult cycle to break. It passes down through generations ... unfortunately, paid domestic work is a door into the work market for black women in our country.'

Through a range of interventions and alliances, Creuza and other domestic workers' rights activists have brought about changes in the law, and fostered the implementation of innovative programmes that seek to change the options open to young black women at the crossroads that take them into domestic work. This chapter considers some of the implications of these intersections, and some of the innovations and conquests that have begun to change the situation of domestic workers in Brazil.

Negotiating the 'traffic': intersections and inequalities

Intersectional discrimination and subordination have distinctly different consequences from those arising from one form of discrimination only, whether based on race, gender, sexual orientation, age or class. The consequences of intersectional discrimination may remain unaddressed by prevailing human rights approaches, because the specific problems or conditions associated with this form of discrimination are often subsumed within one category of discrimination, such as race or gender discrimination (Pradhan-Malla 2005). Brazil's colonial past produces intersections between gender, race and class that emerge from slavery and patriarchal history. It is essential, in this context, to understand the structures that operate to produce and reproduce inequalities that block resources and access to power for those at the crossroads of the intersections of gender, race and social class.

Women of colour are often positioned in the space where racism or xenophobia, class and gender meet. They and other multi-positioned groups who are located at these intersections by virtue of their specific identities must negotiate the 'traffic' that flows through these intersections. This is a particularly dangerous task when the traffic flows simultaneously from many directions. Injuries are sometimes sustained when the impact from one direction throws victims into the path of oncoming traffic, while on other occasions, injuries occur from fully simultaneous collisions. These are the contexts in which intersectional injuries occur – when disadvantages or conditions interact with pre-existing vulnerabilities to create a distinct dimension of disempowerment (Crenshaw 2000).

A vivid example of this 'traffic flowing simultaneously' is provided by an examination of paid domestic work in Brazil. To speak of domestic workers is to speak of women at work: 95 per cent of domestic workers in Brazil are women and 60 per cent are black. The category of the domestic worker is the largest professional category in the country, made up of 6.8 million who work for a monthly salary. They represent 5 per cent of the Brazilian population (IBGE 2007). Almost half a million Brazilian girls are domestic workers, executing all types of housework, working long hours and with little or no financial remuneration. There are 494,002 domestic workers between 5 and 17 years old. Of this total, 222,865 are below the age of 16 (IBGE 2001, 2003). These figures probably underestimate the true scale of the problem, given that employing children under 16 is illegal.

Domestic work in Brazil is part of a pattern of economic development that is strongly influenced by the heritage of slavery, and associated with distinctive forms of gender, race and class exploitation. The legacy of slavery continues to structure the racial and sexual division of work. The exploitation that Brazilian domestic workers face has given meaning to their political mobilization as organizations of domestic workers.

In the 1920s and 1930s, black women organized in the Brazilian Black Front for the first time. They argued for the recognition and status of paid domestic work, with rights and duties as in any other work. This movement resulted in the creation of the first association of domestic workers in 1936, by a black communist activist called Laudelina dos Campos Melo. Born on 12 October 1904, Laudelina started working as a domestic worker at the age of seven. From the age of 16, she became active in black women's associations and went on to join the Brazilian Communist Party (PCB). President of the first Domestic Workers' Association from 1936 to 1949, she initiated a process of organizing that was interrupted by the twenty years of dictatorship (1964–84), and which gathered increasing strength on the return of Brazil to democratic rule in 1985, and the constitutional process of 1988.

The domestic workers' organization at national level began with an informal network of associations from various Brazilian states. This resulted in the creation of a National Front of Domestic Workers in 1981. This Front was institutionalized as the Domestic Workers' National Council in 1985. In the wake of the end of twenty years of dictatorship, the political freedom to organize in the new democracy gave the movement new impetus. The National Federation of Domestic Workers (FENATRAD) was founded in 1997. In 1998, this Federation was affiliated to the National Confederation of the Workers of Commerce and Services (CONTRACS), the Central Workers' Union (CUT) and the Latin American and Caribbean Domestic Workers' Confederation (CONLACTRAHO).

From the first domestic workers' association to the recent conquests of FENATRAD, domestic workers organizing for rights and recognition have arrived at many crossroads and transformed them into moments of choice, and of power. The story of domestic workers' organizing is one of overcoming arduous obstacles, of constructing new pathways for action, and building strategic alliances. It offers rich lessons about the conquest of rights and the construction of citizenship, and about what can be done to avoid getting caught in the 'traffic'.

Differences that make a difference

There is growing recognition that failure to attend to the various differences that characterize the problems and predicaments of different groups of women can obscure or deny human rights protections that all women are due. While it is true that all women are in some way subject to the burdens of gender discrimination, it is also true that other factors relating to women's social identities such as class, caste, race, colour, ethnicity, religion, national origin and sexual orientation are 'differences that make a difference' in the ways in which various groups of women experience discrimination. These differential elements can create problems and vulnerabilities that are unique to particular subsets of women, or that disproportionately affect some women relative to others.

In Brazil, racism divides white men and women and non-white men and women in different categories of income. It aggravates gender inequalities. It makes the female identity of black women inferior to that of the racially hegemonic group of white women. In the face of this inequality, it is necessary to analyse how racism subcategorizes gender, creating different statuses for different women (Carneiro 2003). Black men have social indicators below those of white women in Brazil, and black women even more so. Consequently, black women would require extraordinary social mobility to surpass both racial and gender obstacles.

Despite the expansion of the labour market to include women over the last half century, the fact that 60 per cent of domestic workers are black shows that labour market expansion for women did little to improve black women's reality. When black women are afforded a formal education and therefore social mobility, most of them get jobs with lower salaries in poorly recognized positions in the labour market. The racial discrimination in the selection process is very clear in Brazil; 'good appearance' is an indirect way to obstruct black people and especially black women, because having a desirable 'appearance' means being white.

Racial discrimination in the labour market is reflected in the income of black Brazilians. They have a monthly average income between 50 and 70 per cent less than other workers; they also make up the majority of the unemployed. Black women suffer double discrimination that results in lower wages. According to research carried out by the Institute of Applied Economic Research (IPEA), in partnership with the Special Secretary of Women's Policies (SPM) and the United Nations Development Fund for Women (UNIFEM), black women earn 67 per cent of what black men earn and 34 per cent of the average income of white men. They are at the bottom of the salary pyramid. In average wages according to race/gender in Brazil, on average white men receive US$542 and white women receive US$338 per month; black men receive US$275 and black women receive only US$184.

Black movement activists have succeeded in forcing the Federal Government to take measures to combat racial inequalities and racism. These actions have resulted in the recognition of the existence of institutional racism in our country and the implementation of affirmative action and public policies. With support from international organizations, building on the experience in the US and the UK, this programme against institutional racism brought together the black movement and the women's movement to challenge racial and gender inequality in Brazil. But this crossroads also causes a deep division between women in seeking pathways for collective empowerment as women. The unjust and unequal sexual division of work puts different women on different sides. Domestic workers are on one of these sides.

Between women: the 'sexual re-division of work'?

The relationship between middle- and upper-middle-class employers and domestic workers brings the issue of class relations to centre stage. This relationship of white women in the position of employer and black women in the position of a domestic worker reinforces racial relations of inequalities of power and resources. Women employers often disrespect domestic work as a profession – not respecting the law in terms of payment and hours. Data from the National Institute of Statistics (IBGE) show that in Brazil 72 per cent of domestic workers are without a Worker's Card; 27.7 per cent of them receive half of the minimum salary, and 41.3 per cent receive between half and one minimum salary. Many women employers maintain a relationship based on disrespectful attitudes, on the negation of rights, and on keeping silence in the face of violence and sexual abuse suffered by domestic workers in the workplace at the hands of their employers' partners, husbands, sons, friends or other relatives (Oliveira and Sant'Anna

2002). These patterns of violence have a history; as Oliveira and Sant'Anna note:

> In the past we did not dare to classify the subject as being sexual abuse as today it is considered. It was only domestic-sexual violence. It was a kind of violence that forced black women to remember little had changed regarding the patterns of behaviour established between slave owners and their slaves, between the 'casa grande' and the 'senzala'.

The relationships between women employers and domestic workers are permeated by feelings and situations that confuse a working relationship. In the name of affection or friendship, many domestic workers' rights are forgotten. Creuza reflects on how terms of endearment and talk of being 'part of the family' cloud the very real exploitation of domestic workers, noting that:

> Many domestic workers live for years in the employer's home working without any rights, living an illusion of being a family member and accepting these conditions because they depend emotionally on this relationship, establishing a comfortable situation for the employers.

Most women domestic workers, and especially younger ones, live in the employer's home. They do not have a home of their own. Their room is the smallest in the house. The furniture they use, the food they eat, the used clothes they 'inherit', the day-to-day life they live, are all attached to the family. The assertion that 'She is almost one of the family' not only disguises exploitation, but is used to define a domestic worker's place in the world. The word *criada* means both a person who was raised, and a servant, a term that speaks volumes about the complexities of domestic workers' subjectivities.

The domestic sphere becomes a place where the inequalities between women are reproduced. It remains a 'women's place': a place where the alliance of struggles for women's rights is broken. Confrontation in this environment is established among social classes, with a racial component; a class contradiction without men's participation, because domestic work is cast as 'women's work'. Men's place as employers – as well as employees – is quite different from that of women. Men have a different status. They generally get jobs with defined tasks like being a gardener or driver, for example. Normally, this kind of worker is not referred to as a 'domestic worker'. Nobody says 'I have a domestic worker who drives my car.'

Women in general continue to be responsible for reproductive, devalued and subaltern work. To escape the trap of the unjust sexual division of work, upper- and middle-class women employ other women to carry out reproductive work, and pay them for it. A false idea of autonomy is established for women who employ others: they become employers who can exploit other women, namely their domestic worker. This demonstrates only that they have freed themselves from domestic tasks and can escape from confrontation with men, who are exempt from this responsibility in the home and the family.

This false sense of women's autonomy is found among the privileged classes. To gain this sense they need other women as their domestic workers, who must in turn work to survive and submit themselves to precarious working conditions. Domestic workers are exposed to unequal divisions of work (racial and sexual) and belong to the lowest socio-economic levels – in terms of recognition, income, quality of life and rights – in the work market, while they have the highest workload in terms of duties. This gives rise to tensions between women that have taken shape in recent years in organized reactions to the growing rights that domestic workers have acquired. Domestic Employers' Unions and Housewife Associations have been created in many cities in Brazil with the purpose of organizing and supporting employers' rights. This confrontation is going on in a context where the Federal Government is preparing a Proposal for Constitutional Reform (PEC) to equalize domestic workers' rights with workers' rights in general. The rights that are under discussion would represent a substantial conquest for domestic workers in their struggle for recognition as workers, and include family allowance, payment for overtime, the Obligatory Guaranteed Fund for

Length of Service (FGTS), unemployment benefits, insurance for work accidents and for Repetitive Strain Syndrome (RSS), night shift supplement, a fixed number of working hours – hours/day – and obligatory union contribution. This extension of domestic workers' rights will increase labour costs by more than 100 per cent, in the opinion of labour lawyers.

The Employers' Union president in the state of São Paulo, Margareth Galvão Carbinato, said in one of Brazil's principal broadsheets, the *Folha de São Paulo*, that if all the domestic workers' rights are approved in the Federal Congress, labour costs will be unsustainable for employers. She said: 'Our families are not companies; we cannot pay all the costs because domestic work is a different kind of work that doesn't generate any profit.' There is a proposal to transform paid domestic work into an outsourced service to be organized by companies. According to defenders of this proposal, the end of direct contracting of the domestic workers by the families would be replaced by 'professionalization' of the services given by these workers. In defence of this proposal, the city of Schenzhen in China is being cited as an example. Talking about this model, Marcio Pochmann, President of IPEA, says:

> Each employer organization of outsourced workers offers services to the families who can choose at lower cost and better quality, among other criteria. The companies that offer services to the family only contract the workers protected by the social and labour legislation. (Personal communication)

At this crossroads, the organizations of domestic workers come up against this entrenched position occupied by conservative sectors of society who want to protect their privileges. The solution, Creuza explains, has been to look for alliances. She argues that it is fundamental to establish partnerships with organizations and entities of social movements such as the black movement, both the women's and the feminist movements, as well as the workers' unions.

> The objective is to fortify the struggle of the domestic workers, also incorporating the agenda of these movements, in the struggles

against racism and sexism. It is necessary to make partnerships to construct a common struggle. (Creuza Oliveira, personal comment)

Women in movement: fortifying domestic workers' empowerment

Despite the advances and the conquests achieved by the domestic workers' organization in Brazil, this movement has been led by a small group. Among other reasons, this is a result of the great difficulty they face in gaining visibility for their political activism. The workplace in the domestic environment often obstructs these women's participation. They have no access to information about the unions. Few resources are available from the unions to spread information about the struggle's agenda. For this reason, many domestic workers do not know their labour rights.

One of the most commonly used means of communication for domestic workers in Brazil is the radio. It was through the radio that Creuza found her first group of women to discuss the organization of domestic workers in Salvador in the 1970s. She recounts:

> One day when I was working in a family house, I heard on the radio
> – a great friend in the solitary life of the domestic workers – some
> news that changed my life: a group of domestic workers was meeting
> at the Antonio Vieira School to fight for their rights. They met on
> Sundays. I didn't know how to look it up in the calendar. I asked
> my boss to show me the dates. For the first meeting, I told my boss
> that I was going to church. It was frustrating because there were few
> people there. I did not give up and called other domestic workers
> and this group was the first association in Salvador that became later
> the Union of Domestic Workers, SINDOMESTICO, after the
> promulgation of [the] Federal Constitution of 1988.

Women's participation in social movements – unions, and feminist, black or grassroots movements – has become a vector for significant change in the process of women's empowerment in Brazil. By acting in public, women transcend the limits of the domestic space, creating new situations inside the family, in the informal relationships of neighbourhoods, and in friendships. Women have begun to articulate differentiated struggles in relationship to men inside social movements, organizing around 'women's' issues, and using this as an entry point to question their own condition and the inequalities derived from this condition. In the collective process of empowerment of women there are new practices and new representations: changes of values, new attitudes in relation to work and to the family, and better conditions in which to experience self-esteem. The conquest of women's rights implies transformations that do not only modify the daily relationships between men and women, but also have provoked significant changes in social structures and therefore in the organization of social life. The experience of these rights as part of daily life has brought social transformations of a material and symbolic order.

Women's presence in unions and movements for labour rights has produced achievements that go beyond the general workers' fight for labour and social welfare laws. They illustrate the potential to transform unions into channels of expression and fight for equality in gender and race relations. This potential is increased by the fact that institutionalized channels are spaces which are open for proposals from social movements for public policy implementation in Brazil. The performance of the Workers Women National Secretariat (SNMT) in the national trades' union body (CUT) is an example of transformation in the union movement. What was in the past a space for labour class struggles has become a space that has given rise to active engagement in shaping policies for gender and race equality in Brazil.

Since its creation the SNMT has incorporated all the main campaigns waged by women and feminists – being a vanguard, for example, in the fight to legalize abortion in Brazil. However, the political relationship between workers of different categories and domestic workers within CUT is not easy. Many domestic employers are also affiliated in the same central union. Women who work in banks, or teachers, or civil servants are at the same time employers of domestic workers. This relationship between workers/bosses and domestic workers in the same central union generates a tension in the union movement. The rights claims of domestic workers are often blocked to maintain the privileges of employers.

The old contradiction between the status of productive and that of reproductive work and the consequent lack of recognition of domestic work as work is a crossroads where every woman has to make a choice. Political alliances are unstable: 'If you don't see a light in the darkness, you must light a fire,' Creuza says. 'Sometimes we go along with the women's movement to fight for our rights; sometimes we have to rely on the government.' This kind of strategy has been a characteristic of the history of domestic workers' organizations. During the elaboration of the Federal Constitution in 1988 after the return to democracy, a successful alliance with the feminist and the women's movement resulted in many victories for domestic workers being inscribed in the constitution, including a right to the minimum wage, advance notice (30 days), one day off a week, maternity leave (120 days), paternity leave (5 days) and an extra one-third of a minimum salary before taking holidays. In 2000, these rights were further extended to include the right to unemployment compensation. In 2006, domestic workers gained the right to 20 days' vacation and time off for civil and religious holidays; a job guarantee for pregnant women; and an end to deductions from their wages for housing, food, and personal hygiene products used at the place of work. In 2008, the government prohibited adolescents and children under 18 years old from doing domestic work, in line with the International Labour Organization (ILO) Convention 182 to eliminate all the worst kinds of child labour.

The conquest of public policies

Prior to the election of the Workers Party (PT) government in 2003, the state offered little support to domestic workers in the form of public policies and programmes. Since 2003, domestic workers' organizations have forged a political alliance with governmental sectors. The Workers Party (PT), which was re-elected in 2006, has proved to be a strong ally of these workers. The government has been responsive to domestic workers' demands, but it is important to point out that the legislation on paid domestic work and the conquest of public policies are a result of domestic workers' struggles organized in their unions. For this reason, the organization of domestic workers is an example of collective empowerment in Brazil.

To give greater visibility to their cause and to strengthen their fight, domestic workers' organizations have sought to participate actively in various spaces of power and to seek representation in the legislature, as well as having a presence in a number of organs established by the executive branch of government. FENATRAD is present in various bodies of the government such as the National Council for the Promotion of Racial Equality and the National Council for the Defence of Women's Rights. These alliances with others working for gender and racial equality have become an important part of the strategy of advancing domestic workers' rights as workers, as women and as citizens.

An important achievement in the struggle for racial and gender equality in Brazil was the formal recognition by the government of gender and race inequalities, with the creation in 2003 of the Special Secretary of Women's Policies (SPM) and the Special Secretary for the Promotion of Racial Equality (SEPPIR). Both have ministry status and are linked to the presidency of the Republic. And both have been instrumental in establishing public policies that address the economic marginalization and exploitation of domestic workers. SEPPIR and SPM have made domestic work a priority in the National Policy Plans. Paid domestic work was an important item on the agenda in national, state, and municipal conferences on policies for women and policies for racial equality, which took place in the years 2005 and 2007 respectively.

The government has established a permanent desk for negotiations with FENATRAD to debate the problems and find ways to obtain rights for domestic workers. As a result the campaign

'Rights Cannot Be Less, Only More' was established. Another public policy worthy of note, implemented by the government together with FENATRAD, is the 'Citizen Domestic Work' programme – a proposal made by domestic workers and now transformed into policy – which seeks to improve schooling together with social and professional qualifications, and campaigns to improve social awareness about domestic work with the objective of lessening the informal nature of the work as well as disrespect for domestic workers' rights. FENATRAD and the affiliated unions in the states of Bahia, Pernambuco, Sergipe, São Luiz, Rio de Janeiro and São Paulo – and the public agencies MTE, SEPPIR, SPM, the Ministry of Social Security and the Ministry of Education, as well as the ILO – all actively participate in this process. The validation and management of the Citizen Domestic Work Plan is carried out through meetings and workshops with the presence of grassroots leaders and workers, union representatives and FENATRAD.

Pathways of collective empowerment

All the achievements described in this chapter came after an intensive struggle. FENATRAD knows that there are many crossroads that the organization faces to gain political and labour rights. My relationship with some of the domestic workers' organization's leaders is one built on political activism by the feminist and women's movement, and my work as an associate researcher in the Nucleus for Interdisciplinary Women's Studies at the Federal University of Bahia. For 28 years we have been together in this long and hard journey for the conquest of our rights as women. We fight for labour rights, against women's violence, for sexual and reproductive rights and for more political participation as well. We fight for women's citizenship.

On this journey we take our contradictions and our conflicts; we travel with our 'intersections' and consequently with our in-equalities, our baggage. Many of us, like domestic workers, carry a heavy load. Paradoxically, the heaviest baggage is domestic work itself. Paid domestic work reinforces the unjust sexual division of work and also the premise that women have to be responsible for reproductive work. This 'trap' accentuates the division between women and at the same time maintains men's position of privilege. This kind of devalued work in Brazil is for non-white women. It discloses an unjust racial division of work that relegates the most insecure and precarious work to non-white people. Racism aggravates gender inequalities.

Paid domestic work does not constitute a choice for these women. Many of them start working when they are children, and when they become adults they have no chance of social mobility. Many of these women have grandmothers and mothers who work as domestic workers, revealing the perpetuation of these inequalities. Paid domestic work is the biggest issue at this crossroads of empowerment. Can we fight only for better working conditions for domestic workers, or do we have to fight to change women's social position at work? I can't answer this question. But the domestic workers' organization trajectory can teach us some lessons.

FENATRAD recognizes that it is important to organize domestic workers around the fight for acknowledgement of paid domestic work as a profession, but without forgetting the struggles for women's rights and the other social movements. It also recognizes that the way of addressing some of the pathways of injustice that domestic workers in Brazil end up travelling is to focus on combating child domestic labour as a central strategy to stop this kind of 'destiny', so that children are not denied a chance to make a choice for a different future. Looking back over almost a century of domestic workers' activism in Brazil, we can see that the first actions developed by the domestic workers' leadership in general were then focused as a workers' mobilization around labour rights and social welfare. They started gathering in neighbourhoods, schools and churches. These meetings were strategies to build the organizations in each town and in different states. These groups have been extended and the struggles consolidated.

In subsequent years, and in the years following Brazil's return to democratic rule and the flowering of movements in search of rights and citizenship, this stage was followed by other meetings, seminars and workshops at the local, regional and national levels, for professional and political formation. The creation and consolidation of these associations formed the basis for creating the unions after the promulgation of the Federal Constitution in 1988, which restored to Brazilian workers the right to organize as unions. This was fundamental in giving weight to the domestic workers' struggle. The result was the creation of 45 unions in different Brazilian regions and the formation of the Domestic Workers National Council and of FENATRAD. There were also the union affiliations to national and international labour organizations, which constituted the last step in recognition and consolidation of domestic workers' organizations in Brazil.

The alliances made by domestic workers' organizations range from advocacy groups in Parliament to partnerships with international organizations, such as the ILO, UNIFEM, the United Nations Children's Fund (UNICEF) and feminist NGOs. Other partnerships have been made with domestic workers' unions in Latin America. International cooperation projects have been important to obtain financial resources to develop actions for collective empowerment. Broader perspectives are exchanged in meetings with other social movements, such as the National and Latin American Feminist Meetings, the Women's National and International conferences, the Racial Equality National Conferences and Human Rights conferences. Domestic workers' standpoints are now included in institutions such as the Child and Adolescent Defence Forum, the National Council of Defence of Women's Rights and the National Council of Promotion of Racial Equality, and in many state and city councils where public policies are discussed and monitored.

The movement for empowerment of women traces a collective history made by many anonymous hands and minds. Finally, we can conclude that there is no possibility of individual empowerment for a woman domestic worker without social organization. Personal life histories such as those of Laudelina dos Campos Melo and Creuza Oliveira are closely linked to their organizations' trajectories. They illustrate and reinforce the idea that collective action is the pathway to choose at the crossroads for women's empowerment.

Acknowledgement

This chapter was previously published as an article in the *IDS Bulletin*. We are grateful to Wiley-Blackwell for their kind permission to republish it here.

References

Carneiro, S. (2003) 'Women in Movement', *Advanced Studies*, Vol. 17, No. 49, pp. 117–32.

Crenshaw, K. (2000) 'Gender-related Aspects of Race Discrimination', background paper for Expert Meeting on Gender and Racial Discrimination, 21–24 November, Zagreb, Croatia.

Instituto Brasileiro de Geografia e Estatistica (IBGE) (2001) *Pesquisa Nacional por Amostra de Domicílios*, IBGE, Rio de Janeiro.

—— (2003) *Trabalho Infantil*, IBGE, Rio de Janeiro.

—— (2007) *Contagem Da População 2007*, IBGE, Rio de Janeiro.

Oliveira, G. and W. Sant'Anna (2002) 'No More Nostalgia. The Reality is That ...', *Feminist Studies Review* No. 1 pp. 201–7.

Pradhan-Malla, S. (2005) 'Racism and Gender', in *Dimensions of Racism*, proceedings of a workshop to commemorate the end of the United Nations Third Decade to Combat Racism and Racial Discrimination, United Nations, New York, NY and Geneva.

12
Women's *Dars* and the Limitations of Desire
The Pakistan Case

• •

Neelam Hussain

In recent years growing numbers of women in Pakistan have come to attend classes in which they learn to read and understand the Quran. These classes, known as *dars*, appeal to women across a range of generations and classes, and especially to upwardly mobile women whose desires for a particular mode of observance of Islam are influenced by a wider trend in the South Asia region that has seen the growing popularity of Wahabi Islam.[1] While these gatherings reflect a social and political trend evidenced in the growing approbation of women's 'piety groups', for large numbers of women *dars* also meet a subliminal need for a 'room of their own'. Given the relational nature of their identity as wives, mothers, daughters and sisters – with the insecurities of marriage and the unending routine of nurturing, caring and maintaining social/familial relations – women do tend to be crowded out of their own lives.

Traditionally, the Sufi shrine or *mazar* provided such a space for women across class in South Asia. Drawing upon popular religion and Sufi tradition, the *mazar* culture is eclectic and inclusive. Legitimized by belief in the efficacy of prayer and the existing practice of recourse to Sufis and saints as intermediaries between the desiring subject and the Divine, the *mazar* is both accessible and familiar as a social space where women meet and interact. The supplicant talks to the *pir* – purported holy man or woman; addresses the Divine; makes demands; airs grievances;

228

asks for favours; pleads; reviles; expresses love. For centuries women have gone to *mazars* to ask for the saint's intercession for the fulfilment of desire – for sons; for lovers; for good harvests; for health; for the return of errant husbands. They go to pay their respects to the saint, and for the music and poetry; or they may simply go there for a day's outing with other women. While the popularity of the *mazar* has not waned, for Pakistan's rapidly growing educated middle class and new moneyed elite – including the post-9/11 Pakistani diaspora, comprising university-educated high achievers (doctors, corporate sector executives, IT experts), for whom Islam is both a marker of identity and a coping mechanism, particularly with reference to the West – the indiscriminate egalitarianism and carnival excess of the *mazar* is neither acceptable nor desirable. For this class the air-conditioned comfort of the women's Wahabi *dars* represents a more respectable alternative. As with the *mazar*, the space provided affords women temporary reprieve from the pressures and exigencies of social and familial life. But, beyond this, the immutable certitudes of the *dars* discourse, based on notions of middle-class morality and gender-based stereotypes, also provide guidelines for the mediation of social space in a rapidly changing world, as exemplified in a discussion with students from one of Lahore's upmarket private universities: 'The sense of unease lies in the fact that on the one hand we are taught to value female chastity and on the other the university lifestyle encourages socialization between women and men. We never know when ordinary friendliness may be taken for a "come on".'

This chapter explores the impact that the Wahabi *dars* and its teaching practice have had on women's lives. It draws on a study, undertaken simultaneously in Lahore and Dhaka,[2] that sought to examine both discursive and spatial arrangements of the *dars* in order to understand what was drawing large numbers of women to these meetings. The study tracked the process of change from the traditional practice and eclecticism of popular Islam to the certitudes and rigidities of the *dars* discourse, and sought to mark the moments that initiated the move, if any, from acceptance of the status quo towards the possibility of choice and exercise of agency as a result of this engagement. Using a participatory approach comprising questionnaire-based interviews, life histories, focus group discussions, random cross-class conversations and observations at social gatherings, the research team interviewed about a hundred women. These were mainly college and university students from different social and geographical backgrounds who attended *dars* and *Daura-e-Quran* sessions – dubbed 'Quran tours' with reference to the trendy upwardly mobile attendees – during the month of Ramzan (Ramadan) at two established Lahore institutions, Al Huda and Al Noor, and participated in Al Noor's all-night public prayer and *dars* commemorating Laila-tul-Qadar.[3]

In the main, the *dars* appears to be an urban middle-to-upper-class phenomenon. One reason for this may be that its emphasis on the book and the written word automatically excludes the vast majority of women from low-income sectors who cannot read and who continue to operate within the parameters of the oral religious tradition with roots in folk culture. Al Huda and Al Noor cater primarily to educated middle-to-upper-class women, with lower-middle-class representation being almost exclusively confined to paid employees involved in administrative work. *Dars* meetings are held regularly and other activities include subsidized fee-paying courses for serious students, particularly those intending to undertake *dars* teaching professionally for proselytization purposes.

On course completion, women are provided with teaching materials and are expected to start *dars* classes in their own localities while maintaining contact with the mother institution for feedback and advice. Al Noor also provides day-care facilities and runs summer courses on the Islamic way of life for children. While our findings include some direct experience of private *dars* gatherings and chance conversations and observations at events such as funerals and weddings to assess the impact of the *dars* ethos on social life, they are limited by their sample size and geographical location and do not cover private *dars* sessions and institutions located in either low-income areas or any of the new upwardly mobile middle-class residential areas. As such, they may be seen to indicate or exemplify a trend rather than comprehensively represent the overall *dars* phenomenon.

Recognizing the complex nature of empowerment as well as the shaping power of concurrent discursive contexts and situations in the exercise of agency, this chapter hopes to explore the space provided by women's *dars* so as to highlight the nuanced and complex nature of choice and the impact of this process on the ethical and normative vision of the women. Seeing choice and agency as political acts that cannot be disassociated from their consequences, our concern as feminists was not restricted to the issue of agency alone, but also considered the ideological dimension of women's choices and their implications for gender equality issues. The process of women's empowerment enabled by the piety movement and the *dars* ethos, and the ways in which this interaction is shaping women's subjective and objective world, will be based on Foucault's (1978) notion of power as something other than a commodity that can be acquired and permanently owned – instead, it is what comes into play as 'action' when contending groups and individuals interact and mediate space in specific contexts and relationships. I have also drawn on Deleuze and Guattari's understanding of the power of language as having a direct impact on, and reconstituting, the social and political world.[4]

Dars as religious practice

The *dars* or lecture is not a new phenomenon in Muslim societies, as the term applies to both religious and lay practice. The difference between the older religious practice and the new lies in that the former, based mainly on recitations from the Quran, is a relatively eclectic phenomenon that draws equally on tales of Islamic hagiography and popular religious discourse, while the latter is a modern practice informed by the politics of contemporary resurgent Islam and global neo-colonial interests with a strong Saudi influence. As such, its discursive trajectory is shaped by and contextualized in the literalisms and singularity of Wahabi Islam, with an emphasis on the written word and the book. This is evidenced in *dars*-goers' contemptuous rejection of what they call 'word-of-mouth Islam'.

The impetus of the modern-day *dars* derives from Pakistan's engagement with the ten-year war in Afghanistan. Later it was to gain popularity because of issues of identity raised by the post-9/11 demonization of the Muslim world. Historically the seeds of the Wahabi *dars* may be traced to the 1950s and 1960s when Cold War politics, combined with Pakistan's desperate quest for foreign aid, saw a convergence of interests between the ruling elites of Pakistan and the USA. This led Pakistan's first military – and secular – regime to 'peddle the idea of an "Islamic barrier" against communism and the USSR in the 50s' (Shaheed 2008: 5, citing Jalal 1991), and the USA to mastermind the establishment of the Muslim World League in 1962. Centred on the city of Makah in Saudi Arabia, it included figures to the radical right of political Islam, such as Abul Ala Maududi, the founder of the Jamat-e-Islami in Pakistan (Ahmed 2013) and guide and mentor to the young Abida Gurmani, who was to set up Al Huda and institutionalize upper-class women's *dars* about twenty years later.

Between Pakistan's formation in 1947 and the late 1980s, this interweaving of Pakistani nationhood with Islam as a political leitmotif was to be used time and again by successive governments in pursuit of purely secular interests. The paradigm shift, to Islam as the sole point of reference in social and political discourse, occurred in the late 1970s and 1980s under General Zia-ul-Haq, when Pakistan took on the role of cat's paw in the USA's proxy war against the USSR in Afghanistan and aid from the USA and Saudi Arabia began to flow into the country (Hussain 1991): the former for the 'war effort', and the latter to strengthen its ideological base through a proliferation of *madrassas* (Islamic seminaries), even as the image of the 'unarmed' Afghan mujahid fighting for the religion of his fathers against the godless might of the USSR was blazoned on the international media.

Seeking to divert attention from his illicit regime, Zia forged political alliances between the army and parties of the religious right, particularly the electorally unsuccessful Jamat-e-Islami. Using Islam as a power ploy he set about capturing the discursive field by rewriting the grand narratives of religion, morality, culture, art and the manners of the day in the image most suited to the moment and the army's institutional interests. The Zia regime changed school curricula, rewrote media policy, enacted retrogressive and sexist laws in the name of Islam and, transforming women into markers of national morality, exhorted them to stay within the boundaries of the *chadar* and *char divari* (the veil and the four walls of the home). There was an unremitting focus on public piety, including an attempt to set up vigilante groups to ensure the observance of *namaz* (ritual Muslim prayer) and fasting during the month of Ramzan. Fortunately, this last was not implemented.

South Asians have deep emotional ties to their religion and Pakistanis are no exception to this rule. Zia's patronage of Wahabi Islam, combined with the presence of state censorship and a visibly 'tough' military government, left little room for open dissent, though it fed into the underground repertoire of jokes and irreverent humour about Zia and the mullahs. At the same time, the new religious rhetoric found a resonance among the rising consumer-oriented, tradition-based bourgeoisie of traders and entrepreneurs, as opposed to the earlier Eurocentric post-colonial elite. These *arrivistes* were eager to stake their claim to the fruits of modernity and political power, even as they sought comfort and a sense of belonging in the new state-sponsored religious idiom. They were met more than halfway by sections of the erstwhile liberal elite, comprising feudal landowners, industrialists and bureaucrats whose class interests were best served under authoritarian rule (Hussain 1991). Among the many visible signs of change and expressions of public piety was the almost overnight switch from upper-class ladies' coffee parties to *milads* (festive gathering in honour of the Prophet Muhammed) that later translated into *dars* meetings. Starting in individual homes, the *dars* phenomenon was to acquire institutional status and has continued to gain strength even after Zia's death and subsequent changes in government.

In the pre-Zia years, women's *dars* classes, organized by the Jamat-e-Islami, were localized events for lower-middle-class women and had limited outreach. In its post-1970s avatar, the Pakistani *dars*, unlike its Egyptian counterpart (Mahmood 2005) was not an organic phenomenon. While it shared the approach and focus on visible signifiers of the mosque movement – such as dress codes, terms of speech, public acts of charity in the name of religion and so on – it did not emerge solely due to modernizing pressures and the increasing marginalization of religion as a means of organizing under a secular government (*ibid.*). Shaped in the Egyptian context by the religious right's resistance to a secular state, the *dars* movement in Pakistan enjoyed state patronage, as part of the military government's bid to capture and reinscribe the discursive field in its own interests, and at the same time glorify Pakistan's role in the US war in Afghanistan. Therefore historically the Pakistani *dars*, as a sub-cultural phenomenon, differs from its counterparts in other parts of the Muslim world in terms of its political moorings, as well as its specific focal concerns – particularly its emphasis on a narrowly premised religion-based nationalism and the positing of India as the infidel other. It is typical, however, in that it draws upon the norms, aspirations, patterns of social interaction and status symbols of the parent culture shaped by the combined authoritarianism of patriarchal tradition and military forms of rule inflected by global consumerism.

Two other things need to be kept in mind regarding the *dars*. The first is that despite post-9/11 anti-US sentiment, the *dars* movement has no issue with the neo-liberal consumerist ethic, as this reflects and fits in with the class-based social and material aspirations of the average Pakistani. Secondly, *dars* narratives are shaped by a host of factors including differences of gender, class and social location of both *dars* givers and participants. As such, they not only constitute different sites of power, but are also shaped by the fluidity of group affiliations and discursive categories that locate individuals differently at different points in time (cf. Mohanty *et al.* 1991). This was borne out by the low focus on militant *jihad* among the predominantly upper-class Al Huda attendees, whose vested interests are not served by either armed conflict or civil unrest, as opposed to women from economically under-privileged backgrounds who, having far less to lose materially and perhaps something to gain in terms of status and authority, saw *jihad* as a bounden duty which they would gladly undertake.[5] As one woman remarked, 'My in-laws cannot stop me – I'm doing God's work.'

My argument is that the ideological terrain of the modern-day *dars* and related activities are both the stake and the site of the hegemonic aspirations of what began as an ideology-based, ruthlessly political sub-culture twenty years or so ago, and continues to make significant inroads into mainstream discourse. That the rituals, which include the use of language liberally sprinkled with a mix of Arabic-Urdu phrases such as *Alhamdulillah* (thanks be to God) and *Allah ke Fazal sae* (with God's blessing), the emphasis on Sunnah-based ways of eating and drinking, dress codes such as women wearing the hijab and men having a particular cut of beard and wearing ankle-length shalwars, act as codes of instant recognition and are both strategy for the appropriation of socio-cultural space and makers and markers of a particular Muslim identity that subterraneously links the *dars* discourse to its more radical counterparts on the religious right. It has been argued that the 'latent function of subculture is ... to express and resolve, albeit "magically", the contradictions that remain unresolved in the parent culture' (Cohen 1972: 23). In the Pakistan context – where global power politics combined with years of military rule have created a sense of disenfranchisement and powerlessness among the people – the *dars* philosophy, as a rooting, grounding device that also orders the world around individuals and groups as described by Mernissi (1987), promises just this magical resolution to the contradictions and scarcities of our time, especially as it comes replete with its own imaginary.

The stated aim of Al Huda and Al Noor is to provide tools to approach, understand, and actively engage with religious texts, and to use this learning for character building and moral reform. It is necessary to understand that such an engagement is firmly located within the prescribed limits of an Islam that draws inspiration and guidelines from the Wahabi school of thought. The main focus of the *dars*, according to its students, is on the study of the Quran at three levels: listening to recitations of the Arabic text; literal, word-for-word translation of the Quran to memorize the basic vocabulary; and in-depth contextual explanations of each verse in the light of contemporary concerns. Regular courses on Islam supplement this core of Quranic exegesis with a mix of other subjects so as – in the words of one student – 'to understand the real teachings of Islam and the true practice of the religion'. Other subjects include *Iqballiat*, a study of the establishment's iconic poet Iqbal that forms the basis of nationalist discourse in Pakistan.

When only a small minority understands Arabic, the *dars* pedagogical approach – that focuses almost solely on the denotative dimension of language and discourages, if not explicitly forbids, discussion – reinforces the habit of obedience to authority and at the same time serves to elide Islam's spiritual and reflective dimension by reducing the multiplicity of the word to the singularity of prescribed meaning. In the process it fetishes the Quranic text and closes the doors to its deeper understanding, even as it facilitates the claim of one school of thought (in this case Wahabi Islam) as sole authority and arbiter of 'Truth' – with all other interpretations, nuances of meaning, room for exegetical discussion and debate (including different world-views or philosophies) falling outside the purview of the 'True Faith'. What is especially interesting in this regard is that greater ire and moral condemnation – as compared with critiques bestowed on other religions – are reserved for Shiite Islam and traditional religious practices among Muslims. Singled out particularly fiercely are those associated with popular practices such as *milads* and rituals pertaining to marriage, birth, death and modes of grieving, including those associated with Sufism. Wahabi Islam's focus on visible signifiers of piety, and its concern with the minutiae of daily life such as the injunction against wearing nail polish while praying and the shaping of eyebrows by women, draws attention to the woman's body as a marker of Muslim identity and enables public intervention in the most private areas of personal life. At the same time it makes the observation of religion easier, provides room for pharasaical prevarication, and enables the movement of morality to the surface among things that can be seen, counted and graded for merit. This argument is corroborated by interviews and discussions with Al Huda students. As one put it: 'Al Huda's approach is practical – it provides an exact and precise version of Islam.'

Most respondents stated that they had started wearing the hijab soon after they converted to the Al Huda school of thought as they see it as a marker of identity, and had rejected practices associated with popular religion such as visiting Sufi shrines. Discussions also highlighted the exclusionary dimension of *dars* teaching that is central to Wahabi power politics. All students had an enhanced sense of self-esteem and self-righteous complacency based on the perception that they alone had the understanding/ knowledge of the 'True Faith': 'We now practise true Islam – not the word of mouth Quran and Islam.' Given the Al Huda emphasis on family harmony, it is ironic that the exclusivity that separates true believers from sinners should be the source of family disharmony as doubts have risen among *dars* goers as to the quality and truth of the faith of their mothers and grandmothers (Saigol 2013). This was corroborated by one respondent, a school administrator, who feels strongly that the *dars* culture has created conflict and dissension in family and society. According to her, 'It is making women intolerant and is turning them into bigots who do not want to accept other points of view. Traditional Islam in all its diversity, which is part of our identity as South Asians, is denigrated by them.'

However, for *dars* goers the appeal of the *dars* does not necessarily lie in its larger political dimension or ideological strategy, which in any case remains largely invisible. It lies in the ambience of *dars* gatherings, their comfort level and the opportunity they provide for women to come together in a shared space cut off from the tensions and stress of family and workplace alike; and it lies especially in the seeming simplicity of its approach and narrative technique, where the constant slippage between the *dars* giver's voice and the Quranic text blurs the boundaries between the two to confer authority on the speaker, even as the persuasive tone of the lecture reassures as it exhorts to obedience. This was borne out by our Al Huda experience when the *dars* turned out to be remarkably easy to understand. The text for the day was the familiar story of Joseph and his brothers. Couched as a narrative in everyday language, Joseph's story merged seamlessly with a homily on mainstream notions of morality predicated largely on women's sexuality and the preservation of gender-based roles. Textual translation from Quranic Arabic to Urdu was interspersed by mildly articulated instructions on issues of 'right' (exemplified by honesty and integrity) and 'wrong' (greed and guile). Goodness was equated with obedience and the observation of *namaz* (prayer). The tone of the lecture was conversational and it dwelt on the family as the cornerstone of society and on the woman's role and responsibility as homemaker and preserver of family harmony. Woven into this seemingly innocent narrative, political asides – in this instance NATO's role in Afghanistan in particular and India's perfidy in general – drew attention to and reinforced the official religio-national discourse.

The Al Huda lecture demonstrated that the effectiveness of the *dars* lies in the way assemblages of meaning are evoked through reference to familiar stories from the Abrahamic tradition, while local myths combine with the use of clichés and stereotypes to intervene directly in the social and political world. 'Order words' and 'slogans' (Potter 2010) find a resonance in the existing language and customary beliefs as, with a persuasive ease that belies the imperative mode of speech, the narrator's voice links one ideological trope to the next – the valorization of Islamic norms, the breakdown of the Western family, a passing jibe at US policy in Afghanistan – awakening susurrations of meaning that imperceptibly bind the text as seamless narrative, and makes it seem part of Quranic injunction. Listeners are lulled into the familiar while the iteration of the 'us' and 'them' binary of believers and infidels catches echoes of the eternal conflict between *Dar-ul-Islam* (the Abode of Peace) and *Dar-ul-Harb* (the House of War) of the Muslim imaginary to add weight and legitimacy to the message (Ahmed 2013).

Its effectiveness lies in a narrative that is both familiar and reassuring; that creates an illusion of safety and affirms the listener's sense of place in the world. Above all, it lies in the process of devolution whereby authority passes from the *dars* giver to listeners, effortlessly inserted in the hierarchy of command that grants them an authoritative voice. This becomes evident from women's accounts of the impact of the *dars* on their lives:

Family members and friends listen to our opinions with respect.

Now we take part in family decision making.

Participation in *dars* activities and our work with Al Huda has resulted in increased self-esteem and gained us respect in our families.

The understanding gained at *dars* readings has taught us and other women how to improve family relations and friendships.

It's good for self-esteem and builds confidence.

Now they listen to me.

I found the *dars* experience particularly empowering. As a single woman speaking to older women, I was hesitant and uncomfortable when speaking about sexual matters. However, no objections were raised as my arguments were based on the Quran and Hadith and not presented as my personal opinions. It feels good to be in a position when people listen to you and give weight to what you are saying – it's a happy feeling.

Nor can the role of the *dars* as social space be underestimated. It facilitates mobility: 'Permission to go shopping or visiting friends is often refused. No permission is needed to attend a *dars*.'

It enables women to meet and interact with women outside the family circle: '*Dars* meetings have provided us ... with opportunities to make new friendships.' In a traditionally sex-segregated culture where women's social life is confined to family circles, access to worlds and women outside the family, including those from more privileged economic backgrounds, holds a definite attraction and opens up opportunities for socialization and matchmaking: 'daughters often accompany their mothers to the *dars* – matches are made here'. While interaction with upper-class women does little to narrow the class divide, it does enable a nodding acquaintance with the moneyed elite, and may even provide access to their homes at private *dars* sessions.

Strategic mediations of space and desire

Narratives of two extended interviews and one life history are drawn on in what follows to show how three women, closely associated with the *dars* or piety movement at different stages of their lives, made strategic use of religion to make choices and mediate space and desire in their particular spheres. Though they belong to different age groups, come from different class and social backgrounds, and speak within different sets of discursive constraints, they may be defined as the 'new women': all of them are first-generation university graduates and working women who have significantly reformulated the terms of their lives and relationships.

Samiya has a master's in economics from Punjab University. She is married and has two children – a four-year-old girl and a one-year-old boy. She worked as an A-level teacher but gave up her job on marrying. Now she lectures at *dars* meetings at her house and at Al Huda and Al Noor. She prefers to call herself a Muslim, but says if she had to claim affiliation to any sect it would be Sunni-Wahabi. She says she does not like to follow the teachings of other people but prefers to do her own research. The only religious rituals she observes are those found in the Hadith. The rest, various ceremonies and festivals related to the Prophet Mohammad such as Eid-i-Milad-un-Nabi (the Prophet's birthday), she rejects as being un-Islamic: because they are derivatives from Hinduism or because they set the Prophet on the same plane as God.

There was a time when she had refused to cover her head – even when her grandfather, a conventional man, had insisted she do so especially when visiting their family village. However, this was not an issue for her immediate family. She had been encouraged to go in for higher education – even a PhD. Her interest in Islam goes back to her postgraduate years when she attended a private Quran course. She speaks of it as a

> Call from Allah, which gave meaning to my life. My eyes opened – I found my identity. Earlier my life had been about entertainment and enjoyment with friends – there was no contentment.

Her in-laws are not particularly religious and her *walima*, the wedding reception hosted by the groom's family, was a non-segregated affair. This made her unhappy. Her husband had wanted a conventional, somewhat religious wife, but was not prepared for the hijab. Her in-laws had thought it a passing phase. Now, she says, they have accepted her beliefs and even appreciate them. Initially her husband had problems with her hijab, but has learnt to accept it. 'It took time, but Allah eased things for me.' There had been problems in married life: 'It is not easy to compromise and remain silent, but it becomes easier when I tell myself I'm doing it to win God's grace.'

Samiya uses makeup and is a trendy dresser – only for her husband or at segregated functions – 'never in front of other men'. Her husband teaches A-level students and she used to worry about his being attracted to the girls he taught: 'they are very young and very fashionable'. She dealt with this threat by dressing in the latest fashions. She says her mother-in-law is very broadminded and is open to ideas if presented convincingly: 'The family no longer commemorates my father-in-law's death anniversary with [the ritual] *khatam*.'

Her study of the Quran has brought her recognition and

honour, and she believes that it has made her a better person: 'Now I do things for Allah.' Regarding the role and status of women and men in Islam, she stated that the balance between the two created by Allah cannot be understood in terms of superiority and inferiority. They have their allocated roles to ensure social stability. Men are for the protection of women, she says, citing Mariam Jameelah on Islam and Western society.[6] Islam has given men *ikhtiar* or power so that they may be entrusted as providers and supporters. It would be impossible for them to do their jobs if they did not have authority. The problem, she said, is that today men have *ikhtiar*, but lack *takwa* or self-discipline. Power and *taqwa* (abstinence) are necessary for a fair and balanced system. She says if a husband is a 'normal' person, it should not be difficult to resolve problems as long as it is done 'tactfully'. 'The woman should not try to force her views on a man but bring about change gradually.' In her own case, she says, when there is a difference of opinion between her and her husband, she concedes her point of view to him – but also states her own opinion. She says he often comes around to her way of thinking. It is necessary to point out here that while *dars* teaching emphasizes women's obedience to the husband in all things, the only time it enjoins – indeed insists – on dissent is in religious duty.

Bushra is 21 years old and is associated with the Muslim students' *madrassa*. She is married, has one child and is part of a joint family system. Household expenses are managed by her mother-in-law, and she and her husband get a monthly allowance for personal expenses. Bushra is a *Hafiz-e-Quran* – a person who has learnt the Quran by heart – and her days are spent in teaching, studying and looking after her child. An MBA student at a private institution, she was on a semester break at the time of this interview. She observes all the 'five pillars of Islam' – the five-times-daily prayer, fasting, giving of religious tax for charity, the hajj pilgrimage, and affirmation of belief in the One God. Other than this, she does proselytization work – 'preaching to others what she has learnt'.

At the time of her marriage she had already opted for the

Islamic way of life and her *nikah* (signing of the marriage contract) was solemnized in a mosque. Her husband is the only member of her conjugal family who is practically inclined towards (Wahabi) Islam. Initially there had been trouble with her in-laws, who celebrate birthdays and subscribe to traditional rituals of birth, marriage and death, but now they have accepted her condemnation of these festivities and norms of grieving. She doesn't take part in birthdays of nephews and nieces, even if they take place in her house. She doesn't stint on presents, but makes it a point not to give them on their birthdays. 'Presents,' she says, 'can be given at any time.' Like others who subscribe to the Wahabi school, Bushra rejects the Prophet's birthday celebrations and *milads*, dismissing them as mere 'traditions of elders', and sees hijab as a necessary Islamic requirement.

An urbane and highly intelligent woman, Ameena belongs to a landowning family of the Punjab. About ten years old at the end of British rule and the formation of Pakistan, her education was in keeping with her class and family background – a missionary school in Delhi, where her father was posted before the partition of India, followed by Queen Mary School and then Kinnaird College in Lahore, the first women's college in the Punjab. She read philosophy for her BA degree and professed to a period of atheism: 'Philosophy does make you go a little mad.' She and her sisters have rarely observed purdah although the family's rural/feudal culture was conservative. Her father believed that if his daughters didn't 'observe purdah in the city there was no reason why they should do so in their village'.

Her marriage was arranged by the family soon after graduation; she had met her prospective husband and was under no compulsion to accept parental choice. Her husband came from a 'good' family, 'educated' and 'modern in its outlook', though it did not match hers for wealth. The early years, with her husband moving from one job to another, were financially 'tough'. It was at this time that the principal of a neighbourhood school offered her a teaching job. Excited, she asked her husband if she could take the job. He refused. The following conversation is reported verbatim:

'If you want to teach as a hobby or to pass time, I have no problem with it. You can do whatever you please and I will not discourage you, but *providing for the home and my children is my responsibility.* So do your teaching but as a volunteer – don't take money for your work.' [emphasis added]

So I gave up the idea.

Her marriage led to an association with Maulana and Begum Maududi. Her friendship with the latter sharpened her interest in Islam and gradually led to her holding *dars* classes in her home and then at Al Huda. Ameena's response to the question regarding her formal engagement with *dars* teaching is significant.

> Actually this is a very interesting story. You know sometimes little things can change a whole life. We were in Faisalabad. At that time it was a small industrial town and there was nothing much to do. I am a passionate reader ... but Faisalabad didn't even have a proper bookshop. So I decided to read the Quran. I had read it as a child but hardly remembered what I had read.
>
> One day, when I was taking my afternoon nap I had a strange dream. In my dream, my servant came to me and said, 'Bibi some people have come to see you.' I told him to ask them in.... Then I went to meet them. They said, 'We are arranging a large public gathering and have come to invite you to it.' They said, 'We have invited the Prophet, peace be upon him, to this meeting. He does not know the way to the venue and we would like you to escort him there.' I replied, 'I am a very ordinary person ... and do not merit such honour.' Then [the Prophet] appeared before me in the dream and he took me by the hand and said, 'Come Ameena, let us go!'
>
> I awoke and found I was trembling. I got up and said my prayers. I told my dream to my husband and he said, 'Don't be so upset, I'm going to Lahore and will meet Maulana Maududi.' So he told Maududi sahib about my dream and asked him what it meant.

Maududi had said, she was fortunate in her dream and advised her to do work that would 'please Allah and his Prophet'. After six months of intensive training, Ameena delivered her first *dars*.

These three narratives, each one shaped and inflected by women's voices from different class contexts and generations, show how the strategic use of authoritative texts proved to be an empowering exercise that provided them with space and opportunity for the exercise of agency and choice. However, it would be misleading to see this as a simple process of cause and effect, as these narratives are constructed within the discursive constraints and variables of multiple power nexuses. We see the power of patriarchy which acts upon them as women, exemplified by their submission to family hierarchies and norms, such as the husband's authority illustrated by Ameena's husband's refusal to allow her to take paid work. We see how discourses on femininity and male prerogatives compel Samiya, an intelligent thinking woman, to meet the threat of youthful femininity by reducing herself to odalisque status and dressing up 'only for (her) husband'. We see the power of class as expressed in a narrative focus and strategies for change such as different modes of persuasion and persistence, including assertion of class bias and awareness of status ('I only teach the Quran tour class at the Gymkhana Club'; 'The Quran stresses that your dress should not tempt others but it should be indicative of status and respectability'). We see throughout the power of religion based on the letter-of-the-law adherence to the literalisms of Wahabi Islam. And we see how the discursive deployment of mainstream notions of morality on the one hand acts as a mechanism for regulating female sexuality and, on the other, sanctions women's agency to include that which serves the interests of a particular ideology as exemplified by the defiant, 'I am doing God's work.'

Conclusion

Not for a moment does one doubt the integrity of these women's faith and experience. Yet their moments of empowerment existentially experienced, and the nuanced and complex nature of the choices made by the three women, problematize the processes through which agency and empowerment come into play and highlight their links to the consequences of choice and action. The routes taken and tactics employed, whether of recourse to stereotypical femininity or to the repertoire of the dream-prophecy genre, enable circumvention of authority figures such as fathers, husbands and mothers-in-law – but leave intact the terms of the discourse by which authority is so invested.

The discursive fallout of these actions corroborates Foucault's view that power is intentional only to the extent that it is calculated to satisfy the aims and objectives of the individual, but does not extend to the effects of their actions (Foucault 1978). This is illustrated by the way discursive constraints compel women to take part in an exercise that reinforces stereotypical notions of feminine guile. This grants a dubious legitimacy to the traditional 'backdoor' methods associated with women, while simultaneously diverting attention from the contentious and often painful narratives of embattled authority thresholds (Mernissi 1987) that lie hidden behind the clichés and sanctimonious euphemisms of 'tactful' dealing and 'work that best pleases Allah and his Prophet'. This process also reveals how the banalities of everyday language use serve as repositories and tools for the 'circulation of ideology' (Potter 2010) that shapes social action and relations in ways that reaffirm male prerogatives and locates and defines women's agency and empowerment within the prescribed limits of patriarchy filtered through a Wahabi lens.

It can be argued that if the women's *dars* encounter does not lead to systemic and long-term change, it does open up spaces where agency is exercised, choices made, and battles fought – and that this in itself is a gain. However, it must also be remembered that, if choice is fraught with ambiguity, and empowerment is uncertain and elusive, the consequences of these choices can be far-reaching and certain. They are experienced within the intimacy of the family circle, where they set up patterns of the licit and illicit, of exclusion and control, as well as in public spaces where the *dars* message is carried on the myriad tongues of participants, teachers, listeners. There it gains in strength as it intermingles with countless other voices, generated by other power nexuses that draw inspiration from the same Wahabi agenda of exclusion and control. And ultimately it is this powerful, mingled flow of authority that informs and justifies religious bias and extremist actions.

In a society where over thirty years of military rule have inculcated a fear of difference and dissent and eroded the habit of reflective thought, it is not only women who are 'turning into bigots' as a result of the *dars* discourse. The government's inability to repeal the notorious laws on blasphemy, the public support received by the man convicted for the murder of the Punjab governor who spoke up for the right to fair trial of a blasphemy accused, the small-minded viciousness of the response to Malala's speech at the UN – 'To save myself from ruining my piety during this holy month (Ramzan) I refrained from listening to Malala's UN theatrical presentation'[7] – all bear witness to the dangers of the Wahabi ideology and the perilous cost of its interventions in the social-political world. At a time when Pakistan, as the reputed seedbed and epicentre of global terrorism, is riven internally by religion-based violence, the question that comes to mind is: 'Is this limited and uncertain empowerment that clings to its shackles at the very moment of its enactment worth the cost?'

Notes

1 Muhammad ibn Abd-Al-Wahab, born 1702 or 1703 in Nejd, Arabia, drew inspiration from the late thirteenth-century Sunni jurist Sheikh ibn Taymiyya, known for his literalist interpretations of the Quran, his strictures against innovation (*bidat*), and his attack on the Sufi mystic Al-Arabi. Wahab rose to political eminence by forging links through marriage with Muhammad ibn Saud, the founding father of the Saudi-Wahabi dynasty and future rulers of Saudi Arabia. The Wahabi school upholds absolute monotheism; rejects all innovation; and propounds there be one interpretation of the Quran and Hadith – Al Wahab's. Aiming to restore 'Islam to what it was in the time of the holy Prophet and the great caliphs', it rejects later accretions as forms of paganism

and reserves special ire for the Shiite and Sufi schools of thought. *Jihad* against all those who refuse to share Wahab's vision constitutes a central tenet of Wahabi Islam that targets other schools of thought within Islam as well as other creeds (Allen 2006).

2 The study was conducted by Simorgh Women's Resource and Publication Centre, Lahore, Pakistan and BRAC University, Dhaka, Bangladesh, as part of the Pathways of Women's Empowerment Research Programme's South Asia Hub.

3 Laila-tul-Qadar (Night of Significance) occurs on the last Friday of the month of Ramzan (Arabic *Ramadan*). Traditionally it is a night of private prayer undertaken individually or in small family circles. Its commemoration as a public event is a recent innovation indicative, among other things, of the Wahabi emphasis on public piety.

4 As elucidated by Robert Potter (2010).

5 This observation is corroborated by Rubina Saigol's (2013) research on women's education in religious seminaries.

6 Mariam Jameelah, an American convert to Islam from Judaism. She married a Pakistani member of the Jamat-e-Islami and was herself a strong supporter of the Jamat point of view.

7 Pakistan Feminist Watch Twitter Account: pakfemwatch, July 2013.

References

Ahmed, I. (2013) *Pakistan the Garrison State – Origins, Evolution, Consequences 1947–2011*, Oxford University Press, Oxford.

Allen, C. (2006) *God's Terrorists – the Wahabi Cult and the Hidden Roots of Modern Jihad*, Abacus, London.

Cohen, P. (1972) 'Subcultural Conflict and Working Class Community', *Working Papers in Cultural Studies* 2, University of Birmingham.

Foucault, M. (1978) *The History of Sexuality*, Allen Lane, Harmondsworth.

Hussain, N. (1991) *Military Rule, Fundamentalism and the Women's Movement in Pakistan*, Editora Rosa dos Tempos LTDA, Brazil.

Mahmood, S. (2005) *Politics of Piety*, Princeton University Press, Princeton, NJ.

Mernissi, F. (1987) *The Fundamentalist Obsession with Women*, Simorgh Publications, Lahore.

Mohanty, C. T., A. Russo and L. Torres (eds) (1991) 'Introduction', in *Third World Women and the Politics of Feminism*, Indiana University Press, Indianapolis, IN.

Potter, R. (2010) 'From Clichés to Slogans: Towards a Deleuze-Guattarian Critique of Ideology', *Social Semiotics*, Vol. 20, No. 3, pp. 233–45.

Saigol, R. (2013) 'Reconstructing Patriarchies: Women's Education in Religious Seminaries', in *The Pakistan Project – A Feminist Perspective on Nation and Identity*, Women Unlimited, New Delhi.

Shaheed, F. (2008) *Gender, Religion and the Quest for Justice in Pakistan*, UNRISD, Geneva.

13

The Power of Relationships
Money, Love and Solidarity in a Landless
Women's Organization in Rural Bangladesh
• •
Naila Kabeer and Lopita Huq

This chapter explores the apparent loyalty of a group of landless women in Bangladesh to a social mobilization organization active in the country's southern districts. This loyalty is of particular interest because Saptagram,[1] the organization in question, virtually ground to a halt between 1997 and 2001. Its founder fitted into the 'charismatic' model of leadership discussed in the NGO literature (see, for instance, Gamble 2005; Siddiqi 2001). Her vision was to build an organization for landless women with an explicitly feminist agenda. She was its executive director from the organization's inception in 1976 until her death in 2000. It was widely assumed that her failure to build a second-line leadership, a failure frequently associated with charismatic leadership, meant that the organization would die with her. Instead, Saptagram resumed its work in 2001 with some of its older staff and a new director, although on a much-reduced scale. From over 25,000 group members in its more active period, the organization now has about 2,000 members. Around 700 of its older members have rejoined the organization; the rest are new.

The story of Saptagram is clearly not a story of organizational success. On the contrary, by many criteria, the organization could be said to have failed. We were therefore interested in finding out why, despite its troubled history, some of its older group members had chosen to rejoin the organization. To address this question, we carried out a survey comparing organizational impacts in the lives of 114 of these older members who had been with the organization for an average of 20 years and of 100 new ones who had joined in the previous year. We also carried out detailed interviews with 16 older members to explore their reasons for rejoining the organization.

Our research uncovered a number of issues relevant to the wider community. These include some of the familiar problems associated with 'charismatic leadership' within NGOs and with the influence of donors in shaping civil society. They also include some of the impacts associated with social mobilization organizations.[2] In addition, our work highlighted an issue that does not receive a great deal of attention in the mainstream literature concerned with organizational impact: the significance of social relationships in women's lives and their relevance to the processes of changes that organizations are able to achieve. This chapter explores the importance of social relationships in the feminist literature on women's empowerment before going on to examine the kinds of relationships that underpin the story of Saptagram's survival.

Women's empowerment and development organizations

Studies of women in rural Bangladesh during the 1970s and 1980s were largely preoccupied with the resilience of the structures that constrained women's life choices (Cain *et al.* 1979; Islam 1979). As these writers pointed out, families were organized around patriarchal relationships that placed women in a subordinate position to men, both within the family and in the wider community. Descent and property were transmitted through the male line, leaving women effectively property-less and genealogically irrelevant. The practice of female seclusion restricted their physical mobility to the domestic domain, curtailing their ability to participate in the economic and political life of their communities. Marital practices cut women off from the support of their own families, requiring them to reside with their husband's family after marriage, often in another village. These interacting patriarchal constraints not only limited women's access to resources, but also restricted their social relationships to those given by family, kinship and position within the community. Women remained throughout their lives under the guardianship of men, from father to husband to son.

Subsequent literature shifted the emphasis from structures to agency and to the processes through which these structures could be transformed. This literature ranged from concerns with women's access to resources – such as micro-credit, paid work and education – to the more intangible changes in their consciousness and identity. Given the social isolation of women in the South Asian context, and their greater 'embeddedness' relative to men in family and kinship relations, the feminist literature placed particular emphasis on the importance of expanding women's social relationships, of building their solidarity with other women, and of strengthening their capacity for collective action in pursuit of gender justice (Agarwal 1994; Batliwala 1993; Kabeer 1994). An important dimension of this process of social change is the expansion of relationships in women's lives beyond the 'given' relations of family and kinship within which they occupy a subordinate position, into relationships which they have chosen and which expand their capacity for agency.

Civil society organizations that seek to engage directly with women clearly hold out the potential for making such transitions possible. In the context of rural Bangladesh, development NGOs are the most likely candidates by virtue of their prominence in rural areas and their focus on organizing women into groups. However, as research from the wider South Asian context shows, interventions by development NGOs have had widely varying outcomes (Holvoet 2005; Kabeer 2005). This suggests that group formation on its own does not necessarily bring about the changes associated with women's empowerment. Rather, it is the group formation strategies pursued by organizations – their varying understandings of the causes of gender inequality and their commitment to bringing about social change – that make the difference.

The analysis of efforts to bring about women's empowerment has rarely gone beyond the 'given' relationships in women's lives. The quantitative strands of this research have focused on a fairly narrow set of the measurable changes, with women's roles in household decision making and their mobility in the public domain appearing most frequently. The more qualitative literature has teased out some of the changes in women's sense of identity and self-worth, as well as shifts in power relationships within the family, but neither body of research has paid much attention to the impact of group membership on women's wider social relationships and the implications of this for their capacity to bring about social change.

Yet there is some evidence to suggest that organizational strategies have implications for both the range and the quality of relationships in women's lives (Kabeer 2011; Mahmud 1999; Thornton *et al.* 2000). The significance of social relationships in processes of empowerment[3] was also noted in an early study of Saptagram by Kabeer (1985):

> Perhaps the most important achievement of the women's groups is that of breaking down traditional forms of alliances that are based on a patron–client relationship between the wealthy, *matabbar* families and the poor and landless classes. Traditionally both women and men give their labour and loyalty to their patrons in return for work and protection. The exploitative nature of such relationships is never explicit because it is disguised in terms of patronage or kinship. The groups provide the women with a form of organization that they can *choose* to belong to [unlike those based on family, kinship or patronage where their consent is not required] and that requires them to define and fight for their interests and those of their families, instead of having to accept socially determined priorities. This is an important break with the past for them. (1985: 209, italics added)

However, that study was based on secondary observations during fieldwork Kabeer carried out in 1980 into a very different set of issues and provides little insight into what this 'break with the past' constituted. The interviews carried out with Saptagram group members nearly three decades later offer the opportunity to explore the substance of this break in greater detail.

A brief history of Saptagram

Saptagram was set up in Faridpur district in 1976 by Rokeya Rahman Kabeer[4] (RRK, henceforth) as an organization to be run for women by women. This was unique at a time when all the development NGOs were led by men and focused primarily on problems of class and poverty. This was also a time when the NGO presence was far less pervasive in the villages of Bangladesh than it is today. An evaluation study in the early 1990s noted that Saptagram was effectively the first NGO to move into the areas in which it was working (Arn and Lily 1992: 18).

Saptagram defined itself from the beginning in feminist terms, albeit with a strong class perspective. Its core mission was the empowerment of rural women through a social movement against gender injustice that prioritized, but was not limited to, landless women. It organized women into groups of varying sizes and provided popular education and legal training classes in order to promote their capacity to analyse, question and act on the structures of gender injustice in their lives. In response to requests from its group members, Saptagram also began organizing men's groups, but its male membership never exceeded 10 per cent of the total.

The organization had a range of secondary activities, intended to support its core programme (Howes 1999; Kabeer 1985). These activities were based on the fundamental belief that without some degree of economic security, poor rural women could not be expected to take action against the injustices in their lives. However, it rejected the micro-credit model that was beginning to emerge in Bangladesh at the time of its inception, and opted instead for a savings-led model that would build the collective economic capabilities of its membership.

The savings programme provided the basic rationale for the women to come together as groups and meet on a weekly basis.

The idea of saving was not new to rural women – they had a longstanding tradition of keeping aside a fistful of rice on a daily basis to save for a rainy day – but the idea of collective saving was. As Tamanna recalled:

> We used to borrow money from the rich. They asked us for land as collateral or made us sign a stamped paper in exchange for the loan. Then they would take away our land if we could not pay. I was told that Saptagram worked with *samitis* ... that 10 or 15 women got together and saved small sums of money every week. The money stayed with the *samity* and could be used to meet a need or to generate a profit. I thought to myself, this is not a bad idea.

Women saved on a regular weekly basis and decided how they would use the money. The funds were initially kept by the women members themselves but later were put into joint bank accounts. Saptagram provided loans for collective enterprises to its group members. In addition, it provided training in various livelihood skills and in social development, and linked its members to local government officials and service providers.

Saptagram was unusual at the time in that the majority of its staff was female,[5] young women recruited from the districts in which it worked. Most of these women were married and had children, belying the widespread assertion in Bangladesh that married women were not prepared to take up full-time field work. It also had a much lower staff turnover than other NGOs where women rarely stayed for more than a year (Arn and Lily 1992). The explanation, according to Arn and Lily, was straightforward: 'Saptagram has created working and living conditions to suit the requirements of female field staff instead of demanding that the women adjust and try to behave and work as men, as quite a number of other organizations do' (*ibid*.: 57).

The personal qualities of RRK, her capacity for immense warmth towards her staff and group members, provided a great deal of the inspiration and vibrancy of the organization in the early years. Both staff and group members addressed her as *khalamma,* an affectionate way of addressing an aunt. But she was also seen as a formidable person to deal with by those in authority, able to draw on both her personal authority and her extensive networks to deal with obstacles. As one of her staff members told us, 'Wherever *khalamma* went, whether to the police station or the courts, everyone used to be scared of her. Because of her, they would also fear Saptagram workers.' In a country where women were still largely hidden from public view, she provided a visible and dramatic role model.

RRK made periodic efforts to recruit her replacement among younger women with the qualities widely regarded as essential in the context of Bangladesh, where access to any form of external funding requires English language skills and familiarity with the world of donors. This was a difficult but not impossible task, and a number of women who fulfilled these criteria joined the organization and did what they could to put systems into effect. They did not get very far. As a report by SIDA, one of its funders, noted: 'It requires a certain confidence in one's ability to take over from the founder of an organization, especially one who has managed every facet of its development to date' (cited in Guttman 1993).

The personal qualities that made RRK an effective force in tackling the weight of patriarchal traditions proved to be a major liability when it came to putting the organization on a more professional basis. She was also strongly influenced by the jealousies nursed by some of the longer-standing field-based staff (those she viewed as the 'real' Saptagram) towards the educated, middle-class women who were recruited into the senior management positions. Consequently, the organization continued to be characterized by 'a charismatic leadership, short channels of decision making and flexible decision making' (Howes 1999: 8).

The decline of Saptagram

The implications of this failure to establish proper systems became evident as the organization came under pressure to expand. Until the 1990s, Saptagram, like most of the more radical NGOs of that period, relied on small grants from international NGOs such as OXFAM as well as progressive bilateral donors such as SIDA and NORAD. By the early 1990s, the rise of neo-liberal ideologies within the international donor community had led to a growing focus on NGOs as a preferred private alternative to the state in the delivery of services. There was a massive expansion in official aid flows to NGOs in Bangladesh, along with calls for them to scale up their operations and move towards financial sustainability (Devine 2003). A version of these changes played out in the microcosm that was Saptagram.

Guttman (1993) notes the scale of funding that Saptagram had been accustomed to dealing with: a grant of $50,000 over three years from 1990 from Oxfam, $60,000 from NORAD in 1992, and a grant of $50,000 for two years from SIDA. This changed in the next grant round when a number of its donors came together to scale up their support, a response to the positive evaluations of the organization. A budget of nearly US$3 million was agreed for the three-year period 1993–6, with Saptagram required to raise US$1 million from its own economic activities.

This was a massive increase of funding to a small organization, particularly one that continued to be run, according to its then project director, with the informality of a voluntary organization (Tahera Yasmin, cited in Guttman 1993). A NORAD staff member who knew the organization well highlighted the problems in our interview with her. She pointed to the existence of a serious information gap between the head office in Dhaka and field operations because of the absence of effective monitoring systems. In addition, she pointed out that the organization was being asked to generate funding for its own operations when it did not have a great deal of technical or financial know-how, or any idea about business planning:

> These systems were simply not mature enough.... The problem was that too many resources had already been poured in. Where we should have invested $100, we invested $500 ... when this happens, opportunities for the misuse of funds become inevitable.

A management review commissioned by donors in 1996 found evidence of major mismanagement, lax financial procedures and accusations of nepotism and favouritism. Subsequent efforts to streamline the organization came too late. Divisions between the staff had become openly conflictual and the organization's activities ground to a halt. The donors withdrew and the NGO Bureau froze Saptagram's funds until it could carry out its own audit. RRK's health had been failing for some time and she died in 2000. As noted earlier, it was widely assumed that the organization would die with her.

The discovery that Saptagram had resumed activities, albeit on a much reduced scale, therefore came as a surprise to those who had known the organization's history. It was all the more surprising in view of the fact that there were now many more NGOs working in the areas in which Saptagram had been active. It was to investigate this 'phoenix-like' phenomenon that we decided to include Saptagram in a larger study we were carrying out on the links between development NGO strategies and outcomes.[6] We believed that an understanding of what had led a group of landless women to remain loyal to an organization through its troubled years, including a period of closure, would provide important insights into what they valued about the organization's vision and strategies.

Table 13.1 Characteristics of new and old members

	New	Old
Numbers	100	114
Duration of membership	7 months	20 years
Mean age (years)	34	46
Education		
No schooling	43%	71%
Up to class 5	30%	24%
Up to class 10	25%	4%
SSC or more	2%	0%

Table 13.2 Impacts of Saptagram membership (% of respondents)

	New members	Old members
Cognitive skills/Abilities		
Make oral saline	86	75
Open bank account	26	23
Use mobile	23	8
Recognize risky pregnancy	61	51
Recognize pneumonia	77	70
Bargain for a fair wage	87	90
Know voter eligibility	70	53
Voting behaviour		
Voted in last national election	71	98
Voted in last UP election	69	98
Campaigned in last UP election	1	23
Stood in last UP election	0	2
Encouraged others to vote	50	77
Community participation		
People come to for advice	53	75
Take others to government service	37	56
Give info on government service	58	82
Attended *shalish* in last 5 years	22	28
Participated in *shalish* in last 5 years	12	14
Called to conduct *shalish* in last 5 years	2	7
Participation in protest and collective action		
Ever participated in protest	6	54
On service provision	1	6
On women's rights	2	43
On livelihood issues	0	2
On violence against women	2	34
Perceived improvement in economic and social status since membership		
Land ownership	2	47
Savings	98	100
Housing	1	89
Food	8	72
Marital relations	9	33
Respect in village	3	38
Respect from UP Chairman/Member	3	23

Shalish: Arbitration meeting. UP: Union Parishad (Local Government)

This assumption was borne out by our research. The survey results suggest that Saptagram had an enduring impact on certain aspects of its members' lives. Despite their much lower levels of education compared to new members – 71 per cent of the older members had no schooling at all compared to just 43 per cent of new members – older members were more knowledgeable about their rights and about local politics; they were more likely to demonstrate leadership skills, to act on behalf of others and to command respect from their community and elected officials (see Tables 13.1 and 13.2). They were also more likely to participate in local politics and to engage in collective action to claim their rights and protest injustice.

The qualitative analysis supports the story of positive socio-economic impacts captured by the survey, but it also provides insights – not easily caught by quantitative indicators – into the processes through which these changes came about. For the remainder of this chapter we draw on the qualitative interviews to discuss these changes as they provide an explanation for the members' loyalty to a failing organization. Our analysis is organized around three sets of resources that formed the core elements of the organization's strategy: material, cognitive and relational.

Savings and livelihoods: 'able to stand on my own feet'

Saptagram's group saving and lending strategy, together with the loans and training it provided, had led to discernible improvements in the women's standard of living. Group members talked about being able to build or repair their houses; send their children to school, including their daughters; invest in livestock rearing and paddy husking businesses; purchase land or lease it for cultivation. They learnt how to care for livestock and poultry; to engage in silk worm rearing; to measure the quantity of work they did on public works programmes; and to operate new technologies.

However, it was the more intangible gains bound up with these tangible ones that gave them an enduring value. Jamuna believed that women's enhanced economic capabilities had gained them greater recognition and value within the family:

> No one has ever in their life made a land deed in their wife's name in the village, but now they do DPS (Deposit Savings Scheme) and insurance in their wives' names. I have also done DPS. Earlier husbands used to say, 'I earn money all day, if my money is kept in the bank, the bank will benefit, but what's my benefit?' Now they understand that this money that the wife takes care of will earn them 10,000 takas after 10 years, and that is the benefit. Because they understand this now, they don't stop the women. Now husbands understand that if we both work hard, we both benefit.

Rabeya valued her greater physical mobility and sense of economic independence. She told us how her father had previously forbidden her to work:

> Someone once told my father that he would arrange for a job for me at the local hospital, but he would not even agree to that kind of job. He said, 'What! A woman having a job! What kind of a thing is that to say? I'd rather get her married. If she works, she would no longer have any prestige.'

Now she moved around freely outside the home: 'I learnt this from Saptagram. I have bought a cow, I go to the field and cut grass for the cow myself. I hoe the weed from the land myself. I have been able to stand on my own feet.'

Kohinoor valued her reduced dependence on powerful village families: 'Now I have money, I don't give two hoots about rich people; I can manage without going to their houses. I earn and feed myself.'

Consciousness and capabilities: 'That's how I got the courage'

Transforming women's consciousness and capabilities was the second core element of Saptagram's strategy for social change. It relied on group discussions, training, cultural activities and exposure visits as the means to achieve this transformation.

The courses it developed went well beyond basic literacy and livelihood skills to address its central concerns with gender and class injustice. It had originally used courses developed by other development NGOs but found them to contain too many gender stereotypes to serve its own view of social change. Over time it developed its own course curriculum, which sought to bring a strong gender perspective to the analysis of class and poverty.

Our interviews with Saptagram members suggested that the knowledge they believed they had gained through these courses was transformative in its impact. It changed how they saw themselves, expanded their horizons, altered their behaviour and strengthened their ability to interact with others around them, including those whom they had previously feared. As Jamuna's account suggests, even those lessons that appeared to relate to the practicalities of everyday life contained within them the possibilities of other ways of living:

> They told us how to keep our houses clean, to drink tube well water, to have iodized salt, drink purified water, how to make saline solution for diarrhoea, to use proper latrines.... We also learnt how to keep our children clean and about the problems of child marriage. We were given training on adolescents. What kinds of health problems they are likely to have, how they should move around, how tolerant their parents should be with them. Now I treat my children with trust. I have taught this to others, that instead of always scolding their children, they should handle them with love.

She also told us about the dramas they used to enact to promote awareness about women's unpaid work contributions and the need for husbands to treat their wives with greater respect:

> One was about the abuse of women. A woman is cooking rice, her husband comes home and starts beating her with a stick, asking why the cooking isn't done. The office *apa* got me to take part in the drama. I was the husband and she was the wife. There are many men in this village who abuse their wives. We wanted to send the message that this cannot continue. Both have to work together. Wives don't just sit at home while their husbands work outside. Taking care of

cattle, doing household work, looking after the children; they do it all. If the husband comes home and lends a helping hand, he will be supporting her. Then they can finish the work quickly, bathe, eat together and then rest. Nowadays husbands in villages don't beat their wives so much. They realize that their wives also work.

Hamida believed that she had learnt to value her own contributions to her family's well-being and to demand respect for it from others:

> We were not given any respect by men, no matter how much work we did around the house.... Husbands would come, eat the meals we cooked and then go out again. If there was any change from the norm, there would be abuse and violence. Now I have learnt about our rights. You come home after working outside, I have also been working at home all day. I took the cow out, gave it food, I cleaned the house, cooked, washed the dishes. This is not easy work, I was not just sitting around. On what basis can you get angry with me?

Kohinoor valued the arbitration skills she had learnt and the courage she had acquired to stand up for her beliefs.

> We learnt how to do arbitration in disputes. If a husband is beating the daylights out of his wife, five of us women go there and warn him not to make trouble. Because we took this training for arbitration, we are able to talk like this. I could not have done this earlier; I did not have the courage to talk to people then. Now I am able to tell myself and others what the right course of action should be. Earlier if I saw a group of people sitting together, I did not have the courage to go up to them and say anything. Now even if there are 100 people sitting together, I can go up to them and have my say. Earlier, if we saw a policeman on the road, we would run. Now even if we go to court, we can talk to policemen there. We have achieved this much power.

For Rashida, knowledge of her rights was the lesson that she most valued:

> I have learnt how to stand on my own two feet from Saptagram, the value of unity, how to overcome problems, how to mix with people, how to sign my name. And I have learnt about our rights.

Now I understand that I have the same rights as my husband. I didn't get rights earlier and I cannot say that I get them all even now. But at least I now know what they are and I can teach my children. If I didn't know that we have a right to my father's property then I wouldn't have been able to get it from my brothers. This is also a right.... Whether I get my rights or not, I can still demand them.

The transformative nature of what they learnt from Saptagram, its impact on all aspects of their lives, was summarized succinctly by two of the women we spoke to:

I was an idiot before I joined Saptagram. I didn't know anything about the world.... The office staff educated us.... They told us how to live, to help someone in trouble, to rescue them, things like that. (Safia)

We were in a dark room with our eyes closed. Saptagram came and opened our eyes. It gave us strength. (Rabeya)

Solidarity and social relationships: 'The tree of Saptagram'

The third core element of Saptagram's strategy revolved around building relationships based on solidarity and mutual support among the landless women it worked with. It brought together groups of women with shared experiences of class and gender oppression and used a variety of means to build these relationships up over time. Along with values embedded in all its training programmes, it promoted group-based savings programmes, joint economic enterprises, regular meetings and discussions among its members, and various forms of collective action from the annual celebration of International Women's Day to demonstrations against incidents of injustice. Our interviews with Saptagram group members provided us with experiential accounts of these relational processes.

One striking point that emerged from our interviews was that many of Saptagram's older members had faced considerable hostility from the community in the early years of the organization's life. Their relationships with each other had been forged in the face of this resistance and cemented by their struggles for the right to belong.

As Tamanna recalled, the power of their numbers had helped group members to deal with this resistance:

> There were so many barriers in those days and so much loose talk. Many religious people came to stop us. They said things like, 'Wives and daughters can't go to the field, crops don't grow if women go to the field.' But how many of them are there? We have the numbers. How did Khaleda Zia and Begum Hasina become rulers of this country? Through us. So who do the *matabbars* now come to for their power? To us, right? Without our support, how can they have power?

Similarly, Rashida believed that it was the values that Saptagram had taught its members and the support it provided them that gave them the strength to stay united in the face of the community hostility:

> No other NGOs have taught us the way that Saptragram did, nor did we get it anywhere else in the community. Instead people of this area created obstacles – they wanted to break our legs, they wanted to crack our heads open, ostracize us from society. They said they wouldn't come to our children's wedding. They used to swear at us using bad language. We overcame all the obstacles and we had the strength so long as the organization was with us. Now we are with them, though we had swerved in the middle.

A number of women spoke of the difference that these relationships of solidarity had made at both personal and social levels. For Shathi, it overcame her sense of being alone: 'If I face a problem, then five of us can together solve that problem. Before when I used to go to work in different places, I was alone: I worked, I earned my money and I came home. Here, we are united.'

Jamuna credited their group unity with greater awareness on the part of women and a reduction in domestic violence:

> Women are not as foolish as they used to be. Now everyone realizes their own rights. We didn't know this earlier. By going for

processions, by getting together, becoming united, by becoming members, we have learnt. When we were by ourselves, there was no unity. Now everyone is together. There are 20 members here; can anyone's husband come here to beat her?

Shathi told us how they had used collective action to force the local administration to pay the wages that were owed to them:

Once I was part of a group doing earth work but they refused to pay us. We kept on asking for our payment so that we could buy food. We went to the Member but he said that someone else had taken the money, there is no money. Then we decided that I would go to the TNO.[7] I went with 30 women to the TNO. The TNO was surprised and told us that he had given the money to the Member. We went straight to the Member's house after that, 30 of us surrounded him and told him first give us our money, then we will talk.

It was also evident from their accounts that Saptagram groups extended support not only to each other but also to others within their community. Tamanna told us, 'If anyone faced a problem we would rally together to help them.' Her group would frequently attend the *shalish* (arbitration meeting): 'If justice was served, we didn't say anything. But if not, we would say "Give us a just verdict or we will have something to say".' She gave the example of when they heard that a man they knew ('a smart type') who had not been providing for his wife was now planning to desert her:

We told him, go ahead, but we will fine you 50,000 takas. He said this would not stop him. So our group decided that we would surround his house and teach him a lesson. Before we could go, my nephew came and said we didn't need to go because there was going to be a village *shalish*. We didn't say anything during the *shalish* because we wanted to see what the Chairman and Member would say, what they would do. If their decision was not just, we would have to take the matter up. However, the husband was told to ask his wife for her forgiveness and take her back. She is now very happy. She tells us it is because of us that she is so happy....

Jyotsna and Rashida described how they used their collective clout to ensure a fairer distribution of government services:

If someone needed help, we would give them from our funds to help them. Maybe someone can't take their child to the doctor.... We go to the *shalish* and we would speak out if the judgement was not right. We once went to the Member because our neighbour did not have a proper latrine, 2–3 of us from the group went to speak to the Member on her behalf. That didn't work. But when we gave a written petition, and we wrote that we were Saptagram members, it worked.

We go to the Social Welfare office, to the TNO office to find out when the VGD/VGF cards [Vulnerable Group Development and Feeding cards] are going to be distributed. We have been made aware where our rights lie. We go to the Members to find out how we can get sanitary latrines. We keep in touch with the Chairman/ Member to show where the tube-well should be located so that most people benefit from it. It is through the NGOs that we became acquainted with the Chairman/Member. We know where the blind and the deaf can get an education, where we can get a disability stipend. We know what to do if there is an acid attack. Now we know where we can get justice.

Saptagram's willingness to work with men, and to form men's groups where there was a demand, appeared to have paid off in terms of the support their members received from male members of their family in standing up to the community. Jyotsna said that she was able to go her own way, despite continued comments about her boldness, because she had her husband's backing:

Earlier, neighbours would say 'Look at this woman, she goes here and there on her own, she goes to meetings.' They still say it, but I don't listen to anyone. Even now they ask why I have meetings every day. I say that if I have a meeting I will surely go. No one can stop me. My husband defends me. He says that she is not going for any wrong reasons, she knows the difference between what is good and bad.... A few people say these things even now, but earlier many more people would talk this way. My brother's wife from this house, she says my power has increased from going to different places, that I talk too much.

Shathi related the occasion when she and her group members

had stood up to a fundamentalist preacher in a public meeting and the solidarity they had received from the men in her village:

> Once a mullah came to our village to preach. He said that Bangladesh has been destroyed because of women, that there is more corruption because of women, that poverty has increased because of women, that if women walk across a field it catches on fire. Some of us had gone to hear his preaching. When he started talking about women, a number of us women got together. We confronted the mullah and asked him whether he was not borne by a woman. And does everything happen because of women and nothing because of men? One of our brothers caught me and clapped my mouth shut and sent us home telling us that he won't talk anymore about women. We did go home, but our husbands who had now become aware stood up and warned the mullah not to speak that way about women. They said, the world cannot exist without women. Were you not borne by a woman? They created trouble and stopped the man from preaching. This happened because of our group. If I were alone, this would not have been possible.

Interestingly, an alternative perspective on Saptagram's members from the point of view of fundamentalist leaders is recounted in Naher (2005) in her study of religious agitation against NGOs in Bangladesh. While she had come across a number of women who had stood up to religious agitators in an individual capacity and in unorganized ways, she noted the following account reported in Shehabuddin (2000: 36–7) of the more organized resistance offered by Saptagram members:

> At a *waz mahfil* in November 1995, in the village of Chaita, Jama'at leader Abdur Rahman Azadi began, 'Today I will not talk about Allah but of NGOs.... I have burnt many schools of BRAC.' His tirade, however, was directed at another NGO, Shaptagram, which runs an adult literacy program for women using a unique gender-sensitive syllabus. 'Shaptagram is conducting un-Islamic activities. They are forming cooperative with women. They are educating women not the men; they are making women immoral. The books used by Shaptagram talk of divorce and dowry and include anti-Islamic teachings – these will turn people into Christians and

send them straight to hell.' He referred to the staff of the NGO as 'offspring of traitors and dogs', who deserved to be tied up with a rope and their tongues cut off. When village women involved with Shaptagram heard about this *waz* they banded together, brooms in hand, and confronted Azadi. They warned him, 'In your next *waz*, talk about Islam only, do not say such filthy things about women. If you do this again, we will beat you with our brooms.'

The flourishing of 'chosen' – as opposed to 'given' (family/kin/patronage) – relationships in women's lives was not confined to each other but also encompassed their relationships with the staff of Saptagram. Obviously, the material gains they had made through their membership of the organization played an important part in their positive assessments of the organization. But their loyalty to its staff was also based on the affection they felt for women who had come into their lives before any other development organization, who had lived amongst them over the years and who had offered them an unconditional form of support that was very different from the benefits on offer from most NGOs today.

Jyotsna spoke of her regret at the setbacks the organization had experienced and the love that brought her back to it, despite her disappointment that it failed to live up to its initial promise:

After the trouble, this office became drowsy. The other NGOs came: PP, BRAC, ASA. I had thought Saptagram would be the one to shed light here but the others have done that. Saptagram missed out. I had wanted Saptagram to be the one. That is why we want it to come back.... Saptagram came here first. We were a part of its groups. Then the useless organizations came. But when we loved someone first, is it possible to love someone else later? Their office was close to our homes, the office *apas* would come and talk to the people in the village, they did a lot for the people in this village. They would come and husk paddy with my aunts.

Tahera was one of four or five in her group who had not joined any other organization when the Saptagram office closed. She spoke of her affection for the organization and its staff and her decision not to leave it:

When such a good organization left the village, we did not want to join anyone else.... When RRK came to our house, we gave her a chair to sit on, but she would sit on the floor with the rest of us. When she died, I felt that I would leave the organization.... But then Latifa came to talk to me and so I stayed, she has been here from the beginning and I have a soft corner in my heart for her.

Golapi pointed to a tree in her homestead and told us: 'After the 1988 floods, Saptagram distributed saplings for us to plant, guavas and amra. This jackfruit tree is a symbol of Saptagram for me: it bears wonderful fruit.'

Hamida recalled the past in words that eloquently summarized the deep sense of well-being that the organization had aroused in those whose lives it had touched:

If there was a programme at that time, there would be so many people, the Saptagram field would get filled with men and women. People used to feel the same kind of peace there that they felt during Eid prayers.

Holding on to the organization: staff perspectives

While we had set out to explore the factors which explained the loyalty of Saptagram's group members to the organization, our fieldwork suggested that the loyalty of the staff to the group members also played a role in the organization's survival. It had changed their lives as much as they in turn had changed the lives of the landless women with whom they worked. Consequently, their accounts were as much a part of the story of Saptagram's survival as those of its group members.

Saptagram's staff were described by Arn and Lily (1992: 56) as 'one of the strongest points of the organization', but the failure to establish proper systems of rules, regulations and accountability had served to erode this strength. By 1997, divisions and conflicts within the staff, and the corruption of some of its members, brought about its near-collapse.

At the same time, it was the efforts of other staff that prevented the organization from disappearing altogether. There were a number of reasons for their determination to keep it alive. Saptagram still had property and assets that could provide the organization with a modest basis for future survival. The staff were convinced that they would be able to raise further funds on the basis of the networks they had established over time, and they knew that they had the support of some of the organization's older groups. In addition, the significance of Saptagram in their own lives emerged as a powerful factor in explaining their efforts to sustain its life. It was their source of livelihood but it was much more than that. This was apparent from Latifa's account of why she had fought to save the organization:

> I have to start from the beginning because I have worked in Saptagram from the beginning. It is not only that we sought to raise awareness in other women – I myself gained a lot of experience and awareness. I fell in love with Saptagram and with its people. Because of these changes in myself, I wanted to hold on to the organization. There have been so many conflicts, but we did not leave, we held on. We held on to it in spite of all these problems because of love. I have gained understanding, knowledge, I have been able to stand on my own two feet and given advice to others.... I thought that if I could hold on to it, then 10 other people will benefit the way I have been benefited.... No one will benefit if the organization is no longer there. If we let it go, then who knows who would take over? Both the motivation of money and love worked in this. These are the two reasons why we held on and this is why we are still standing today.

During the period when the organization was dormant, it was this small group of field staff members who continued to work without any salary. They paid their own travel expenses to visit their branch offices each day to keep their lines of communication with the existing groups alive, in the hope that the organization would one day resume activities. Those who had savings invested them in the organization. They also continued negotiations with the NGO Affairs Bureau. They finally managed to persuade it that they were capable of managing the organization's affairs.

In 2001, the Bureau agreed to unfreeze the organization's funds and authorized the staff to resume operations. Around this time, they received a small grant from ActionAid that allowed them to resume their work on a more formal basis. Since then they have taken funds from a number of other organizations. The organization that has survived has retained its commitment to women's empowerment through participatory education, but it has also internalized the lessons of its past. It has rules, regulations and regular audits. In addition, it adopted the more conventional micro-credit model in 2002 in order to generate some of the funds it needed to keep going.

Conclusions

While many of Saptagram's problems can be explained in terms of the problems of charismatic leadership, they are also the product of the haste of donor agencies to push organizations to go to scale. It is significant that, among the better-known development NGOs in Bangladesh, typically it has been organizations committed to social mobilization that have foundered in the move to large-scale funding. This suggests a certain disjuncture between the capacity of these organizations and their way of working, on the one hand, and the pressures associated with handling large amounts of donor funding and the bureaucratic imperatives that go with that on the other. Even the 'new' Saptagram – with its more decentralized structure, pragmatic leadership and focus on micro-finance – has problems dealing with the 'short-term' approach of most donors. Efforts to promote women's agency and empowerment within the typical three-year project cycle were described by the current director as 'the problem of the monkey climbing the oiled bamboo'.

In any case, it is not clear whether there is space for an organization like the 'old' Saptagram in the current era. The ease with which women can now gain micro-credit from other NGOs has made the more collective, savings-based approach associated with the old Saptagram difficult to sustain. Saptagram emerged at a particular point in the history of Bangladesh, when the barriers to women's empowerment as individuals and as citizens appeared to be insurmountable. In the face of a male-dominated order that had deep roots in the country's tradition, culture and religion, the disruptive power of the charismatic leadership provided by Saptagram's founder, and her willingness to take on patriarchal authority, clearly held a strong appeal for the many women around her who had been brought up to accept their subordinate position without question.

But for the organization to survive and expand, it would have had to develop rules and procedures, to 'routinize' authority and develop a more decentralized style of leadership. This is not something that charismatic leaders find easy to do. In retrospect, the commitment and capacity of those who struggled to save their organization suggest that the organization had succeeded in building a second line of leadership after all, but at the grassroots level rather than at the centre.

Returning to the question that this chapter set out to address, the findings from our case study tell us that there were many reasons why women opted to return to Saptagram, despite the problems it went through. While the older members we spoke to had by no means become affluent as a result of their membership, they had achieved a degree of economic security that had helped to diminish their reliance on patronage relationships. They also spoke of the knowledge they had gained, their greater voice and influence within their households and communities, the respect they received from others. Weaving through these various changes was the organization's ability to carve out a social space in which new kinds of chosen identities and relationships had been able to flourish in the lives of landless women. The bonds of solidarity between group members had been forged and strengthened through many years of dealing with adversity together. It was the power of these social relationships that they drew on in confronting relationships of power within the community.

In conclusion, we would say that, for all its failings and limitations, there was clearly something about the way that

Saptagram had worked that set it apart from most other NGOs in Bangladesh. The overwhelming majority of NGOs work with women and the vast majority seek to organize women into groups. To that extent, they all provide the possibility of expanding the range of 'chosen' relationships in women's lives. But it is evident from the existing research that the substance and quality of the relationships these organizations build vary considerably according to their vision, values and strategies. The provision of micro-finance has been found to create a business relationship – but little beyond that. Social mobilization organizations create a more enduring set of relationships, a sense of loyalty and solidarity of the kind we have noted in this chapter. However, in the course of our research into a number of development NGOs in Bangladesh, it is only in the case of Saptagram that both staff and group members spoke of 'love' in describing their relationship to an organization, based on a sense of ownership that was deeply personal.

The organization had come into their lives at a time when there were very few NGOs around. It had taught them to value themselves as human beings when society expected them to accept their inferior position without protest, and it had given them unconditional support in their efforts to better their own lives and the lives of women around them. It stood out in their memories as a beacon of light in very dark times. The difference it made to their lives endures to the present day.

Acknowledgement

This chapter is an expanded version of an article which was previously published in the *IDS Bulletin*. We are grateful to Wiley-Blackwell for their kind permission to republish it here.

Notes

1 The full name of the organization is Saptagram Nari Swanirvar Parishad or the Seven Village Women's Self-reliance Organization, so called

because the original intention had been to work in the seven villages that separated the founder's own village in Faridpur district from the village of her husband. In fact, it later covered many villages in a number of districts.

2 Some of the quantitative impacts associated with social mobilization organizations are discussed in greater detail in Kabeer *et al.* 2012.

3 Although a re-reading of this article for the present chapter revealed that, while it covers some of the same ground covered here, the word 'empowerment' does not appear in it.

4 Rokeya Rahman Kabeer was the mother of Naila Kabeer.

5 100 out of 140 employed in 1993 (Howes 1999).

6 The larger study of eight NGOs in Bangladesh was part of the Development Research Centre, led by the Institute of Development Studies, Sussex, and funded by DfID. The Bangladesh component of the research was carried out in collaboration with BRAC Development Institute, Dhaka.

7 Sub-district administrative officer.

References

Agarwal, B. (1994) *A Field of One's Own: Gender and Land Rights in South Asia*, Cambridge University Press, Cambridge.

Arn, A.-L. and F. B. Lily (1992) 'Evaluation Report of Saptagram Nari Swanirvar Parishad', OXFAM, Oxford.

Batliwala, S. (1993) *Empowerment of Women in South Asia: Concepts and Practices*, Food and Agriculture Organization – Freedom From Hunger Campaign/Action for Development (FAO–FFHC/AD), New Delhi.

Cain, M., S. R. Khanam and S. Nahar (1979) 'Class, Patriarchy and Women's Work in Bangladesh', *Population and Development Review*, Vol. 5, No. 3, pp. 405–38.

Devine, J. (2003) 'The Paradox of Sustainability: Reflections on NGOs in Bangladesh', *Annals of American Academy of Political and Social Science*, Vol. 590, pp. 227–42.

Gamble, J. (2005) 'Thought and Action: Perspectives on Leadership and Organizational Change in the Indian Voluntary Sector', consultancy report, McGill University, Montreal.

Guttman, C. (1993) *In Our Own Hands*, Education for All Innovation Series No. 2, UNESCO, Paris.

Holvoet, N. (2005) 'The Impact of Microfinance on Decision-making Agency: Evidence from South India', *Development and Change*, Vol. 36, No. 1, pp. 75–102.

Howes, M (1999) 'NGOs and the Development of Membership Organisations: The Case of Saptagram', IDS Discussion Paper No. 370, Institute of Development Studies, Brighton.

Islam, M. (1979) 'Social Norms and Institutions', in Women for Women (ed.), *The Situation of Women in Bangladesh*, Women for Women, Dhaka.

Kabeer, N. (1985) 'Organising Landless Women in Bangladesh' *Community Development Journal*, Vol. 20, No. 3, pp. 203–11.

—— (1994) *Reversed Realities: Gender Hierarchies in Development Thought*, Verso, London and New York, NY.

—— (2005) 'No Magic Bullets: Gender, Microfinance and Women's Empowerment in South Asia', *Economic and Political Weekly,* Vol. 40, Nos 44 and 45, pp. 4709–18.

—— (2011) 'Citizenship Narratives in the Face of Bad Governance: The Voices of the Working Poor in Bangladesh', *Journal of Peasant Studies*, Vol. 38, No. 2, pp. 325–53.

Kabeer, N., S. Mahmud and J. G. Isaza Castro (2012) 'NGOs and the Political Empowerment of the Poor in Bangladesh: Cultivating the Habits of Democracy', *World Development*, Vol. 40, No. 10, pp. 2044–62.

Mahmud, S. (1999) 'Informal Women's Groups in Rural Bangladesh: Group Operation and Outcomes', paper presented at workshop on Group Behaviour and Development at the World Institute for Development Economics Research, Helsinki, 10–11 September.

Naher, A. (2005) 'Gender, Religion and Development in Rural Bangladesh', unpublished PhD thesis, University of Heidelberg.

Shehabuddin, E. (2000) 'Beware the Bed of Fire: Gender, Democracy, and the Jamaat-i-Islami in Bangladesh', *Journal of Social Studies*, No. 87, pp. 17–45.

Siddiqi, M. S. (2001) 'Who Will Bear the Torch Tomorrow? Charismatic Leadership and Second-line Leaders in Development NGOs', CCS International Working Paper No. 9, London School of Economics, London.

Thornton, P., J. Devine, P. P. Houtzager, D. Wright and S. Rozario (2000) *Partners in Development: A Review of Big NGOs in Bangladesh*, prepared for DfID, Dhaka, Bangladesh.

14
Women Watching Television
Surfing between Fantasy and Reality

Aanmona Priyadarshini and Samia Afroz Rahim

Young Bangladeshi women's lives are greatly influenced by urban culture and popular media. They occupy and are visible in public spaces in ways not previously seen. Far more women are attending university or becoming wage earners than before. The private spaces that these women inhabit have also been transformed. Homes that were considered secluded are now made more public through technology and media. Television in particular has captured imaginations across economic, socio-cultural and political boundaries in Bangladesh. Television is a powerful means of conveying ideas and norms, and a pivotal tool for shaping identity. While reflecting values, television as part of the media also reconstitutes them; this interplay fashions women's subjectivities.

This chapter will outline how women in urban and peri-urban areas in Bangladesh engage with television and attach meaning to images and representations that may or may not have been the producers' intention. The pleasure involved in watching television will be explored, and we will attempt to highlight the notions of femininity, sexuality and self that are experienced. We ask what are the dominant narratives? How are they interpreted? And do the interpretations shape viewers' values and sense of self? Does the influence of images end with the 'off switch', or does it last beyond this into daily lives? And does television viewing open up new spaces for women, emotionally and psychologically: are these moments of escape and recognition crucial to experiencing new realities, or do they simply reinforce the limitations within which women live?

Our analysis draws on research on television viewing with women aged 15 to 45, from different economic and social backgrounds, occupations, marital status and locations. Most belonged to the lower-middle and economically lower class. Some were housewives; some were students; some were day labourers, garment workers or domestic workers. At the confluence of migration from rural areas, negotiation of new spaces and relationships, and instability and mobility in their employment, such women represent the majority of women in Bangladesh. We also interacted with middle-class university students, a group undergoing immense transition as they engage in a process of learning, often having to travel miles from their homes to pursue their studies. Through focus group discussions, we were able to get a broad picture of what the viewers watched and why, as well as the different kinds of relationships they had with television viewing. To understand this experience, we undertook household interviews. We also conducted participant observation, watching television with the viewers to note who possessed the remote control; with whom women watch television; whether and how what they watch changes according to who is present; what interruptions there are; and which activities take place simultaneously. We also analysed popular television programmes and films to understand the leading narratives around gender, sexuality, romance and social relations.

Dominant narratives

Our research found that women predominantly view Indian and Bangladeshi channels. The linguistically varied, nationally separate and religiously different narratives offer a very interesting space for identity formation. The depiction of class dominates Bangladeshi, Indian Bangla and Hindi serials, with Hindi programmes in particular focusing on the upper classes in shows like *Kasamh Se*. In contrast, the Bangladeshi serials predominantly portray the middle class, but with an upper-middle-class veneer – *Dainik Tolpar*, for example shows a middle-class family living in a modern apartment in an exclusive area, something this class could not afford in reality. However, in Bangla films, both Indian and Bangladeshi in origin, class identity often shifts through the course of the film and depictions of characters moving up the social ladder are common.[1]

Family is an important issue. Hindi programmes tend to depict large, extended families and focus on the private sphere. Bangladeshi ones often show small nuclear family life, with less demarcation between public and private worlds. This urban, nuclear middle-class family is a new and increasingly common image, replacing the rural–urban joint family that would have been depicted a decade ago. Bangla films, on the other hand, represent a broader spectrum of family structures, including single-parent, adopted and foster families. Within the family, heterosexual marriage is the basic relational structure. However, representations of sexuality previously embodied by married couples through symbolism are becoming more diverse and explicit, particularly in Hindi serials and Bangladesh movies. These include extra-marital affairs – whether initiated by husbands or wives – and polygamous marriages.

It is usually through the narratives of romance, jealousy and revenge that portraits of the main characters in serials and films are framed. Whether male or female characters are portrayed as socially acceptable or not depends on their enactment of family duty. Binaries maintained between gender roles are further distinguished by posing an opposition between the good and bad character. The good woman is depicted as a devoted wife and mother with limited ambition. In contrast, the bad woman is aggressive in the pursuit of her interests and dominating over her family. Her wickedness often manifests itself physically in arched eyebrows, long painted fingernails and a cold, hard stare.

A good man must earn enough to sustain his family adequately. He is usually the head of the family, making all the important decisions, and is portrayed as sensible and dependable. However, extra-marital affairs, considered taboo for women, are more acceptable for the leading male character. Rationalizations for his actions include his wife being uncaring, irresponsible or unable to bear children. The bad man is shown as gaining his wealth through ill means, or is unemployed and scheming. Any loss of income, even if it is unexpected, is seen as failure on the part of the man.

These narratives that make distinctions in class, depict family relations, delineate gender roles and stereotype the characteristics of good and bad individuals represent dominant accounts of broader social values. This is the process of 'encoding', through which values are embedded in the texts and images to represent and re-create social contexts.

Power dynamics and negotiations while viewing

The entire experience of viewing is strongly moderated by power relations and negotiations between viewers. In most households, we found nuclear families negotiating their viewing preference around a single television. Women were always extremely busy with household duties but managed to carve out some time for viewing during the afternoons – working women in the weekend afternoons, and those who are housebound, daily. During this time, female neighbours visit one another and women mostly watch television together. At other times, television viewing has to be negotiated with family members, whose preferences often override theirs. When male members of the household are present, they assume control over what is shown on television.

Negotiation over viewing also takes place in different kinds of familial relationships. Decorum is maintained between mothers and sons and sons-in-law, and sisters in the presence of their brothers. In the lower-middle-class neighbourhood of Agargaon, a family was watching the Hindi film *Main Prem Ke Diwani Hu* together when Bollywood actress Kareena Kapoor appeared wearing a swimming costume – something that seemed inappropriate for the mother to watch in front of her sons. The mother left the room and beckoned her daughter to follow. The sons had no qualms watching these scenes in front of their mother and sister, and did not move their eyes from the screen. Regardless of age difference, this decorum is always maintained by women – the male members, however young, do not have to censor their viewing in front of anyone. Age is relevant, however, when viewers, especially women, are watching television in the presence of *murubbis* (older, respected persons); or in university halls, where juniors acquiesce to the viewing preferences of senior students. At Dhaka University we saw senior students controlling the remote, despite the presence of an overwhelming majority of students in other academic years. Marital status also creates distinctions between viewers by giving those who are married the licence to view more than those who are not. In the slum area of Korail, one married woman said, 'Romance and bed scenes should not be seen too much by young, unmarried women, otherwise, they will become bad. We can see all of this because we have husbands.'

Other factors impinge on women's viewing patterns. Attempts to create time in hectic routines to indulge in television are thwarted by electricity cuts, forcing women to rearrange their next-day schedules to catch re-runs. Another issue is religious events – during Ramadan, women read the Koran, break their fasts and say the supplementary *Tarabee* prayers when they might otherwise watch television. All these practical and socio-religious realities influence their viewing patterns and entail negotiation for women viewers.

Viewers' interpretations

Despite these negotiations and codes of conduct, television opens up different worlds, both familiar and unfamiliar. Intersections of class, gender, social position, language, age, religion and other dimensions of identity all play a role in determining how women interpret the narratives they watch on screen, and associate meaning to them.

Some theories of popular culture see media as omnipotent and people as merely passive consumers (Adorno 1991); others maintain that people can have an active and creative engagement (Fiske 1989). In our research, we have found a significant engagement and negotiation between media producers and consumers to create meaning. The manufacturing of this meaning is a complex process, involving the producers representing certain dominant images for imagined audiences, and consumers interpreting these texts via multiple identities, whose allegiances vary according to time and space (Hall 1997). Meaning is not created uniformly or distinctly. It is forged by producers and consumers of media, and in this uneven process they constantly feed off one another. Viewers are in a state of constant negotiation as they watch television – continually judging what they view, assimilating the new values they encounter and using them to reshape their own, and rejecting narratives that are alien to them. The tropes of propriety and impropriety that allow viewers to relate to what is on television are also influenced and affected by how they interpret these.

One of the tropes that frame viewers' reception of images is their idea of masculinity and femininity. Social values and representations of masculinity on screen favour athletic, good-looking men, educated and earning sufficiently for their family, 'A hero should have a muscled, tall body like Salman Khan or Hrithik Roshan!' chorused many female respondents, spanning both middle-class and lower-income groups. But in some cases muscled bodies are celebrated in women. 'We love watching female wrestling! That women have so much physical strength, we couldn't imagine it. It gives us great *foorti* to watch them!' said a married woman in the semi-urban area of Koitta, Manikgonj. Many women however, still adhere to conventional models of femininity, perceiving female wrestling as despicable. For example, a woman from Gerua commented, 'Such activities do not suit women at all! It is bad!' While traditional models of gender are still being upheld by some, other respondents want to see a transformation of these in the media. Jahangirnagar

University students said that they want to see new images of women on screen, such as career-oriented women engaging in professions dominated by men, like business management. One group of students agreed:

> We should break with the stereotypes that are portrayed in the media: married women are always shown as busy making a home and tending to children; the good wife is the one looking after her in-laws and tolerating all manner of injustice; dark women are constantly shown trying to become fair and pretty – all this should change and new images and stories of women need to be depicted.

They added:

> We see on television a nuclear family where the man is the bread-winner, or sometimes the husband and wife together maintaining the family, but we want to see serials where it is the wife who is the sole breadwinner. In scenes that show men driving around in their cars and motorbikes, they have their wives next to them; we'd now like to see women in the driver's seat.

They also said that instead of the tradition of man proposing marriage to a woman, romance should show the woman proposing to a man. Some students said that traditional mother-in-law/daughter-in-law tensions are shown too often, and that harmonious relationships between in-laws should be portrayed. These comments reveal that women want to see a change in women's representation on screen, while they may or may not simultaneously subscribe to certain gender norms and relations.

Another criterion that viewers take cues from to define proper femininity is clothing. Clothing is a means to relate to the characters on screen – our viewers preferred to see actresses who play a married role in saris, perhaps reflecting their own values about the appearance of a married woman. But this does not necessarily reflect how the viewers dress in reality. Viewers enjoy seeing unmarried female roles exhibiting a wider array of clothing, ranging from the sari to *shalwaar kameez*, *lehengas* and Western wear. Satellite television has made the *lehenga* and Western wear familiar to viewers who did not have a culture of wearing them even two decades ago. Bodily form also changes the parameters of modesty; our respondents spoke derisively of over-weight women wearing fitted clothing or clothing that does not cover their 'fat' bodies, and deemed them vulgar. But when they see slender women on screen dressing similarly, they appreciate their style. Notions around modesty regarding clothing are also mirrored in ideas around romance.

The construction and meaning of romance varies according to changing times and contexts. Some older participants commented that they preferred the depictions of romance screened during their youth – a boy and a girl riding a rickshaw together and wooing with sweet conversation; the most intimate physical contact was a touching of hands. Our younger respondents, particularly female factory and household workers, said that 'Romance should involve glancing at each other coyly, holding hands, going out to eat at restaurants, hugging, and kissing – these are so natural!' But some of these younger respondents added that 'Everything should have a limit [matra].' Scenes depicting sexual foreplay and intercourse are not considered permissible; some modesty must be maintained.

The notion of modesty varies, though, among women of different ages and educational background. While younger women in the lower-income group preferred a censoring of explicitly sexual scenes, university women claimed they would like to see all physical expressions of love and romance on tele-vision. One Jahangirnagar University student commented:

> Whenever we hear the word 'sex' we sit up straight. We think it is something that only happens in the bedroom between a husband and wife. Sexual scenes give us pleasure. I am not saying that we will like all sexual scenes. But scenes that are heterosexual or show husband–wife relations excite us. Whoever denies this is a hypocrite. Just because we are not married doesn't mean that we have no sexual feelings.

Another added, 'Sex is a part of life. Among those of us who are at university and having affairs, many are having physical relationships. This is no longer the era where women remain virgins until marriage.' Some students considered sex to be an area of learning as well:

> I think that sex is an art, you can't enjoy sex if you lie like a dead person; you have to play an active role. And if anyone wants to learn and have sex in different ways and positions, then society should not stop this in the name of values and morals.

The comments by the Jahangirnagar University students indicate a shift in attitudes towards sex and sexuality among the middle-class younger generation. Where dominant narratives portray women passively in matters of sex, these young women advocate an active role and an exploration of pleasure. Traditional values frown upon premarital sexual relations, but these seem to be an ordinary part of their lives. While university students are defying certain norms and values, some identities and relationships remain important to them. The male–female union was seen as an ideal by all the Jahangirnagar University respondents, as it was by all our other respondents.

That the Jahangirnagar University students were so open to watching sexually explicit material may be due to their distance from their families outside of Dhaka. The Dhaka University students, on the other hand, did not think it was appropriate to view intimate scenes. One student commented about a serial: 'The actress was lying on the bed and her husband caressing her belly; this relationship between a husband and a wife needn't be shown on television; children may see this and how bad is that!' Dhaka University respondents in general seemed more conservative in their preferences than their Jahangirnagar counterparts, and this may relate to their living in the capital, often with family around, compelling them to be cautious about the values they hold. However, although these students made strong statements about appropriate viewing, our experience from participatory observation showed they watch anything and everything that is screened. Steamy music videos showing provocative male and female dancers were the mainstay of their viewing, but they also watched Hindi and English movies, and never switched channels when intimate scenes were displayed. Our research has revealed time and again that what people say when asked about viewing habits is often very different from what they actually do, perhaps because in detailing what they watch they are also self-censoring to provide answers that seem more 'proper'.

Notions of propriety and impropriety are strongly influenced by what individuals experience as their reality. People's immediate living situations influence what they are drawn to on television, in terms of both their direct physical reality and their fantasy. A Jahangirnagar University student commented:

> I find my surroundings reflected on television. Whatever is surrounding me on four sides, that has made up my existence; that is what has made me. Therefore when I see all this reflected on television, I feel as if I am looking at myself.

Students liked watching serials reflecting university life – romances between students, hours whiled away with friends – all of this finds resonance in their lives.

A few programmes found a following among viewers across all classes. One is the news. A woman in Korail slum area, Dhaka, commented:

> We can find out all that is happening in Bangladesh through the news. For instance, there is flooding in the South, near the Bay of Bengal. It is not possible for us to go there personally and see. We don't even have the money to go if we wanted to. If the television is there, we can get news daily, as and when it happens.

As our research was being conducted just prior to elections, the news was watched frequently and the topics debated with much passion. The political context during this time was unsteady, with politicians being charged with corruption, the rising prices of goods, and preparations for the elections all making the media important to our respondents. The political environment affects people's lives in direct ways, as can be seen by a woman from a Hindu household in Koitta, Manikganj, who said:

Of course we watch the news! There is tension because we are wondering when the elections will be held. We are tense because our community is very vulnerable. If the government changes, if Hasina comes, our situation might be better. See today, Khaleda got released from jail; now her cronies here will flex their muscles. My husband's business will suffer then.

But politics does not just affect minority communities: every Bangladesh citizen is affected by the political and economic situation. The women we talked to said that they watch the news to learn about food price fluctuations and keep abreast of economic conditions facing the country. Thus, the very real circumstances affecting people's lives also draw them to television, besides the pleasure and fantasy it offers.

The depiction of reality is important for forming connections with viewers. But sometimes in representing the realities of the majority, television can make the lives of minorities more invisible, compelling them to seek mediums that express their lifestyles even if this belongs to a different region, country or language. During our field research in Koitta, we found Hindu households there forsaking Bangladeshi Bangla channels for West Bengali Bangla and Indian Hindi ones such as Akash Bangla and Star Utsav – channels that some of our researchers had never seen before.[2] We were researching in Koitta during the week preceding the Hindu festival of Durga Puja and our participants were engrossed in watching the Puja programmes these channels were airing. Sitting in those households we felt as if we were inhabiting another world; the images and narratives on screen – of Hindu mythological symbols and rituals – were distinct from anything we had witnessed our other respondents watching over the past three months of field research. One woman commented that they enjoy watching Akash Bangla and Star Utsav because

it shows women dressed well, wearing a *sindoor*, maintaining a nice family.... These channels show the Puja and the temple; when someone is in trouble, they show the person falling on [the goddess] Ma's feet and praying to her, just the way we do; you can see brass utensils being used – do you ever see them depicted in the channels here? Never!

It is because the Bangladeshi channels seldom portray their daily lives and religion that this member of the Hindu household in Koitta is watching Indian channels, rather than what the majority of viewers in Bangladesh are watching. Television has made it possible to find elements of one's identity in narratives spanning different nation states, cultures, ethnicities, classes and gender. Technology, and in particular the media through narratives, enables one to transcend geopolitical boundaries in affirming identities and gaining a sense of belonging.

While some women watched television because it affirmed certain aspects of their lives, others were watching television precisely because it offers such different realities. Women living in the slum areas of Korail and Bhasantek told of how they enjoyed watching serials showing the lives of those who live in very different circumstances. 'By watching all this, we can learn what happens in other women's lives; so what if none of this happens in our own lives, we can hope for it for our children,' said a young mother in Korail. A woman in Bhasantek, watching a West Bengali film that showed a couple going to a dance party, commented 'Eesh! Look at rich people dancing! It's most absurd!' To her, going to dance parties was something so alien that it aroused only incomprehension and rejection. It resembled nothing she would ever do in her life, but she enjoyed the film by distancing herself and imagining it occurring in other people's lives. It is by relating to their own reality and imagining the realities of others that viewers become so engrossed in television. This envisaging of other ways of existence, both for oneself as well as for others, provides viewers with a rich landscape for fantasies.

Analyses of the relationships women share through fantasies have been complicated historically. The pleasures that women get through indulging in fantasy – whether through reading romance novels or watching films – have often been dismissed as a source of false consciousness and pandering to patriarchal norms. Authors such as Janice Radway (1991) and Ien Ang (1982) have challenged this, arguing that fantasies – because they do not simply re-create the status quo but instead offer space to reimagine social relationships in ways that may even challenge them – need to be given importance in order to understand women's realities fully.

The space for fantasizing that television offers is limited only by one's imagination. During our research, we watched television in one-room homes, with walls of corrugated steel containing so many holes that old newspapers were pasted over them to provide some privacy, among viewers who watched the opulent lives on screen mesmerized. 'We love watching the lives of the rich,' said one young woman in the slum area of Korail. The glamorous ambience and world of luxury seem to represent their fantasies and express their fascination with realities out of their reach. The poverty and distress in their lives seem to evaporate as they are transported from their world to experience plenitude and privilege, however vicariously and fleetingly.

The television offers space to feed emotions and desires that satiate a viewer's fantasies so that fissures in representation are filled in seamlessly by the power of imagination. A favourite theme is the battle between a mother-in-law and daughter-in-law. Our respondents enjoyed this narrative because it gave them pleasure to see a nasty daughter-in-law taught a lesson, or a conniving mother-in-law getting her come-uppance. A respondent from Gerua commented:

> A daughter-in-law is abused by her mother-in-law; after that the mother-in-law is taught a lesson. She (the mother-in-law) then starts to feel sorry and thinks 'Why did I do this? I shall never do it again.' When she understands, it makes us feel very good.

A married woman in Bhasantek said, 'We don't just like rebellion. At first she must try to be tolerant. If the situation pushes her against the wall, only then should she revolt.' This woman enjoyed narratives showing the dilemma of putting up with abuse, and the tensions that this builds until the moment when tolerance wears out and the protagonist stands up for herself and reclaims her ground. Watching these conflicts on screen may perhaps offer hope for women who have to endure such injustices themselves. An unmarried respondent in Bhasantek said:

> Seeing women protest is a matter of learning. It shows that women can stand up against injustice. These should be shown much more on television. Then we can learn that women will not tolerate injustice silently. And those who oppress will learn that women will not stand for it.

That the unmarried woman spoke so plainly against any oppression by in-laws, while the married respondent was much more careful about rebelling, highlights the tenuous position of the wife, who has to balance her role as a good daughter-in-law with any injustices she suffers.

Television is a terrain that harbours dissent and unfulfilled desires, so that desires that cannot be had off-screen can be experienced vicariously. Respondents from all ages, classes and locations said they loved watching romance, particularly courtship and love between a husband and wife. The story of Salma,[3] a young married woman in Gerua, highlights the influence of on-screen romance in her life. She and her two-year-old son live mostly in her parents' home, as her husband is away with the army. Salma told us how she and her husband met and got engaged – he came to see her at her parents' home and fell in love at first sight. They got engaged quickly and, at the ceremony, her fiancé sang a romantic song. During their engagement they wrote frequently; she saved every letter from him, and reads them often. He once gave her a red rose, which she kept. Many years into their marriage, following their son's birth, she showed him the rose, and he was taken by surprise: 'You have saved so many things from me? You truly do love me! I think I fail to appreciate you sometimes. But you truly love me!' Salma said, 'See, wasn't it good to have saved that memento from him? I now have my husband's love.'

The influence of romance as depicted on television is palpable in Salma's life and it seems to have charted expressions of love for her. When their romance was just budding, she had sent a letter, sprayed with perfume, saying 'You are only mine!' to her husband-to-be. She says he still carries that note from her in his wallet. She told of the hours they talk on the phone when her husband is away, often singing songs from Hindi and Bangla films to each other, and how these infuse their long-distance relationship with passion. Salma's exuberant recounting of the romance they share was punctuated by sighs about the girlfriends he had, about his tendency to place confidence in his mother more than her, and the fact that he never brought her any gifts when he came to see her. On one of our visits, she sat red-eyed and glum, saying how carefree her life had been when she was unmarried, and how fortunate we researchers were to be single. That her life was such a contrast between the romance she said she shared with her husband and the reality of it – her husband's absence for ten months of the year, her suspicions of his being with other women – was striking. It seemed as if fantasizing about romance sustained her while she dealt with her missing husband and the tensions that her conjugal life brought. Salma loved watching romance on screen as it seemed to offer her experiences that may have been missing in her life. To us researchers, it seemed as if watching television was offering Salma a substitute for life itself, allowing her to experience pleasures that she may not be able to experience otherwise.

Television provides an escape from sorrow, where viewers can harbour dissenting desires, imagine alternative existences, and vicariously experience other lives. The envisioning of new realities facilitates an engagement with the narratives on screen that occurs not only while viewing, but even when the television is switched off. During our research, we found women incorporating dialogues heard on-screen into their own conversations. In Bhasantek, one household had young women gathering every afternoon to watch television together while doing piecework embroidery. While chatting, they would pick up on dialogue from the Hindi movies. When one of the girls asked another to pass along a spool of thread, she replied, '*Nahe, nahe, kabhe nahe* (no, no, never)!' in mimicry of a Hindi film.[4]

We found narratives on television incorporated not only in the everyday speech of our respondents, but also in what they wore. In each of our field sites, respondents said they tailored clothing according to the fashions portrayed on screen. Our middle-class respondents purchased these designs from local fashion houses, but buying outfits from shops is beyond the means of the lower-middle and lower-income groups, so they made copies of the designs themselves, often purchasing a cheaper variety of material. In assimilating the screen designs, viewers have to negotiate with their own realities and customs. For instance, a participant in Bhasantek wore a tank top underneath a *shalwaar kameez* that she requested to have tailored with a big neck so that the tank top straps could be seen. She had seen the Indian actress Katrina Kaif wearing this and wanted to emulate her style. The young woman explained that, during the day, she wraps herself with a big *dupatta* so that her straps are concealed, and she can walk about with modesty; when she is at home or with friends, she removes the *dupatta*. Through such assimilation of the styles and aesthetics on screen, young women are able to exercise their choice strategically and straddle between what is presented on television and what is acceptable to their own society.

New spaces

Women experience different worlds, escape from their own realities and harbour dreams through the space that television opens up. This enables the woman to become a subject – choosing, judging, and discarding the narratives seen on-screen – rather than an object, viewing without participation. The television has blurred the boundaries between the public and the private. Spaces that for long were kept separate now lie close together, often overlapping, their distinctions erased. Stories of the private are made public to mass audiences, while viewers encounter the public sphere through television in the confines of their home. The boundaries of viewers' knowledge are expanded through the information, narratives and representations on screen. Besides presenting universes previously unknown, the television also offers opportunities for a temporary escape from the realities of life. It lays open a world of fantasies in which women can experience vicariously all that they desire, kindling hopes and allowing the imagining of new realities. The pleasures of viewing television do not only remain in the realm of fantasy, but are translated into reality through the myriad ways that women incorporate the narratives on screen into their daily lives.

Our research has found that it is possible for women to imbibe different subjectivities through watching television. Even though viewers may find comfort in narratives that reinforce existing power structures because they are so familiar to their realities, the spaces that television offers for escape, fantasy and participation all lead to a reconfiguring of their lives through women's conscious and active selection and enactment. The potentialities of empowerment remain nascent now but can be realized through further engagement. For a start, we can begin by breaking stereotypes, replacing dominant narratives with a diversity of representations, and having media producers cater to the pleasures of women's viewing. Time and further research might show whether engagement with television will lead to new ways of being or simply reconfigure the existing parameters of their lives.

Acknowledgement

This chapter was previously published as an article in the *IDS Bulletin*. We are grateful to Wiley-Blackwell for their kind permission to republish it here.

Notes

1 For instance, Amma Jaan, Hira, Shanto Keno Mastaan.
2 Akash Bangla is not offered by many cable operators in parts of Dhaka,

perhaps because the cable operators do not anticipate much demand for it and therefore leave it out of their selection.

3 Not her real name.

4 From the Hindi film *Sangam*, starring Boijonji Mala and Raj Kapoor.

References

Adorno, T. W. (1991) *The Culture Industry: Selected Essays on Mass Culture*, Routledge, London.

Ang, I. (1982) *Watching Dallas: Soap Opera and the Melodramatic Imagination*, Routledge, London.

Fiske, J. (1989) *Understanding the Popular*, Unwin Hyman, London.

Hall, S. (1997) *Representation: Cultural Representations and Signifying Practices*, Sage, London.

Radway, J. A. (1991) *Reading the Romance*, University of North Carolina Press, Chapel Hill, NC.

15

Family, Households and Women's Empowerment through the Generations in Bahia, Brazil
Continuities or Change?

Cecilia M. B. Sardenberg

Those who visit Plataforma today may not realize that, in the past, it was a *vila operária* (a workers' village), on the outskirts of the city of Salvador, Bahia, and home to Fábrica São Braz (a large factory). Nowadays, visitors are likely to arrive by bus or by car, taking the access road from Avenida Suburbana, which leads into the square where the Church of São Braz is located. Standing on the church steps, at the top of the hill, one has a view of the ocean peeking behind mango and banana trees that edge the alleyways going down to the Bay of All Saints. No spot on the square offers the slightest hint of the contours of the large buildings that once housed Fábrica São Braz. At the foot of the hill on the waterfront, the remains of the factory are now hidden away from the eyes of visitors. And in the absence of the well-known signs of factory activity – the tall chimneys puffing smoke up into the sky, the loud whistles sounding in the early morning calling people to work or sending them home in the afternoon – nothing here offers any clue to the visitor that Plataforma was once home to one of the largest textile mills in Bahia.

Until the late 1950s, first impressions of Plataforma were very different. Not only was the factory still in operation, but there was no Avenida Suburbana cutting across north-western Salvador, allowing cars and buses to manoeuvre their way into the Subúrbio Ferroviário area where Plataforma is located. Access to the neighbourhood was by train or by boat, and either way the incoming visitors disembarked at the gates of the old factory. When I began my research in Plataforma, a newspaper article suggested the possibility of getting there by train, and I was thus able to see the community from a totally different angle. Dominating almost its entire front view, from side to side, rose Fábrica São Braz, its dirty yellowish façade framed by immense palm trees hovering along the waterfront. Everything else – the church, the school, the roofs on the rows of little houses encrusted in the hillside – crept behind the old factory, as if they were merely outgrowths on the upward slope of its backyard.

During the late 1980s and early 1990s, I was often in and out of Plataforma conducting the research that formed the basis of my doctoral dissertation (Sardenberg 1997a). That research dealt with issues regarding gender, class, and power in Bahia that arose, in particular, from the testimonies of former factory workers, both women and men, and their memories of work in the factory, their families and everyday life in the neighbourhood in the past. Aware that the great majority of the labour force in the factory was represented by women, one of my major interests in that study was to learn more about gender, work and family-household organization, including women's participation in decision making. Plataforma and other similar *vilas operárias* were not simply places for people to find employment, but also settings in which 'men and women fell in love, married, reared their children, and retired in old age' (Hall *et al.* 1987: 114). Moreover, for those living or seeking factory-owned housing in such settings, a family labour system usually applied. Housing would be available so long as tenant families provided labour hands to the mill. But who and how many in these families should actually work in the mills to comply with these stipulations, or who would share in the fruits of their labour, taking care of the other needs of the household, was an arrangement that has varied considerably. It has depended not only on the whims and vagaries of global economies and how they reflect on local labour markets, but also on the composition of the households in question and on the needs, capabilities and preferences of their members (Parr 1990).

Bourgeois family morality sustains the basic principles of the patriarchal family model, with the husband/father as head of the household, assuming the role of the provider, while wife and children remain dependent and subordinate, sharing the fruits of his labour. Decision-making power and authority within the family household are invested in the patriarchal hierarchical structure. Men should have authority over women, elders over younger; husbands should have authority over their wives, fathers over daughters, brothers over sisters (Borges 1992: 47).

At Fábrica São Braz, these principles were observed in so far as the chain of command and the payment of lower wages to women and youngsters were concerned (Sardenberg 1997a). However, by relying primarily on the employment of women and youngsters, policies at Fábrica São Braz contradicted and undermined patriarchal authority in the domestic sphere. Because more women were likely to work at the mill than men, most company houses in Plataforma were rented out to women. Likewise, it was usually women who provided basic food staples acquired at the company store. In these households women assumed *de facto* positions as heads, particularly as men were more likely to have irregular incomes. Yet, while employment at the factory guaranteed more regular income for women, wages were never high enough to meet household needs. Children also had to seek employment. To borrow Karl Woortmann's words (1984: 35), workers' families then became 'true working families'. This contributed to the weakening of conjugal ties and to the formation of matrilocal extended households where women played a central role. Nevertheless, in Plataforma, the 'traditional' gender divide with its ensuing distinct roles for men and women – though often transgressed and/or redefined – was the basic principle in the organization of the family households, as well as for the socialization of children in the community (Sardenberg 1997a).

My original work in Plataforma focused on the testimonies of the older generations – the people who worked in the factory – and only on a small sample of families. Would these forms of family and household organization be true for younger families as well? During 2004 and 2005, I had the opportunity to coordinate another study in the same neighbourhood, based on a survey of 259 families that, unlike my previous study, were headed by men and women of different age brackets (Sardenberg and Gonçalves 2005). Between 2007 and 2009, I coordinated a third project in the neighbourhood, in which 353 women of different generations were interviewed (Sardenberg et al. 2008). Many of these women were members of the same family households surveyed in the 2004–5 study, and some of them had also been part of my original research in Plataforma.

Although these three studies had distinct objectives, timelines and data bases, it is worth drawing some comparisons, particularly in so far as change and continuities in family-household organization and gender relations through the generations are concerned. This chapter seeks to do so, focusing in particular on identifying processes of women's empowerment – that is to say, the processes by which women gain autonomy and make important decisions concerning the course of their lives and those of their families (Kabeer 1999).

Family-household organization and female trans-generational solidarity

The records of the Fábrica São Braz reveal a predominant presence of women in the workplace. In 1945, women represented 85 per cent of all workers, rising to 91.2 per cent working on the production lines. The female contingent of workers in the factory was quite homogeneous: 84.5 per cent were black, 49.7 under 25, 82.8 resided in Plataforma, and 40.3 per cent were born in that neighbourhood (Sardenberg 1997b: 22–3). Successive generations of women – mothers and daughters – worked at Fábrica São Braz, sometimes side by side.

Interviewing former factory workers, women and men alike, it came to my attention that close to 80 per cent lived in houses inherited from their mothers – some even from their grandmothers – who had taken possession of these homes at a time when only families working at the factory could inhabit them. It became evident that, in addition to homes, some women also inherited the position of head of household. When I met them in the 1990s, more than half were responsible for households that brought together two or more generations of mothers and daughters, whose partners and sexual mates passed through their lives, and who bonded to bring mutual help and support in raising their children and grandchildren.

In Plataforma, this type of household seems to have a long history among the families of the former factory workers interviewed, the ownership of the houses and responsibility for the families passing from mothers to daughters even when husbands and partners were integrated into the domestic groups involved. More important, from the information I was able to obtain from the testimonies, these groups could be characterized as *matrifocal extended families* of more than two generations, constituting what we may identify as informal *matrilineages*.

Given the importance of women's work in the factory and for the households in question, it would be fair to say that female-headed households, whether matrifocal or not, or with or without the presence of husbands and male partners, probably found significant expression throughout the history of the factory in the neighbourhood. As Katia Mattoso (1988) and other historians (Borges 1992; Santos 1993; Ferreira Filho 1994) focusing on Salvador have shown, female-headed households were already common in the poor parishes of the city back in the eighteenth and throughout the nineteenth centuries. In the case of Plataforma, these households were often formed by the desertion of mates, and expanded by children of their daughters' children, who remained at home and sometimes had their partners coming to live with them – thus becoming part of a female-headed extended household.

Several factors seem to have been at play in the formation of these households. The basic one was the financial inability of men to set up households of their own. Rental facilities were not easy. The company had ceased to build new housing for workers and the existing ones were usually occupied. Land was available for the building of houses, but this was a project to be accomplished over a period of many years, sometimes over a lifetime, and difficult for young couples to start. It was easier to build an extension – a room for instance – to an existing house, even a company house. This course of action also figured as a strategy for abiding by company rental policies. Moreover, these households had previously depended on the pooling of financial contributions of all able members – sons and daughters – and could not afford to do without them. This was increasingly so as the mothers aged and their productivity slowed, gradually drawing lower earnings. At the same time, daughters now had children of their own. If they were to continue working at the factory – as nearly all women like them did – and guarantee the company house and the wages to maintain it, they would need the help of their mothers in caring for house and children, establishing a trans-generational cycle of mutual help between mothers and daughters. While daughters often assumed their mothers' tasks so that these mothers could work at the factory, now it was the mothers who would fill in for the daughters. This mutual dependence of mothers and daughters contributed to the formation of matrilocal – and matrifocal – extended households.

While all these arrangements tended to the needs of the households and individuals involved, they were not immune to conflicts on gender and generational lines as related roles became muddled. The roles of *pai de familia* (husband, breadwinner, decision maker) and of *dona de casa* (housewife, home maker) figure as complementary roles, realized through the nuclear family household. In a situation of matrilocal extended households, however, there would be more than one individual to fulfil each of these roles, and thus a cause for dispute and conflicts. In Plataforma, mothers remained as heads of their households and the central figures of authority in their families. This strained relations between the conjugal pairs living under their authority and affected household administration. Their daughters' mates could not fulfil the role of *pai de familia* expected of them, especially as their unstable jobs and meagre earnings did not enable them to become the sole providers. This contributed to the weakening of conjugal ties and the greater dependence of women on their female kin group.

Plataforma in the twenty-first century: women and families

As noted, my study in the early 1990s focused on former factory workers, and thus on the older population of Plataforma. Most of the homes I visited then were female-headed extended households. However, it was a very small sample on which to make generalizations regarding contemporary family life in Plataforma, and it centred primarily on workers' memories of family life, when the factory was still in operation. It was over a decade later that the opportunity arose to conduct a larger survey in the same neighbourhood (Sardenberg and Gonçalves 2005), with members of 259 dwellings. This permitted the identification of some trends regarding household composition and organization in Plataforma. All the dwellings surveyed consisted of private units. Only three of them included more than one family living within the same premises. All of them were 'family households'; they had kinship ties as their major organizing principle. However, households varied considerably in terms of their internal organization, from single-dweller households to those comprising three generations or collateral extended families.

Three-generation extended families were still very common in the neighbourhood, constituting 27.4 per cent of the households surveyed. Not surprisingly, we found some very large households in our sample. One of them, headed by a 69-year-old retired woman, was composed of 14 people, including her husband, eight children and three grandchildren. At the time, the household head's eldest son (39 years old) was unemployed, as were three of the couple's daughters, all of them forced to live with the parents because of financial need.

Although such large households were exceptions – households in our sample averaged only four to five people – close relatives, adult daughters and their families often lived in the same building, or in an extension. This is a common arrangement in poor neighbourhoods in Salvador; as children grow up and begin their own families, the houses 'grow' either up, with new floors being added, or 'out', that is, by extending the house into the backyard. The new additions eventually become independent dwellings. As a popular saying affirms, 'Those who marry want a home away from home' – even if, due to economic constraints, 'away' means just a different floor of the house (Sardenberg 1998). Nevertheless, it is important to note that the 'nuclear family household', composed of a heterosexual couple and their children, the traditional ideal model of the family in Brazil, corresponded to less than a quarter (24.3 per cent) of the households visited.

Our 2004–5 survey confirmed some socio-demographic trends that have been observed for Brazil as a whole among the working classes: (1) a significant proportion of female-headed households and their greater vulnerability; (2) the tendency for female household heads to live without partners, and to be older and have fewer years of formal education than their male counterparts; (3) the sizeable percentages of these women who are retired or receiving pensions; and (4) the equally considerable proportion of these women who have to support unemployed adult children and their spouses as well as grandchildren, out of their meagre retirement and pension benefits. Within the past three decades, the marked increase in the percentage of households headed by women represents one of the major changes that have been observed in census data as well as in official household surveys (PNAD) in Brazil. For instance, whereas in 1992 these households represented only 19.3 per cent of the total, by 2002 this percentage had risen to 25.5, an increase in the order of 32.1 per cent. This increase was much more pronounced in urban areas, and particularly marked in metropolitan areas in the north-east and north regions, where the proportion of women-headed households was 35.1 per cent and 35.2 per cent, respectively. Among the metropolitan regions surveyed, the RMS – Metropolitan Region of Salvador – showed the highest proportions: 32.9 per cent (IBGE 2002). Similar studies have shown that even though increases are to be found in all strata of the urban population, these proportions tend to be even higher among the poor population (DIEESE 2004). Our 2004 survey of Plataforma confirmed this trend. Women-headed households represented 44 per cent of the sample, a figure much higher than the national average of 25.5 per cent (IBGE 2002), even for Salvador (32.9 per cent).

Our survey included a set of questions about such arrangements as division of labour, distribution of financial responsibilities, and decision-making authority within the family households – who decides about children's education, where to live, who should work within the group, how should the earnings of household members be spent? The results obtained indicated that, whereas financial responsibilities and decision making were commonly shared almost equally by women and men, even in those households that had a 'male head', domestic tasks – including caring for children, those ill, and the aged – were still treated as women's responsibility. These trends remain. However, women are now complaining about this unfair situation.

Women's empowerment?

During 2007–9 we conducted a new study in Plataforma as part of the Pathways of Women's Empowerment Research Programme Consortium (RPC). This study aimed to identify and analyse changes in women's lives over the past three generations, and how these changes relate to processes of women's empowerment, looking at educational opportunities, paid employment, political participation, family relations, and exercise of sexuality, as well as how changes in each of these aspects of women's lives may bring changes to the others. We went back to our sample of households surveyed in the 2004–5 study, but instead of taking households as our basic unit of analysis, we interviewed only the women, working with a sample of 353 women of all ages, ranging from 15 to over 90 years old.

Of these women, 25.8 per cent were identified as household heads without a partner, 36 per cent as spouses, 30 per cent as mothers or daughters, 6.7 per cent as other relatives, and 1.4 per cent as non-kin-related members. Among those identified as 'spouses or partners', nearly 66 per cent affirmed that in their homes they and their husbands/partners shared the position of being heads. These findings gain greater relevance when we consider that, until 2003, it was still stipulated in the Civil Code (sanctioned in 1916) that the husband/father was the head of the household.[1] The new Civil Code, sanctioned in 2003, establishes the possibility of shared household leadership. Were the women interviewed simply responding to the change in legislation, or is the Code merely catching up with a change of values and attitudes regarding women's roles in the family?

Our survey also included sets of questions regarding distribution of financial responsibility and authority within the households. Our findings indicated that the women interviewed are not only sharing decision making within their households, particularly with husbands/partners, but also seem to exercise a high degree of 'autonomy' regarding the course of their own lives. Although 15.3 per cent affirmed that they faced resistance on the part of family members (48 per cent of them from husbands and partners) when they decided to find work outside of the home, they did it anyway. In addition, 70 per cent stated that their economic contribution to their families is highly regarded, and 58.9 per cent believe that this contribution has made a difference in the way other household members regard them. Moreover, over half of the respondents (50.4 per cent) believe that their financial responsibilities to their families have earned them respect within their communities.

A significant proportion – 54.4 per cent – of the respondents stated categorically that they have 'total control' over their lives, while 34.4 per cent affirmed that they had 'considerable control'. For the majority (59.5 per cent) of the interviewed women, marriage is no longer a 'safe port', 98.3 per cent affirming that it is very important for women to have economic independence. Yet, while nearly 60 per cent believe that work does not affect a marital relationship or may have a positive effect on it, an equally high proportion (60.1 per cent) are ambivalent in so far as relationships between 'working mothers' and their children are concerned, thus expressing traditional beliefs regarding work and motherhood.

This is consistent with the finding that 96.6 per cent of respondents affirmed they were responsible for performing domestic tasks in their homes, including caring for the children. Although an equally high proportion stated that they share the responsibilities for these tasks with members of their families, the overwhelming majority (90.4 per cent) of them do so with other women, with mothers and daughters in particular. As in the case of the former factory workers, so too the women interviewed more recently are closely bonded to mothers and daughters for mutual help and support in accomplishing chores, caring for children and the elderly, and finding assistance in moments of need.

Three generations of women and their pathways to empowerment

Although it is possible to find a significant correlation between age and values in that the younger generations tend to express more 'progressive' values and attitudes regarding women's empowerment, this is not necessarily always the case. 'Dona' Nora constitutes such an example.[2] At 63 and now retired, she is still very vocal about women's rights and has sought a college education for her daughter and the means for her 14-year-old granddaughter to continue a successful career in international karate competitions.

A native of Plataforma, daughter of a canoe boatsman (*canoeiro*) and a laundry woman (*lavadeira*), she was raised in a family that included factory workers. She started work young, helping her mother with the voluminous weekly wash. She earned pocket money carrying lunch meals to factory workers from their homes, some of them leaving her leftovers in the pots. 'We were very poor,' she states, and 'sometimes I went to bed on an empty stomach'. Dona Nora went to live with her older sister who worked at the factory to care for her children. This allowed her to witness her sister falling victim to constant acts of domestic violence at the hands of her brother-in-law, a situation that, she claims, made her never want to be married herself. And she never was. But she loved children, she says, and eventually adopted as her own daughter her brother's little girl – now a grown woman with a daughter of her own – with whom Dona Nora lives.

Although she barely completed elementary school, Dona Nora took over a pre-school formerly founded by one of her elder sisters, staying as head of this school for nearly 40 years. She says that in spite of the fact that she could barely make ends meet (and could not even buy a house for herself with her meagre earnings), she is proud to have been able to give her daughter a college education, and thus the means for her daughter's empowerment. Nevertheless, unlike her adopted mother, Lara, the 36-year-old daughter, married young and lived in an abusive relationship. When her own daughter 'Dora' was seven, she finally decided to walk out. By then, she had finished college with her mother's support, earned more than her husband, and could not find any reason to remain by his side. She left, carrying only her clothes and her daughter's, and went back to live at her mother's home. At present, she supports her mother, ever since Dona Nora was forced to close the school. Dona Nora and her daughter Lara are both now directing all their energies towards finding sponsors for Dora. 'She is going places,' affirms Dona Nora, 'she will be an Olympic champion.'

Change or continuity?

In considering changes in women's lives in Plataforma over three generations, it must be stressed that what we found here was not unique to this area – not at present, nor in the past. Despite the absence of systematic studies of working-class families in Bahia during the first half of the twentieth century, there is much to indicate that home life among the populace departed in many important ways from the model of the family upheld by the local elites. Contrary to the general principles of this model, for instance, 'illegitimate' births resulting from consensual unions predominated among the working classes of Salvador. Consensual unions were the rule, not the exception among the working classes (Borges 1992). The precariousness of men's jobs made it difficult for them to establish their own households and/ or to assume the role of sole providers. Women's contribution to the domestic budget thus became fundamental, granting them greater economic independence, which laid the basis for a more symmetrical relationship (Chalhoub 1986: 137–44). Studies of working-class families in Rio, for instance, have shown that women there also contested the authority of the husband/father (Besse 1989), often counting on the support of other women in their families in staging their insubordination (Chalhoub 1986: 150). And, as in Plataforma, this situation was more common in those instances in which the young couples were forced by economic need to live with relatives. As Claudia Fonseca observed, 'the nuclear units were diluted in these consanguineous groups where strong, long-lasting loyalties contrasted sharply with the precariousness of conjugal ties' (1989: 105, my translation).

Families thus tended to be organized primarily around a mother and her children. 'The mother was the centre of this family, though the father might visit, or even live with them in the household' (Borges 1992: 48).[3] Matricentrality and matrilocal residence were mutually reinforcing, giving rise to matrifocal families and granting women greater relative autonomy and independence than women of the elites. The relatively high frequency at which they seemed to occur among the urban working classes all over Brazil has engendered speculations concerning the socio-cultural dimensions of the observed patterns. Even if, on the one hand, they can be seen as adaptations to socio-economic conditions (or as 'strategies for survival'), the regularity with which they seemed to occur suggests, on the other hand, that some principles for organization were in play. Dain Borges (1992: 48), for example, suggested that these arrangements constituted a distinct model of the family that 'had a long tradition in Brazil' – one that has been especially strongly associated with the Afro-Brazilian population (Landes 1947). But he is not clear as to what kind of 'model' it would be: a simply statistical model or a normative model – that is, a recognized, conscientiously upheld set of principles for family-household organization?

Claudia Fonseca reflects: 'Where [one finds] certain practices which are regular, renewable, and frequently pre-visited by the members of a group, there is [always] a logic guiding these practices and granting them specific meanings' (1989: 96, my translation). That being the case, she continues, one would be dealing with a 'reasonably coherent symbolic universe, resulting from experiences accumulated through (different) generations' (1989: 97, my translation).

One could say, then, that among the urban working classes, an alternative model of family-household organization was at play. Yet this model needed not be 'normative' but instead a *modus operandi* – or 'habitus' (Bourdieu 1977: 72) – of urban working-class families in Brazil. In this case, this 'alternative model' would not imply a rejection on the part of the working classes of family ideals (and the ensuing gender roles) espoused by the elites. As Maria Clementina P. Cunha suggests: 'It is more likely ... that the same claustrophobic role of the bourgeois woman operated as a parameter of aspiration and of vindication for the popular classes, earmarking a horizon of rights to be conquered' (1989: 144, my translation).

Indeed, evidence to that effect is to be found in the discourse and struggles of organized labour. From the late nineteenth century onwards, for instance, labour unions in Brazil and other spokesmen for the working classes – whether actually espousing these ideals or instead putting them to work in their service – have consistently fought for a family wage, thus claiming the right to constitute stable, conjugal families organized around the gender divide instilled by the bourgeois model. Of course, the thesis that the 'alternative' model of the family put to work among the working classes in Brazil represented in the past a conscious rejection of bourgeois ideals is certainly enticing to socialist feminists (such as myself). Nevertheless, as Eunice Durham poignantly indicates, all available studies and records suggest that, to the frustration of Brazilian radical intellectuals, workers in Brazil have been not only 'extremely attached to the family', but also

> express a generalized preference for a sexual division of labour on traditional modes, that is, that which subordinates women to men and tends to restrict female activities to the domestic sphere. At the same time, they also tend to appreciate the traditional virtues of respect and obedience of children towards their parents. (Durham 1980: 201–2, my translation)

From the perspective of women workers, the non-fulfilment of bourgeois gender role ideals has often been translated into the burden of a double day. For these women, in particular, the constitution of matrifocal families, without a stable male provider, has represented 'a result of poverty, an overload of misery, the impossibility to achieve a minimally decent life instead of a sign of better and freer forms of relations between the sexes' (Durham 1980: 203, my translation).

This seems to have been the case of the women of Plataforma in the past. Among the factory workers I interviewed back in the 1990s, even those women who were raised in and constituted their own matrilocal extended households and assumed the role of heads as major providers, enjoying a certain independence, were still betrayed in their discourse, which revealed unfulfilled aspirations for the realization of those ideals. They were not unaware of the contradictions between these ideals and their own life experiences. Indeed, when women asked, 'Why do I need a man that can't even bring me a bag of flour?' they were justifying the 'alternative' paths their lives have taken, precisely in terms of the gender roles intrinsic to bourgeois family ideals.

This does not seem necessarily to be the case of women we have interviewed in our last survey. Women in our sample have chosen to end abusive relationships, and some not to marry at all. In the case of Dona Nora and her daughter (and granddaughter), for example, the formation of their female-headed household appears to be the result of gender resistance and rebellion. Professional, middle-class women in Salvador are exercising agency, both in ending unsatisfying relationships and in constituting female-headed (and matrifocal) families (Macêdo 2008), as well as in choosing to remain single and live alone (Tavares 2008). Our study in Plataforma suggests that similar trends may also be making their mark among working-class women.

However, in the case of Plataforma as well as in other poor neighbourhoods of Salvador, processes of women's empowerment regarding family relations are being slowed, if not entirely diverted, by the growth of evangelical churches. Over the past decade, much has changed in relation to religion. The 2000 Population Census showed Brazil as primarily a Catholic country − 73.8 per cent of the Brazilian population. Yet it is considerably less Catholic than it used to be. Along with Catholicism, Afro-Brazilian religions have lost much ground to Evangelical Christian churches, which − particularly among the poorer and dispossessed − have gathered a faithful flock especially among women (Prandi 2003; Bohn 2004). In the survey conducted in Plataforma in 2004, we found that 36.9 per cent of women heads of household, as opposed to 26.1 per cent of male heads, were Evangelical Christians. Among the women interviewed more recently, the figure had risen to close to 40 per cent. These religions tend to preach fundamentalist values and be much more conservative than the others, especially in so far as gender relations are concerned: most of them advocate women's obedience to their husbands and a traditional division of labour.

Final considerations

Taking into consideration the findings from the different studies discussed here, it is possible to see some patterns continuing over time regarding women's empowerment in the sphere of gender relations within the family. The most obvious, of course, is the relevance of women's economic independence to their participation in decision making within the home, as well as in terms of autonomy. That is to say, both in the past as well as in the present, economic independence, particularly from partners, seems to have contributed significantly towards women gaining the *power to* assert control over their own lives, including in ending relationships that fall short of fulfilling the established ideals. To this end, female solidarity, particularly from women kin, has also played a special role: it has propitiated the growth of the exercise of *power with* to bring about the desired changes in one's lives, as witnessed in the case of Dona Nora's support to her daughter and granddaughter. However, despite their relevance, neither economic independence nor female solidarity alone seem to have led automatically to conscious 'gender rebellion' and a break with traditional roles in the family. I contend that this only becomes possible when new values and attitudes in favour of alternative models gain greater expression. Indeed, as indicated in the responses of the women we interviewed more recently, a new discourse – a feminist discourse – about women's roles and women's rights seems to be finding expression among working-class women in Brazil. This, we may say, is contributing to the growth of self-esteem and self-confidence – of the *power within* – among these women as well, of which Dora's Olympic aspirations are a good example. But only time will tell if this new discourse will stand its ground against the rise of religious fundamentalism in the form of Evangelical Christianity in the neighbourhood.

Acknowledgement

A version of this chapter was previously published as an article in the *IDS Bulletin*, and we are grateful to Wiley-Blackwell for their kind permission to republish it here.

Notes

1 This clause was maintained, even though the 'Statute of the Married Woman' passed in 1962 granted married women greater autonomy.

2 In order to preserve the privacy of everyone interviewed in the course of this research, their names and other identifying characteristics have been changed.

3 This was illustrated in a report prepared by a famous local paediatrician for the governor of the State of Bahia in 1924. The report indicated that among 3,091 youngsters registered with the agencies assisting poor children run by the Bureau of Child Hygiene of the City of Salvador, 54.28 per cent were illegitimate. In addition, 31.28 per cent had fathers who were either absent or unemployed, while the overwhelming majority – 94.17 per cent – had working mothers (Ferreira Filho 1994: 23–34).

References

Besse, S. K. (1989) 'Crimes of Passion: The Campaign Against Wife Killing in Brazil, 1910–1940', *Journal of Social History*, Vol. 22, No. 4, pp. 653–66.

Bohn, S. R. (2004) 'Evangélicos no Brasil. Perfil Socioeconômico, Afinidades Ideológicas e Determinantes do Comportamento Eleitoral', *Opinião Pública*, Vol. 10, No. 2, Campinas.

Borges, D. (1992) *The Family in Bahia, Brazil, 1870–1945*, Stanford University Press, Stanford, CA.

Bourdieu, P. (1977) *Outline of a Theory of Practice*, Cambridge University Press, Cambridge.

Chalhoub, S. (1986) *Trabalho, Lar e Botequim: O Cotidiano dos Trabalhadores no Rio de Janeiro da Belle Époque*, Brasiliense, São Paulo.

Cunha, M.C. P. (1989) 'Loucura, Gênero Feminino: as Mulheres do Juquery na São Pauldo do Início do Século XX', *Revista Brasileira de História*, Vol. 9, No. 18, São Paulo.

Departamento Intersindical de Estatística e Estudos Socioeconômicos (DIEESE) (2004) 'A Mulher Chefe de Domicílio e a Inserção Feminina no Mercado de Trabalho', *Boletim DIEESE*, DIEESE, Salvador.

Durham, E. (1980) 'Família Operária: Consciência e Ideologia', *Revista Dados*, Vol. 23, No. 2, pp. 201–14.

Ferreira Filho, A. H. (1994) *Salvador das Mulheres. Condição Feminina e Cotidiano Popular na Belle Epoque Imperfeita*, Mestrado de História/ Universidade Federal da Bahia, Salvador.

Fonseca, C. (1989) 'Pais e Filhos na Família Popular', in M. A. D'Incao (ed.), *Amor e Família no Brasil*, Contexto, São Paulo.

Hall, J. D., J. Leloudis, R. Rodgers Korstad, M. Murphy, L. A. Jones and

C. B. Daly (1987) *Like a Family: The Making of a Southern Cotton Mill World*, W.W. Norton and Company, New York, NY.

IBGE (2002) *Pesquisa Nacional por Amostra de Domicílio – PNAD*, Instituto Brasileiro de Geografia e Estatística, Brasil.

Kabeer, N. (1999) 'Resources, Agency, Achievements: Reflections on the Measurement of Women's Empowerment', *Development and Change*, Vol. 30, No. 3, pp. 435–64.

Landes, R. (1947) *The City of Women*, MacMillan, New York, NY.

Macêdo, M. (2008) *Na Trama das Interseccionalidades: Mulheres Chefes de Família em Salvador*, Tese de Doutorado, Programa de Pós-Graduação em Ciências Sociais – Faculdade de Filosofia e Ciências Humanas, Universidade Federal da Bahia, Salvador.

Mattoso, K. de Q. (1988) *Família e Sociedade na Bahia do Século XIX*, Corrupio, São Paulo.

Parr, J. (1990) *The Gender of Breadwinners: Women, Men, and Change in Two Industrial Towns, 1880–1950*, University of Toronto Press, Toronto.

Prandi, R. (2003) 'As Religiões Afro-Brasileiras e Seus Seguidores', *Civitas, Revista de Ciências Sociais*, Vol. 3, No. 1, pp. 15–34.

Santos, M. A. da S. (1993) 'Habitação em Salvador: Fatos e Mitos', in S. Bresciani (ed.), *Imagens da Cidade. Séculos XIX e XX*, Marco Zero, São Paulo.

Sardenberg, C. M. B. (1997a) 'In the Backyard of the Factory: Gender, Class, Power, and Community in Bahia, Brazil', UMI Dissertation Services, Ann Arbor, MI.

—— (1997b) 'O Bloco do Bacalhau: Protesto Ritualizado de Operárias na Bahia', in A. A. Costa and I. Alves (eds), *Ritos, Mitos e Fatos: Mulher e Gênero na Bahia*, Núcleo de Estudos Interdisciplinares Sobre a Mulher/Universidade Federal da Bahia, Salvador.

—— (1998) 'Mães e Filhas: Etapas do Ciclo de Vida, Trabalho e Família entre o Antigo Operariado Baiano', *Caderno CRH*, No. 29, pp. 21–48.

Sardenberg, C. M. B. and T. Gonçalves (2005) 'Enabling Urban Poor Livelihoods Policy Making: Understanding the Role of Energy Services', Brazil Country Report, Winrock International, Salvador, Bahia.

Sardenberg, C. M. B., F. Capibaribe and C. Souza (2008) 'Tempos de Mudança, Vidas em Mutação: O Empoderamento de Mulheres na Bahia Através das Gerações', Trabalho Apresentado no *Fazendo Gênero 8*, Instituto de Estudos de Gênero-UFRGS, Florianópolis.

Tavares, M. (2008) *Os Novos Tempos e Vivências da Solteirice em Compasso de Gênero: Ser Solteira e Ser Solteiro em Aracaju e Salvador*, Tese de Doutorado, Programa de Pós-Graduação em Ciências Sociais – Faculdade de Filosofia e Ciências Humanas, Universidade Federal da Bahia, Salvador.

Woortmann, K. (1984) *A Família Trabalhadora, Ciências Sociais Hoje*, Associação Nacional de Pós-Graduação e Pesquisa em Ciências Sociais (ANPOCS)/Cortez, São Paulo.

About the Contributors

∙∙

Hussaina J. Abdullah, an independent researcher and consultant, is a member of the Board of the Agency for Research and Cooperation in Africa (ACORD). She has recently completed a multi-sectoral Country Gender Profile of Liberia for the African Development Bank and is consulting with the Millennium Challenge Cooperation Compact in Sierra Leone as a social and gender constraints analyst.

Mulki Al-Sharmani is an Academy of Finland research fellow and lecturer in the Faculty of Theology at the University of Helsinki. From 2005 to 2010, she was a joint research/teaching faculty member at the Social Research Center of the American University in Cairo. Al-Sharmani's research interests and work are in Muslim family laws, gender, Muslim feminist engagements with Islamic textual tradition and religious discourses, and transnational migratory family life. She is the co-editor of a volume in this series, *Feminist Activism, Women's Rights, and Legal Reform.*

Akosua Adomako Ampofo is a professor of African and gender studies and director of the Institute of African Studies at the University of Ghana, Legon. An activist-scholar, her work addresses issues of African knowledge systems, higher education, reproductive health, identity politics, gender-based violence, women's work, masculinities, and popular culture (music and religion). Recent publications include 'Changing Representations of Women in Ghanaian Popular Music: Marrying Research and Advocacy' in *Current Sociology* (with Awo Asiedu, 2012) and *African Feminist Research and Activism: Tensions, Challenges and Possibilities* (co-edited with Signe Arnfred, 2009). She is currently working on an edited volume with Cheryl Rodrigues and Dzodzi Tsikata, *Transatlantic Feminisms: Women and Gender Studies in Africa and the Diaspora.* In 2010 she was awarded the Sociologists for Women in Society Feminist Activism award.

Awo Mana Asiedu is a senior lecturer in the Department of Theatre Arts at the University of Ghana. Her research interests are in the areas of contemporary African theatre and performance, the sociology of theatre, theatre for purposes other than enter-tainment, and women and popular culture. Her publications include articles on the plays of Ama Ata Aidoo, Tess Onwueme, Efo Kojo Mawugbe, Mohamed Ben Abdallah and Tracie Chimo Utoh-Ezeajugh, West African theatre audiences as well as on women and popular culture. She is currently on sabbatical leave and is working on a book on contemporary Ghanaian theatre.

Ana Alice Alcantara Costa holds a PhD in political sociology from UNAM (Autonomous University of Mexico). She has been active in the Brazilian and Mexican feminist movements since the late 1970s. A member of the Faculty of Philosophy and Human Sciences of the Federal University of Bahia (UFBA) since 1982, she was one of the founders of UFBA's Nucleus of Inter-disciplinary Studies on Women (NEIM/UFBA), and is its current director. She is the present coordinator of the master's and PhD programmes on interdisciplinary studies on women, gender and feminism at NEIM/UFBA, where she teaches gender and power and gender and history. She has worked in the area of gender and public policies in Brazil, both as a practitioner and researcher, for over twenty years, with several articles and books published on feminist studies in Brazil and abroad.

Akosua K. Darkwah teaches in the Department of Sociology at the University of Ghana, where she is also director of the Centre for Gender Studies and Advocacy. Her primary research interest is in the ways in which global economic policies and reforms affect Ghanaian women's opportunities for work that can be defined as empowering.

Rosalind Eyben is a feminist social anthropologist with a background in development policy and practice, convening the global policy research stream in the Pathways consortium. Until she retired in September 2013 she was a professorial research fellow at the Institute of Development Studies and is now associate faculty at the University of Sussex. New publications include *Feminists in Development Organisations* (with Laura Turquet, 2013) and *International Aid and the Making of a Better World* (2014).

Terezinha Gonçalves is a feminist economist and chief of staff to the minister for the promotion of racial equality in the Brazilian government. Since 2000, she has been a research associate of Nucleus of Interdisciplinary Studies on Women (NEIM) at the Federal University of Bahia, representing NEIM in the Salvador Women's Forum and in the Feminist Network for Sexual and Reproductive Health Rights. She has been active for over thirty years in women's movements in Brazil and was a founding member of the Feminist Group Brasil Mulher. Gonçalves has also worked as special superintendent for women's policies in Salvador. She has a master's in agrarian sciences, focusing on rural development.

Lopita Huq is a research fellow at the Centre for Gender and Social Transformation (CGST) at BRAC Development Institute, BRAC University. Her research is mostly qualitative, involving gendered analysis of social norms, attitudes and practices related to early marriage, dowry, work, education and rights. Her interests also include citizenship and rights, and organizational strategies and practices around grassroots mobilization. Her current work is on unpaid care work, women's access to justice, and home-based workers. Huq studied cultural anthropology at the New School for Social Research, New York, and political studies at Jawaharlal Nehru University, New Delhi.

Neelam Hussain has worked at Simorgh Women's Resource and Publication Centre since 1995, as editor, writer, researcher, translator, sporadic publisher and project coordinator. Prior to that she taught English at Kinnaird College, Lahore, for twenty-two years. She combines academic work with activism and is a member of the Women's Action Forum, Pakistan. She also teaches English literature to A-level students at Lahore Grammar School. Hussain read English literature at the universities of Punjab, Leeds and Sussex.

Naila Kabeer is professor of gender and development at the Gender Institute at the London School of Economics and Political Science. She has had over twenty-five years of experience in teaching, training and advisory work in the related fields of gender, poverty, social exclusion and labour markets and livelihoods. She is the author of, among other publications, *Reversed Realities: Gender Hierarchies in Development Thought* and *The Power to Choose: Bangladesh Women and Labour Market Decision-making in London and Dhaka*, and she co-edited a volume in this series, *Organizing Women in the Informal Economy: Beyond the Weapons of the Weak*. She is on the editorial boards of *Feminist Economics*, *Development and Change* and *Gender and Development*.

Ayesha Khan is a social science researcher who has been working in Pakistan for the last twenty years. Her areas of focus are poverty, gender, reproductive health and conflict issues. Recently she has participated in a number of field-based research projects exploring the theme of empowerment, particularly with regard to its linkages with paid work for women in different local contexts. She also conducted a survey on women's experience of induced abortion. Ayesha studied at Yale University and the School of Oriental and African Studies in London.

Eileen Kuttab is a tenured assistant professor in sociology at the Institute of Women Studies in Birzeit University, Ramallah, Occupied Palestine. She is a founding member of the institute, and was its director from 1998 to 2008. She is also a founding member of the Arab Council for Social Sciences, based in Beirut, and a core member of the Arab Families Working Group, a collaborative group of researchers working on Arab families in the region. She has been involved with grassroots women's organizations and served on the boards of trustees of human rights and development research centres. Kuttab was the first elected woman in Palestine to head the Teachers and Employees Union at Birzeit University, from 2011 to 2013. Her publications focus on feminism and nationalism, social movements (particularly women's movements), gender and development, youth, and political participation. Currently, she is working on youth groups in the Arab uprisings.

Sohela Nazneen is a professor of international relations at University of Dhaka and a lead researcher at the BRAC Development Institute, BRAC University. She has a PhD in development studies from the Institute of Development Studies, University of Sussex. Her research mainly focuses on institutional analysis of gender, particularly in the areas of governance, rural and urban livelihoods and feminist movements. She is currently leading research on gender and political settlement in selected South Asian and sub-Saharan African countries for the Effective States and Inclusive Development RPC, based at the University of Manchester. Nazneen has published many articles and book chapters. She is the co-editor of a volume in this series, *Voicing Demands: Feminist Activism in Transitional Contexts*.

Aanmona Priyadarshini is currently studying at the University of Pittsburgh for her PhD in cultural anthropology. In the Pathways programme she did research on media and women under the 'Changing Narratives of Sexuality' theme. She worked intensively in Rangamati and Dhaka, while doing her master's thesis on population policy. She has published work related to media, gender roles, population policy and sexuality. Her research interests focus on ethno-religious violence, gender, identity politics, nationalism, globalization and governmentality. Apart from research she is interested in teaching. Priyadarshini completed her master's from Jahangirnagar University, specializing in anthropology. She received a Fulbright Scholarship for her second graduation in gender studies in the USA.

Samia Afroz Rahim worked at the Pathways programme at BRAC Development Institute, where she was involved with research investigating the practice of religion and the role of television-watching in everyday life and facilitated the first digital storytelling workshops in Bangladesh. Her interests lie in using technology in creative ways to share personal stories and community histories so that they may be drawn upon as sources for learning and knowledge. Her current research pursuits seek to explore the cultural links shared by Muslim traders between Kerala and the Bay of Bengal region and how the politics of nation-making in the twentieth century has shaped these linkages.

Cecilia M. B. Sardenberg is a Brazilian feminist activist and since 1982 has been a member of the faculty of philosophy and human sciences of the Federal University of Bahia (UFBA). She is also a visiting professor at the Institute of Development Studies. She was one of the founders of UFBA's Nucleus of Interdisciplinary Studies on Women (NEIM), where she teaches feminist theory and where she helped create the master's and PhD programmes on interdisciplinary studies on women, gender and feminism. She has worked in the area of gender and development in Brazil, both as practitioner and researcher, and has published several articles in Brazil and abroad on feminist and gender studies. She is the convener of the Latin American Hub in the Pathways of Women's Empowerment Research Programme Consortium, and national coordinator for OBSERVE — the Observatory for the Application of Maria da Penha Law, the new domestic violence legislation in Brazil.

Hania Sholkamy is an anthropologist with a PhD from the London School of Economics and Political Sciences. Her research interests and publications are on reproductive health, gender, population and qualitative methods. She is co-editor of *Categories and Contexts: Anthropological and Historical Studies in Critical Demography* (with S. Szreter and A. Dharmalingam) and *Health and Identity in Egypt* (with F. Ghanam). She was regional co-ordinator of the Pathways of Women's Empowerment Research Consortium in partnership with the Institute of Development Studies.

Maheen Sultan is one of the founders of the Centre for Gender and Social Transformation at the BRAC Development Institute, BRAC University, a regional centre on research, teaching and policy related to gender and social transformation. She is a development practitioner with over twenty-five years' experience working for NGOs, donors, the UN, Grameen Bank and the Bangladeshi government in a range of capacities, from direct programme management to policy formulation. She has worked on issues of social development, poverty, civil society and community participation, and gender equality in various capacities – including a close engagement with government structures in the post-Beijing conference period when her work addressed gender mainstreaming and CEDAW reporting. Maheen is a member of Naripokkho, a Bangladeshi women's activist organization, a board member of Caritas Bangladesh and Utsho Bangladesh, and the chairperson of the ADB External Forum on Gender and Development. She co-edited *Mapping Women's Empowerment: Experiences from Bangladesh, India and Pakistan* (2009). She is the co-editor of a volume in this series, *Voicing Demands: Feminist Activism in Transitional Contexts*.

Index